Yale Studies in English, 180

KILLING THE KING

Three Studies in Shakespeare's Tragic Structure

by Maynard Mack, Jr.

New Haven and London, Yale University Press

Designed by John O. C. McCrillis
and set in Fairfield type.
Printed in the United States of America by
The Murray Printing Company, Forge Village, Massachusetts.

Published in Great Britain, Europe, and Africa by
Yale University Press, Ltd., London.
Distributed in Latin America by Kaiman & Polon,
Inc., New York City; in Australasia and Southeast
Asia by John Wiley & Sons Australasia Pty. Ltd.,
Sydney; in India by UBS Publishers' Distributors Pvt.,
Ltd., Delhi; in Japan by John Weatherhill, Inc., Tokyo.

For Old Maynard and his Queen
and my ravishing mad Ophelia

Preface

The Arden editions of Shakespeare's plays are used throughout as the basic reference, despite the unfinished revision of the series. I am, therefore, particularly indebted to the following editors for their careful work: Peter Ure, *Richard II* (1956), Edward Dowden, *Hamlet* (1912, third edition), and Kenneth Muir, *Macbeth* (1951).

The weight of the past on anyone who writes about Shakespeare would be intolerable were it not that such critical debts paradoxically enrich the one who owes them; such burdens lift up the beast. My rifling of the vast published criticism has been extensive, probably indiscriminate, certainly incomplete. Only the more memorable or startling instances can possibly be included in the footnotes. My thefts—petty and major—from the unpublished stores of mentors and friends may be fewer and more easily acknowledged, but they are no less important. Professor Alvin Kernan is probably the rightful owner of more of this book than I can at present see. His advice has always been valuable; his example through the rugged clarity of his own writing has been nearly overwhelming. Professor Louis Martz read an earlier version of my essay, and his comments were extremely helpful in some extensive rewriting. Professor Alice Miskimin also read the manuscript and made many helpful suggestions, including the reference to Edward Peter's book. I am still benefiting from the incisive and exhaustive reading done by Professor Eugene Waith. His service was "in every point twice done, and then done double," since he read my work a second time when it was offered to the Yale Studies in English series. The energy, keenness of mind, and generosity with which he helped me at every stage create debts that only imitation can properly repay.

Two friends, Bartlett Giamatti at Yale and Keith Stavely at Boston University, have listened patiently and helped me learn to tell a hawk from a handsaw. Patricia Woodruff of the Yale Press has cheerfully and effectively cut through much of the underbrush of my writing. The remaining weeds I insisted were flowers. And finally to the three to whom I have dedicated my book and whose contributions lie too deep for words, I can only claim that you put me up to it, and now will, I hope, put up with it.

M.M., Jr.

Cambridge, Massachusetts
May 1972

Contents

Introduction

Kings are everywhere in Shakespeare: from Scotland to Rome to Antioch, from the days of Priam and Caesar to those of Henry VIII, in every condition, in every degree of wisdom and power. Kingship is a major thematic element in half of the plays. From the beginning of his career, with the three parts of *Henry VI*, to the end, with *Henry VIII*, Shakespeare returned time after time to write about kings, kingship, and the problems of rulership in general. Six of the eight major tragedies written throughout his career incorporate questions of who rules and how as an essential part of the tragic development. And this emphasis on kingship serves not merely as a background for the action or as an embodiment of the exalted state from which the hero falls and against which his fall can be measured, as in much medieval tragedy, but, in many of the plays, as what Eliot called an objective correlative for the central imaginative issues and forces Shakespeare was dealing with.

The reasons for this preoccupation with kings are many, and in a short essay like this, one cannot stop to explore them in detail. In an age of kings, and especially in an age of political and social revaluation of the traditional role of kings, it is not surprising that a writer for the public theater should have turned his attention to one of the most important intellectual and political questions of the day. Likewise, in a culture like that of Elizabeth's reign, when the Tudor propaganda machine was in high gear, with many of the most popular books being histories of England's kings, with Machiavelli's startling views on rulers and ruling circulating widely in manuscript,[1] bowdlerized translation, and hearsay, with *A Mirror for Magistrates* offering its solemn warnings in four editions from 1559 through 1587 (each larger than the one before), with Spenser writing and presenting long sections of a

1. See Felix Raab, *The English Face of Machiavelli* (London: Routledge & Kegan Paul, 1964), pp. 30–76.

huge epic to the virgin Queen—in such a culture,[2] Shakespeare's preoccupation with kingship seems reasonable, almost inescapable. Furthermore, the history of the English theater before Shakespeare is full of plays dealing with kings and kingship, from the morality tradition to the chronicle tradition. Shakespeare was influenced by the tradition he was reshaping.

In the general uncertainty of our knowledge, however, one aspect of kingship stands out as probably the most significant factor in drawing Shakespeare back to kings even when they were the essentially fictional ones of Denmark, France, Troy, early Britain, Bohemia, and Naples. For kings could have a value for a dramatist more important than simply supplying him with plots or lending the splendor of high office to his play. They could be seen, and in the real world were seen, as complex "fictions" made of two different entities or functions. One part was the public function, the ruler, who was the center of the political structure; the other was the private man, who was no different from his fellows. This "twinned" conception of kingship—royal "gemination" as its historian calls it[3]—had its roots, of course, in the more general split in Western thought between the public and private aspects of man. But it stresses two characteristics of kings that are naturally appealing to a dramatist.

The first is the simple fact that as leader of his people a king occupies a position that makes his experience uniquely important, exemplary, and symbolic, and therefore immediately attractive to the artist, who is a creator of symbols. A complex conception of kingship is, therefore, an ideal vehicle for conveying and exploring complex conceptions of other people and values. The other appealing aspect of twinned kingship is the drama automatically implicit in a twinned but single creature. This use neither supposes that the king is really two different functions nor claims that he is in fact unified. It stresses the tense middle ground bound to exist between the two functions and marks this middle position as the "reality" of kingship.

2. This context, and much more, has been fully documented by E. M. W. Tillyard, *Shakespeare's History Plays* (London: Chatto & Windus, 1944), pp. 3–126.

3. Ernst Kantorowicz, *The King's Two Bodies* (Princeton: Princeton University Press, 1957), p. 24.

During Queen Elizabeth's reign, and while Shakespeare was growing up, there emerged in England a specific formulation of the idea of the king as a twinned entity called "the King's Two Bodies." Of course this was by no means the beginning of complex ideas of kingship, which in effect go back to the earliest kings. As far as Europe is concerned, ever since the last Merovingian king was deposed by Pope Zacharias in 751 intellectual circles had been constantly aflame with debate over the powers and status of kings. And this debate was widened, heated, and complicated even further in 1245 when Innocent IV avoided deposing King Sancho II of Portugal but instead publicly and officially separated the royal powers, giving the effective power, or *administratio*, to Sancho's brother, leaving Sancho himself merely the *dignitas*, or trappings of the kingship. Splits like the common medieval one between the *potestas* and the *nomen* of the king, with terms and concepts like *dignitas, ministerium, inutilis, idoneus* floating loosely between them, have a long and complicated history. But by the sixteenth century the debate had become sophisticated to the point where, as Edward Peters puts it, "such new fictions as that of the body politic, the mystical body of the realm, and the king's two bodies [encouraged] the official belief that the king could do no wrong because the suprapersonal perfection of the body politic wiped away the imperfections of the individual ruler." [4] But *official* is, of course, the key word in that assessment, for both history and literature show that such a solid belief in the perfection and sanctity of the king was by no means universal. Unlike constitutional ideals, the dramatic facts—on the stage throughout the period, and on what Marvell calls "the tragic scaffold" for "the royal actor" in 1649—the dramatic facts were quite different and immensely more interesting. As a way into these dramatic, theatrical struggles as Shakespeare saw them, it will be helpful to consider briefly this Elizabethan doctrine of the king's two bodies.

4. Edward Peters, *The Shadow King*: Rex Inutilis *in Medieval Law and Literature, 751–1327* (New Haven: Yale University Press, 1970), pp. 28–29. Though dealing with an earlier period, Mr. Peters raises many fascinating questions about the complexities surrounding kings in any period, as does William A. Chaney in a chapter entitled "Sacral Kingship in Anglo-Saxon Law" in his book *The Cult of Kingship in Anglo-Saxon England* (Manchester: Manchester University Press, 1970).

In Edmund Plowden's law *Reports*, collected and written under Queen Elizabeth, there is a famous case of 1562 concerning the disposition of lands claimed by the Crown. In supporting the Crown's claim, Elizabeth's lawyers argued:

> The King has in him two Bodies, viz., a Body natural, and a Body Politic. His Body natural . . . is a Body mortal, subject to all infirmities that come by Nature or Accident. . . . But his Body politic is a Body that cannot be seen or handled, consisting of Policy and Government, and constituted for the Direction of the People . . . and this Body is utterly void of . . . natural Defects and Imbecilities, which the Body natural is subject to.[5]

Therefore,

> what the King does in his Body politic, cannot be invalidated or frustrated by any Disability in his natural Body.[6]

In short, the Crown still owned the lands in question even though Edward had leased them while a minor. This formulation obviously appealed to the lawyers and they went on in their theological style to explain the relation between the two kingly bodies.

> The Body politic includes the Body natural, but the Body natural is the lesser. . . . So that [the King] has a Body natural adorned and invested with the Estate and Dignity royal, and he has not a Body natural distinct and divided by itself . . . but a Body natural and a Body politic together indivisible.[7]

Some sentences later, they "clarified" the relation.

> His Body politic, which is annexed to his Body natural, takes away the Imbecility of his Body natural, and draws the Body natural, which is lesser . . . to itself which is the greater, *quia magis dignum trahit ad se minus dignum.*[8]

5. Edmund Plowden, *Commentaries or Reports,* 212a (quoted by Kantorowicz, *Two Bodies,* p. 7).
6. Ibid.
7. Ibid., 238 (Kantorowicz, p. 9).
8. Ibid., 213a (Kantorowicz, pp. 9–10).

To put it in the language of another case in the preceding year, "the Body politic wipes away every Imperfection of the other Body." [9] So thorough, in fact, was the dominance of the body politic according to this doctrine that it persisted through all natural changes, including death. Justice Southcote ruled, for example,

> as to this [natural] Body the King never dies, and his natural Death is not called in our law . . . the Death of the King, but the Demise of the King, not signifying by the Word (*Demise*) that the Body politic of the King is dead, but that there is a Separation of the two Bodies, and that the Body politic . . . is transferred . . . to another Body natural.[10]

Statements of this sort might be multiplied from Plowden, Coke, and Blackstone,[11] but the main outlines would come no clearer. The precise status of conceptions of this kind in the minds of men long dead can never be evaluated accurately, and very possibly the idea of the king's two bodies was taken with varying degrees of seriousness by the lawyers themselves, not to mention the spectators or the litigants, who always seemed to lose the judgment when the Crown's defense invoked this splendid fiction. Nevertheless, the doctrine became the official English way of dealing with the king in certain situations. In case after case in which the Crown had an interest, the concept was invoked, usually to assert the king's special power, though on at least one occasion to assert his obligation: it was ruled that he must continue to pay as king the servants he had hired as a private individual before coronation, because his body natural continued to need attention in his new kingly ways.[12]

Whatever its oddities to a modern eye, the view that the king is both a fallible mortal *and* an immortal, hereditary, and perfect ruler was widely available and popular by the time that Shakespeare wrote. From legal textbooks and dictionaries, quoted by

9. Ibid., 238 (Kantorowicz, p. 11).

10. Ibid., 233a (Kantorowicz, p. 13).

11. Sir Edward Coke, *Les Reports de Edward Coke* (London: Wight, 1600–59); Sir William Blackstone, *Commentaries on the Laws of England* (Oxford: Clarendon Press, 1765–69).

12. Plowden, *Reports*, 455a (Kantorowicz, p. 14).

Coke and Bacon, it quickly penetrated, as Ernst Kantorowicz
points out, "into political and popular parlance and its verbal
formulations were repeated over and over again." [13] The pop-
ularization of the idea was no doubt accelerated by its analogies in
religious doctrine. Kantorowicz, in his careful study of its origins,
concludes that it is fundamentally different from classical parallels
such as Aristotle's distinction between friends of the prince and
friends of the princedom, or Alexander's between friends of
Alexander and friends of the king.[14] Augustus did get himself
in the position of being both the performer and the receiver of
sacrifices, but this too lacks the peculiar English Tudor metaphor
of *bodies.* The corporeal emphasis appears to stem directly and
only from early Christianity, from the two bodies of Jesus Christ.
In fact, Kantorowicz amusingly reviews the ways in which the
legal doctrine of the king's two bodies was subjected to the same
interpretations that centuries earlier had led to Athanasianism,
Arianism, Nestorianism, Sabellianism, and Monophysitism.[15] The
religious extension of the idea to tomb art is well known. In
both England and France numerous tomb sculptures survive which
show the dead man in all his robes of earthly state lying on or
praying before a casket containing another marble figure of his
decayed and naked corpse.

In the Middle Ages, the need to clarify what happened to a
state when its ruler died lent political and legal urgency to the
developing conception of twinned kingship. Throughout this
period of history, the problem of succession had remained difficult.
One solution—to regard any interregnum as a period during which
only Christ officially ruled—ceased being satisfactory when popes
like Innocent III and Innocent IV claimed the rulerless lands in
their capacity as Christ's Vicar. Hence, it became imperative to
make a distinction between the dead ruler and the immortal state,
to find quickly a new body natural for the body politic to rest on,
and to claim that the body politic was still alive in the meantime.

In England, three factors appear to have hastened the peculiarly corporeal formulation of the ruler's double status. First was

13. Kantorowicz, *Two Bodies,* p. 405.
14. Ibid., pp. 496–506.
15. Ibid., pp. 16–18.

the simple fact of Parliament. While France was heading steadily toward absolutism, Parliament in England was asserting its claim to a role in government. Although it did not officially question its status as a body called and dissolved by the king until the Civil War, long before it had made its presence and will felt in a way that prohibited mistaking the king for the whole government. Probably even more important was the growth of the legal fiction of the corporation sole, the one man corporation. As F. W. Maitland has shown,[16] this developed first in decisions concerning bishops, abbots, and parsons as they acquired and held lands for their churches. The working thesis of corporation sole provided more than normal stability, and such stability was clearly a prime concern of the churches and their lawyers. Kantorowicz suggests that in the sixteenth century, when the Continent was tending to see the State as a fictitious person—"which was not only above its members, but also divorced from them"[17]—England, in contrast, assigned to the king what had been developed by the Church lawyers for clerics, compressing into the doctrine of two bodies united in one being the faceless permanence of an institution and the character of a man.

A third factor that lent support to the developing double conception of kingship appears to have been the increasing movement of royalists toward the theory of divine right. While Parliament could see in the king's two bodies proof of its essential participation in the government as part of the body politic, the kings themselves could see in the conception an assertion of their godlike infallibility, for the perfect body politic wiped away all mortal imperfections and limitations of the body natural. The comparison of the king's double nature with Christ's was flattering and useful.

Most of the legal uses of the king's two bodies occurred, as I have already suggested, when the established king sought to assert his claim to some ambiguous right. In the time of the Civil War, however, when the greater power, the army, wanted to establish

16. F. W. Maitland, "The Corporation Sole," in *Selected Essays* (Cambridge: Cambridge University Press, 1936), pp. 73–103.
17. Kantorowicz, *Two Bodies*, p. 382.

its legitimacy, the tradition of the two bodies was used to limit rather than to assert King Charles's powers. Whether or not the Puritans intended on any given occasion to evoke the specific legal doctrine, they continually exploited the double view of kingship that the legal doctrine requires. The Puritan ballad of the 1640s that ran

> 'Tis to preserve his majesty
> That we against him fight[18]

only exaggerated slightly Parliament's officially admitted purpose of raising armies in 1642 against the king "for the safety of his majesty's person, of kingdom, and Parliament." [19] It would be hard to separate what is simple deceit and self-deception here (Parliament having been carefully pruned by this time of all the king's supporters) from what is or may be an appeal to the doctrine of the king's two bodies. In the Declaration of the Lords and Commons of May 27 of the same year, however, the situation is clearer.

> If judgments should be given by [the king's courts and ministers] against the king's will and personal command, yet are they the king's judgments. The high court of parliament is . . . likewise a council to provide for the necessities, prevent the imminent dangers, and . . . to declare the king's pleasure in those things requisite thereto.[20]

If nothing else, this proved that two could play at twinning. If the Tudors and Stuarts could use the two bodies to connect their kingship with Christ—a "genuine Royal Christology" Kantorowicz calls it[21]—and to increase their means of obtaining and conserving power, Parliament could use it in turn as a hedge against that power, as a way of legitimizing naked military force.

18. Quoted by Ethyn Kirby, *William Prynne* (Cambridge, Mass.: Harvard University Press, 1931), p. 60.
19. "The Militia Ordinance, 1642," in *Sources of English Constitutional History,* ed. Carl Stephenson and F. Q. Marcham (New York: Harper & Row, 1937), p. 486.
20. *Sources of English Constitutional History,* p. 488.
21. Kantorowicz, *Two Bodies,* p. 16.

This fact was recognized and stated in a poem supposedly written by Charles I along with *Eikon Basilike.*

> With my own power my majesty they wound,
> In the King's name the king himself uncrowned.[22]

At his trial the king challenged the court's authority, saying, "No earthly power can call me, who am your king, in question as a delinquent . . . , no learned lawyer will affirm that an impeachment can lie against the king . . . [for] one of their maxims is that the king can do no wrong." [23] Charles hoped to invoke the full power of the long tradition of the king as a reality more than human. The parliamentary court, however, simply skirted the issue. Making use of the distinction that underlies the legal doctrine of the two bodies, it found the king guilty as "Charles Stuart . . . a tyrant, traitor, murderer, and public enemy," [24] and proceeded to cut the head from his natural body. Only later, as Parliament, did essentially the same men kill the king in his body politic with the formal Act Abolishing Kingship.

In a passage which Kantorowicz overlooks, but which Shakespeare must have read, Holinshed reports in his history of Richard II that "parliament [was] called by the Duke of Lancaster, using the name of King Richard in the writs." [25] Thus, like Charles I, Richard II was officially destroyed in his own name, by his own power. Deceit this no doubt was, but deceit of a kind invited by conceptions like the twinned nature of the king and by the power of such conceptions on men's imaginations. Paradox it certainly was. For the rebel who had overwhelmed Richard deliberately appeared to submit to the traditional laws and ceremonies in calling Parliament to judge him. But the rebel is still slave to what he rebels against, even after his victory, and hence simply murdering Richard and taking his throne was neither sufficient nor even possible for Bolingbroke. He was to be made king because he led an overwhelming power, but it is proof of the claim on

22. Ibid., p. 41. This was almost certainly not written by Charles himself, however.
23. *Sources of English Constitutional History*, p. 517.
24. Ibid., p. 519.
25. *Holinshed's Chronicles*, 2 vols. (London: J. Johnson, 1807–08), 2:859.

men's minds of ideals of order, legitimacy, and tradition, and of the power of certain patent fictions that he felt he had to proceed as if he had not just shattered these ideals and these fictions. The ceremonies, deceitful as they must have been, were necessary if Bolingbroke was to be king in body politic as well as in body natural.

Though there is considerable circumstantial evidence that Shakespeare was personally familiar with the doctrine of the two bodies in its legalist form,[26] it is not to my purpose in this essay to claim that he was. Kantorowicz says all that needs to be said on the point, and says it well: "The poet's vision of the twin nature of a king is not dependent on constitutional support, since such a vision would arise very naturally from a purely human stratum. . . . [The] image of the twinned nature of a king, or even of man in general, was most genuinely Shakespeare's own and proper vision." [27]

I have dwelt on the legal doctrine for two reasons. First, it establishes that awareness of a twinned nature in kings was widespread during Shakespeare's lifetime. However much we allow to monolithic doctrines like the Tudor myth, we must not imagine that such official thinking resolved all doubts about the status of the ruler. The kinds of concern and the views of human experience and institutions that were precariously reconciled in the legal doctrine were familiar to Shakespeare from other areas of thought and became, as I hope to show in detail, one of the major structural resources in his plays.

26. It was noted long ago that the gravediggers' speeches in *Hamlet* bear a close resemblance to the Tudor lawyers' arguments in the case of *Hales* v. *Petit*. (The first reference to this appears to be a note by J. Hawkins in Johnson's revised edition of 1771.) This case is one that Plowden uses to clarify the idea of the king's two bodies. Kantorowicz (*Two Bodies*, pp. 24–26) points to the last line of the play *Woodstock* ("I have plodded in Plowden and can find no law") as a specific place in which Shakespeare might have encountered Plowden.

27. *Two Bodies*, p. 25. This view was not only Shakespeare's: Spenser's famous letter to Raleigh about his *Faerie Queene* describes Elizabeth as bearing "two persons, the one of a most royall queene or empresse, the other of a most vertuous and beautifull lady."

A further reason for pausing to look briefly at the doctrine of the two bodies involves the central questions of Shakespeare's dramatic technique that I mean to explore. What emerges from a study of the legal fiction is a sense not of resolution and order but of constant tension and conflict. The fiction of the king's two bodies appears less a stable element of social order than a momentary stay against political and intellectual confusion. Viewed from behind, the ordered surface of disparate functions harmoniously united turns out to be a conceptual mask covering a confused tension of opposed and isolated interests. In simple terms we are here facing the difference between doctrine and fact, between theory and history—differences that occupied Shakespeare's imagination throughout his career. As our glance at the depositions of Richard II and Charles I has made clear, the settled, creative subordination of body natural to body politic, by which the former is cleansed and the latter made real, did not hold up in practice. In fact, Kantorowicz's thorough study unwittingly, I think, establishes that the idea of the two bodies tends to become most visible and clear when it is most fiercely threatened by conflicting interests.

What happened in history in 1649 is not finally much different from what had often happened in Shakespeare's plays fifty years earlier: the breakdown of the complex unity of idea in which the king is both perfect eternal ruler and real sympathetic man. The aspect of kingship that captured Shakespeare's imagination most was precisely this breakdown, and the king killing that resulted from it. In the history plays, and in many of the tragedies, too, killing the king is the central action, the touchstone, that tests the reality of all the other acts and the characters. The chapters that follow will undertake to study in some detail what might be called the imaginative structure of killing the king, the environment or pattern in which the action is placed and from which it takes its special significance. As the two bodies of the king split apart in open war, opposing conceptions of kingship emerge and polarize, gathering around them other basic oppositions and conceptions of both a political and psychic nature. Through plot, character, and poetry, these crystallized views of kingship then develop into what can only be called competing visions of the nature of all action and indeed of all life.

Western drama opened with defiance of the king. When Prometheus challenged Zeus and when Clytemnestra struck down Agamemnon, they set a pattern that, despite temporary resolutions, has continued through much of the history of drama. When Tamburlaine strode over the stage, marking a renaissance in the English theater his path was strewn with dead kings. Although Shakespeare's early Henry VI plays tell the complicated, detailed story of one regicide, it is not until *Richard II* that killing the king begins to acquire in Shakespearean drama the central, symbolic function it had in *Agamemnon* two thousand years before. In *Richard II, Julius Caesar, Hamlet, King Lear,* and *Macbeth,* Shakespeare makes the attack on the ruler the central action of the play. (In innumerable others as well—some comedies included—metaphoric extensions of king killing play decisive roles.)

I have chosen three of these plays for their representiveness, their variety, and their range: *Richard II, Hamlet,* and *Macbeth.* To follow the action of killing the king from *Richard II* to *Macbeth* is to watch the action become increasingly a symbolic act of drama, almost *the* dramatic act. Progressively, national politics, social consequences, personal experience, psychic tension, religious dimensions, mythic structures, and metaphysical implications are examined until, in *Macbeth,* where all of these are present, the killings of Duncan and Macbeth contain almost the full meaning of action in a tragic world.

Plays before *Richard II,* namely 3 *Henry VI* and *Richard III,* do not develop the clear, symbolic confrontation that makes killing the king such an important action later. In the former, the death of Henry VI is almost lost in a clutter of schemes, plots, and counter plots. In *Richard III,* the focus is so completely on the protean villainy of Richard that none of his opponents is allowed more than momentary dramatic development, least of all the other kings, Edward IV, Edward V, and Henry VII. I do not include *Julius Caesar* for two reasons: first, Caesar is not a king; and second, the play, like other Roman plays, deals with a thoroughly political climate in which all characters are qualified by irony almost from the start and every ideal is immediately tested in the fire of actual events. The plays considered here all have a common structure of an old, lyric, "green" world of a glorious past being challenged by a new, dramatic, political world of the ambiguous present, and this is lacking in *Julius Caesar*. It is as if an ideal, even religious, dimension of politics disappeared when Shakespeare left kings for caesars and emperors.

King Lear is plainly not about killing the king. It may be the archetypal story of the death of a king, but it does not dramatize the same issues. The structure of regicide is to a large extent replaced with a complex, mythically enriched structure of something resembling suicide, giving the play a very different shape and color. In his chapter on "Killing the King," John Danby sees *King Lear* as exemplifying a type of action that many of the earlier plays stumble toward. Killing the king is clearly for him, however, a different action from the regicide I intend to consider.[28] Furthermore, all four of the particular aspects of regicide that he asserts have their genesis in *King Lear* can in fact be found fully developed in *Richard II*, of which he makes no mention.[29]

But Mr. Danby has at least put a finger on the right spot, even if it is the wrong finger. Killing the king *is* a central fact of the tragic—and historic—world in Shakespeare, but it must not be simplified or sentimentalized into a struggle between the good man and the bad world, between the helpless poet and the evil politicians.[30] All of these simplifications are hinted at in the plays, but none of them are allowed to stand unqualified. Killing the king is a central fact because it offers a rich image of conflict and change *without*, for example, labeling the old good or the new bad. Indeed, regicide served Shakespeare so well because of the inescapable complexity of the act, its unavoidable political, religious, social, personal, and metaphysical reverberations. Reg-

28. John Danby, *Shakespeare's Doctrine of Nature* (London: Faber and Faber, 1948), pp. 141–67. Included among his king killing plays, with no explanation, are *Troilus and Cressida* and *Othello*.

29. Mr. Danby claims that *King Lear* is the first king killing play in which the death of the king does not open the action (he excepts *Henry VI* but not *Richard II*), in which the king is not "marginal to the main concerns," in which the "rightful king" is transferred "from the wings into the center of the stage," and in which the slain king is not a figure of "putative goodness—model Kings like Caesar [*sic*] or Hamlet's father or Duncan" (p. 165). Obviously *Richard II* satisfies all four criteria.

30. These are Mr. Danby's terms in *Shakespeare's Doctrine*, pp. 209–24.

icide is historically an act of painful ambiguity worthy of Shake-speare's infinite variety. And always, in his plays, both sides, old king and new king, speak to something real, alive, fascinating in the world and in human nature. Criticism must at least attempt to respect this vital variety.

This Royal Throne Unkinged

Richard II tells the very simple story of the deposition and death of the last Angevin king. The first act sets the situation as the king exiles his cousin, Bolingbroke, because of a mysterious dispute relating to the murder of their famous uncle, Thomas of Woodstock; the first scene of the next act supplies the motive for Bolingbroke's return, when Richard seizes his inheritance. The rest of the play shows Bolingbroke rising and Richard falling until the deposed king is murdered at Pomfret Castle.

Many of Shakespeare's plays tell of the death of kings, some of two or more deaths in one play,[1] but no other play deals so thoroughly and exclusively with the subject—politically conceived. There is hardly a scene that does not cast its political weight directly on Richard's shoulders; not a single character in the play remains isolated from the central political action. Nor are there the many probing soliloquies and supernatural elements that in *Hamlet* and *Macbeth,* for example, expand the central action of killing the king to a general philosophic and intensely metaphoric concern. In its fundamental outlines, therefore, *Richard II* is above all a play about political struggle.

To say only this, however, is to leave out what is most interesting in the play: the background of images in front of which, and often in terms of which, the conflict is waged. This is what in the Introduction I have called the structure for king killing, the imaginative setting in which the action occurs. To this setting I now turn.

Gaunt's deathbed eulogy of England, the royal throne of kings, has always stood out from the rest of the play—partly because it is a remarkable piece of writing, and partly because it is

---

1. Both *Hamlet* and *Macbeth* are about double king killings. Three kings die in *Richard III.*

carefully set in a context calculated to give it maximum resonance.[2] Richard, fresh from having stopped the combat between Boling- broke and Mowbray, receives the news that Gaunt is dying. As he leaves the stage with the brutal comment "Pray God we may make haste and come too late!" (i.iv.64), he and his companions are replaced by representatives of a different world: "*Enter* John of Gaunt *sick, with the* Duke of York." Gaunt asks:

> Will the king come that I may breathe my last
> In wholesome counsel to his unstaid youth?
>
> . . . .
>
> O, but they say the tongues of dying men
> Inforce attention like deep harmony.
>
> [ii.i.1–6]

Gone here are Richard's confident jests and nasty ridicule, and in their place is a helpless question followed by a different kind of confidence, the quiet confidence of age that has seen much. Though Gaunt is physically weak and politically helpless, he feels himself filled with the spiritual power of the "prophet new inspir'd" (31). He speaks a formal, frequently rhymed verse that we have heard before in the ceremonious accusations of treason. But there is a new note of rhetorical pattern, sententiousness, and adage-making. As Gaunt talks with York, he piles up pithy phrases as if he were seeking the precisely correct statement.

> Where words are scarce they are seldom spent in vain,
> For they breathe truth that breathe their words in pain.
> He that no more must say is listened more
> Than they whom youth and ease have taught to glose;
> More are men's ends mark'd than their lives before.
> The setting sun, and music at the close,

---

2. Modern audiences inevitably nod knowingly when Gaunt begins, and at least one Elizabethan must have noted the speech as something special since it was already anthologized by Robert Allot in 1600 in *England's Parnassus*. Significantly all seven of Allot's "beauties" from *Richard II* (three of them by Gaunt) come in the first half of the play and describe the older, simpler world that is shattered in the course of the action. (The passage in question is, however, wrongly attributed to Drayton.)

As the last taste of sweets, is sweetest last,
Writ in remembrance more than things long past.

[ii.i.7–14]

Or else he repeats proverbial wisdom, apparently willing it to be true through the cumulative power of the rhetoric.

His rash fierce blaze of riot cannot last.
For violent fires soon burn out themselves;
Small showers last long, but sudden storms are short;
He tires betimes that spurs too fast betimes;
With eager feeding food doth choke the feeder;
Light vanity, insatiate cormorant,
Consuming means, soon preys upon itself.

[ii.i.33–39]

Then suddenly in the next line the tone changes, and the rhetoric, though no less formal, breaks free of its didacticism into the rhythm of pure hymn.

This royal throne of kings, this scept'red isle,
This earth of majesty, this seat of Mars,
This other Eden, demi-paradise,
This fortress built by Nature for herself
Against infection and the hand of war,
This happy breed of men, this little world,
This precious stone set in the silver sea,
Which serves it in the office of a wall,
Or as a moat defensive to a house,
Against the envy of less happier lands;
This blessed plot, this earth, this realm, this England,
This nurse, this teeming womb of royal kings,
Fear'd by their breed, and famous by their birth,
Renowned for their deeds as far from home,
For Christian service and true chivalry,
As is the sepulchre in stubborn Jewry
Of the world's ransom, blessed Mary's Son.

[ii.i.40–56]

These lines place England in an optimistic but complex perspective. The heavy emphasis on royalty shows kingship to be the central issue of Gaunt's thoughts, as of the play in general. England's insularity is also stressed and this underscores both the precariousness of its natural and political situation and its symbolic status as a nation isolated from lesser breeds and destined to stand or fall alone. Two further aspects of Gaunt's words are especially important. One consists in the suprapolitical images which tie his thoughts about England's kings to a long-standing natural and religious tradition. From "Eden, demi-paradise" Gaunt's thought flows on uninterruptedly to "This fortress built by Nature for herself." Two traditions, one Christian, one possibly but not necessarily pagan, are here blended to mark England as the choice of both God and Nature. The Christian tradition is picked up ten lines later in "Christian service" and "blessed Mary's Son," while the close connection with Nature underlies the image of England as "This nurse, this teeming womb."

The idea that brings the whole speech to its climax is that of a Christian heroic service. It is, we notice, a service rugged, fierce, and energetic, based on a tough-minded conception of the world and of England's place in it. In Gaunt's view England is great because of its great strength both at home and abroad. "This other Eden" is first of all "this seat of Mars," a fortress; its insularity serves it as a "wall," a "moat" against assault. It is an order fiercely defended. Its fame is based not on its justice or its culture, as the modern audience might prefer, but on its deeds of strength, specifically in the Crusades—though these Crusades no doubt serve here as expressions of all three national virtues. So long as its kings are *feared,* the precious jewel is safe. Such is the England Gaunt praises, the kind of Christian service he remembers. And it is from this exalted state that England is falling.

> This land of such dear souls, this dear dear land,
> Dear for her reputation through the world,
> Is now leas'd out—I die pronouncing it—
> Like to a tenement or pelting farm.
> England, bound in with the triumphant sea,
> Whose rocky shore beats the envious siege
> Of wat'ry Neptune, is now bound in with shame,
> With inky blots and rotten parchment bonds;

> That England, that was wont to conquer others,
> Hath made a shameful conquest of itself.
>
> [ii.i.57–66]

These may be the words of a weak and dying man, but there is nothing weak or helpless in their conception of the world. Even Neptune is apprehended as an "envious" attacking force to be resisted. And now the rugged power, the spare frugality suggested even in Gaunt's name (73–83), is being destroyed from the inside by foolish waste and shameful bonds that commit England's revenues to favorites of the king. The harmony of discipline that made this other Eden both God's and Nature's chosen home is threatened by the discord created and allowed by a willful misled king. Richard is a king but no Mars renowned for his deeds; he is Christian but has failed in "service"—because he has also failed in strength.

What Gaunt says in this speech and the lost ideals he stands for inform the whole play. From its very first line he is "Old John of Gaunt, time-honoured Lancaster," who like an ancient landmark chiefly functions to measure change. Later in the first scene he loyally obeys his king in trying to calm the angry disputants, and in the second scene with the Duchess of Gloucester, he reveals the yet fiercer loyalty that has kept him obedient to Richard though he knows the king is responsible for his brother Woodstock's death. His manner of refusing the Duchess's demand that he avenge her reveals a firmly established hierarchy of loyalties and priorities, surviving from a world now all but gone. He rates the fact that Gloucester was his brother above the widow's "exclaims" (i.ii.2), but rates his duty to Richard higher still because of his supreme duty to God, whose deputy Richard is.

> Put we our quarrel to the will of heaven,
> Who, when they see the hours ripe on earth,
> Will rain hot vengeance on offenders' heads.
>
> [i.ii.6–8]

His words may appear at first evasive and inadequate to the situation in the light of the angry charges of treason in the preceding scene, in which all parties have invoked heavenly support.

But Gaunt's conservative faith cannot be rejected as merely "poignant impossibility" [3] unless we are prepared to ignore a good deal of evidence. The necessary criticism of his view is already implicit in the Duchess's comment "Call it not patience, Gaunt, it is despair" (1.ii.29), and Shakespeare provides no easy judgment between the two claims. Like the royal widows in 3 *Henry VI* and *Richard III*, she invokes images of the specific natural womb that bore both the murdered man and Gaunt (1.ii.22), while his thoughts tend toward God and the more general teeming womb that bears England's kings.

When Richard arrives to see Gaunt die, the old man is quick to warn him in clear terms of what is happening to England, though, in the king's presence, his style changes significantly. The prophetic rhetoric of his earlier hymn to the royal throne of kings takes second place to an ironic wit that seems to come, with Richard, from the preceding scene of jests against "high Herford" (1.iv.3). But the substance of his address is the same: "Thy deathbed is no lesser than thy land" (11.i.95). Apart from one indirect mention of his son's banishment (79–81), his thoughts are filled solely with the health of England and the potential greatness of both country and ruler. In this vein, he evokes his memories of Edward III and the Black Prince:

> O, spare me not, my brother Edward's son,
> For that I was his father Edward's son.
>
> [11.i.124–25]

And York evokes similar memories as soon as news of Gaunt's death is announced.

> I am the last of noble Edward's sons,
> Of whom thy father, Prince of Wales, was first.
> In war was never lion rag'd more fierce,
> In peace was never gentle lamb more mild,
> Than was that young and princely gentleman.
> His face thou hast, for even so look'd he,
> Accomplish'd with the number of thy hours;

3. Wilbur Sanders, *The Dramatist and the Received Idea* (Cambridge: Cambridge University Press, 1968), p. 193.

> But when he frown'd it was against the French,
> And not against his friends.
>
> [II.i.171–79]

Here is an image of the good prince that hovers in the back-ground of every scene. It is a picture of energy and also of order. It is an ideal of rigorous balance between opposites, not necessarily subtle but reliable and restrained. In this prince, as in imagined England-Eden, lamb and lion lie down together.

The view of kingship held by Gaunt and York, and, we discover later, by Carlisle, corresponds, in one way of understanding it, to the very order of the universe. As Tillyard, C. S. Lewis, and so many others have shown, kingship was simply another dimension of the general hierarchical order that prevailed in the Elizabethan world-picture.[4] York voices the pure doctrine when he warns Richard that rebellion in one area will cause trouble in others.

> Take Herford's rights away, and take from time
> His charters, and his customary rights;
> Let not to-morrow then ensue to-day:
> Be not thyself. For how art thou a king
> But by fair sequence and succession?
>
> [II.i.195–99]

Three vastly different areas of experience are here linked. Inheritance, time, and kingship are all presented as analogical.[5] As one critic has described this kind of thinking, "Everything was like everything else; beneath the diversity in degree there was a remarkable likeness in kind."[6] York exploits this view as a means

---

4. E. M. W. Tillyard, *The Elizabethan World Picture* (London: Chatto & Windus, 1943); and C. S. Lewis, *The Discarded Image* (Cambridge: Cambridge University Press, 1964). A wonderfully brief but penetrating survey—often overlooked—is that by Norman Holland, *The Shakespearean Imagination* (New York: Macmillan Co., 1964), pp. 1–49. I am using the term "world-picture" in the special sense defined by Tillyard; there were, of course, many Elizabethan world views.

5. Latent here also is a fourth area of experience, the deepest problems of personal identity: "be not thyself." I will return to such matters.

6. Sigurd Burckhardt, *Shakespearean Meanings* (Princeton: Princeton University Press, 1968), p. 59.

of ordering and imaginatively controlling the rapidly changing facts that confront him. Spotting Richard on the walls of Flint Castle, he says:

> Yet looks he like a king. Behold, his eye,
> As bright as is the eagle's, lightens forth
> Controlling majesty; alack, alack for woe
> That any harm should stain so fair a show!
>
> [III.iii.68–71]

The heavy use of simile and the word "show" may hint at an imaginable breakdown in the analogies by which the king can appropriately be signified as God on earth, or the eagle among birds, the lion among mammals, the diamond among stones, and so on. But the lines alert us also to the whole implicit structure of royal correspondences that run throughout the play and define one conception of kingship.

This structure of correspondences emphasizes primarily unity and power. On the highest level the king is seen as closely linked with God, as "God's substitute, / His deputy anointed in His sight" (I.ii.37–38):

> the figure of God's majesty,
> His captain, steward, deputy elect,
> Anointed, crowned, planted many years.
>
> [IV.i.125–27]

God's aid is invoked lest "in a Christian climate souls refin'd / Should show so heinous, black, obscene a deed" (IV.i.130–31) as killing his vicegerent. "Stirr'd up by God thus boldly for his king" (IV.i.133), Carlisle utters the famous prophecy of the disastrous effects for England if the divine and natural hierarchy is disturbed.

Richard himself of course relies on the connection between God and king throughout. He claims that "God for his Richard hath in heavenly pay / A glorious angel" (III.ii.60–61); he asks Northumberland to "show us the hand of God/That hath dismiss'd us from our stewardship" (III.iii.77–78); he asserts that his "master, God omnipotent" (85) will prepare armies of pestilence in his defense. In the deposition scene he explicitly calls upon God to pardon the oaths that had been broken in the transfer of power from old to new king. His frequent comparisons of himself to Christ in the hands of Pilate and Judas further enlarge the web of divine connections that in this play surrounds the idea of the king.[7] Even at the moment when the nature of Bolingbroke's demands is at last revealed, Northumberland continues to invoke the sanctity of the royal person: "The King of heaven forbid our lord the king / Should so with civil and uncivil arms / Be rush'd upon" (III.iii.101–03).

The imagery of relationship between God and king is paralleled on a less specifically Christian level by imagery of relationship between the king and Nature. The most obvious imagery of this sort, as many critics have pointed out, is the traditional comparison of sun and king which Richard frequently makes, calling himself "the searching eye of heaven" (III.ii.37), describing how thieves and robbers who thrive during the night "Stand bare . . . trembling at themselves" (46) when the "day"—both sun and king—dawns.[8] Other images implying sympathy between the political and natural worlds abound. Richard imagines a powerful conspiracy of the elements to help him in the face of danger (III.ii.4–26). He animates the earth, expressing sympathy for the pain she suffers from the hooves of rebels' horses. He calls upon the earth to oppose to Bolingbroke her spiders, toads, nettles, adders. He supposes that her very stones, like the dragon's teeth in the Jason story, will turn to "armed men" to protect his throne. When Bolingbroke says at their first encounter "be he the fire, I'll be the yielding water" (III.iii.58), the comparison sets the conflict of king and rebel in a context of hierarchic natural elements that comments tacitly on Bolingbroke's own soon-to-be-accomplished inversion of hierarchy in the human world.

When the Welsh captain alludes to withering bay trees and falling meteors as foreshadowing Richard's doom, his words take

---

7. All the characters are forever referring their claims to God ("God defend the right," etc.), and hardly an action is performed without reference to His will and power.

8. The Welsh Captain sees Richard's doom in terms of the setting sun (II.iv.21). Elsewhere Richard is described as "the blushing discontented sun" (III.iii.63), and "a mockery king of snow . . . before the sun of Bolingbroke" (IV.i.260–61); he asks of his image in the mirror, "Was this the face/That like the sun did make beholders wink?" (IV.i.283–84).

us again into that web of sympathies which secretly embrace the
anointed king. The Queen's striking description of her husband—
"Ah, thou, the model where old Troy did stand" (v.i.11)—looks in
a similar direction. Though it emphasizes his fallen state, it does
so in an image genealogical, architectural, geographical even, that
glorifies and magnifies his mysterious significance. The conception
of London as "New Troy" lies of course behind her conceit, but
into it seems to flow also some of the feelings that the Renaissance
had absorbed from Vergil about the ruined city beside the sea that
fathered Rome and thereby civilization.

In this particular play, which comes early in his career and
rather quickly on the heels of his earlier historical tetralogy, it
is not easy to exaggerate the role that Shakespeare's imagination
assigns to these and other standard fixtures in the lore of kingship.
Richard asserts his power, for example, by comparing himself to
the king of the beasts, "lions make leopards tame" (1.i.174), and
his Queen urges him on reminding him that "the lion dying
thrusteth forth his paw / And wounds the earth" (v.i.29–30).
Later he discovers that his horse Barbary has betrayed him by not
protesting against a new rider, the usurping Bolingbroke, and
exclaims: "'Would he not stumble? would he not fall down?'"
(v.v.87). But he catches himself: "Forgiveness, horse!" (90). The
episode is revealing. It tells us something about Richard, who
has obviously gained in self-knowledge, for while his questions
presuppose the sympathetic support of nature, his answer recog-
nizes that he has forfeited such support precisely by not behaving
like a king, or even like a man.

> Forgiveness, horse! why do I rail on thee,
> Since thou, created to be aw'd by man,
> Wast born to bear? I was not made a horse,
> And yet I bear a burthen like an ass,
> Spurr'd, gall'd and tir'd by jauncing Bolingbroke.
>
> [v.v.90–94]

Perhaps the passage also tells us something about Shakespeare.
"Forgiveness, horse!" is a phrase that today actors find themselves
inclined to muffle, cut, or throw away. Its appeal to an equine
moral sense touches modern risibilities. To the extent that the
effect was different for Shakespeare and his Elizabethan audience,

as we have reason to believe it was, it must have been made so by the seriousness with which the system of sympathetic forces joining natural, human, and divine could still be taken. At another level, the dogged loyalty of the groom who appears in Richard's cell for no other reason than "To look upon my sometimes master's face" (75) makes the same point. Even in prison, the king's face merits a pilgrimage.

Most important, however, of all the dimensions of ideal kingship is not the divinity that doth hedge it, but its capacity to maintain a stable, just, and energetic order through ordinary political acumen and force. Carlisle seconds Richard's faith in divine support but urges too that "the means that heaven yields must be imbrac'd" (III.ii.29). The brief lyric glimpse we get of Mowbray later in the play (IV.i) celebrates his having fought "Many a time . . . For Jesu Christ in glorious Christian field" (IV.i.92–93), only after which, "toil'd with works of war," he "retir'd himself / To Italy" to die (96–97). Similarly, in York's memories the Black Prince is "that young Mars of men" (II.iii.100). In his own image of himself, Richard was "not born to sue, but to command" (I.i.196); "the king's name" is "twenty thousand names" (III.ii.85); "Ten thousand bloody crowns of mothers' sons" (III.iii.96) must stain the land before his throne can be usurped. In short, to borrow a phrase from the Duchess of York, the efficient king who roots out traitors and resolves civil and familial strife is "A god on earth" (v.iii.134). When he is less than this it is because "The king is not himself, but basely led / By flatterers" (II.i.241–42), and the country must "shake off [its] slavish yoke, . . . And make high majesty look like itself" again (II.i.291–95). As we saw earlier, only in the king's own name can the king himself be uncrowned.

In all these forms, Shakespeare keeps the official lore of kingship before us throughout the play. It is not, of course, *all* that he keeps before us, for there are crosscurrents of irony and qualification on every page, which will be noticed in their proper place. All that needs to be said here is that though these crosscurrents qualify the system of references at which we have been looking, they do not cancel them out. In poetry, no strand of meaning ever wholly disappears however much it may be colored by other elements in the context. Hence, though the official lore I have just now summarized, the idea of a divine, natural, and human axis with the king its center, is often enough objected to in the play, and either undercut with ridicule or overlaid with disbelief, it is never entirely obliterated from our apprehension of the play's imaginative meaning. Though it fails to find again so clear a spokesman as the dying Gaunt, it survives him to become, in its turn, an ironic comment on a new kind of kingship. To put this matter more succinctly, all the images and actions of kingship we have traced, the network of correspondences and dynamic energies, establish a definition of kingship which, for want of a better term, we might call nostalgic. It is a definition filled with imaginative power, but embodied primarily in warriors either dead or dying. Like the Golden Age it seems most visible when it is moving away, into the past. This vision of kingship, focused most clearly in the figure of Gaunt, is also touched with an elegiac idealism that has encouraged critics to sentimentalize it. If we are to avoid following their example, we must now consider its character more closely.

It is frequently asserted that the essential expression of the "old order" of kingship in *Richard II* is ceremony: the ceremony we see broken by Richard in the third scene of the play, the ceremony we see dominating the deposition scene despite Boling-broke's impatience, the elaborate ceremony of style that Shakespeare gives the gardeners in their conversations with each other and with the Queen. Needless to say, the vision of kingship we have been examining has a major place for ceremony; indeed, it is based on the conception that all movement and order in the universe is ceremonially arranged. The pattern of "time's charters" in the succession from king to king is ceremonial, as is the whole view of the cosmos as hierarchical. Tillyard has shown in detail that the play is filled with ceremonial speech and action which reflect this cosmic order.[9] But this ceremonial way of life— Shakespeare's conception of medievalism, Tillyard asserts[10]—is easily abused and turned into a mere ritual, empty of meaning or power. Such abused, ritualistic ceremony is by no means the

9. Tillyard, *History Plays*, pp. 244–59.
10. Ibid.

central feature of the nostalgic definition of kingship. The image of the old order in this play is, as we have seen, much more a function of power and energy than of ceremonies. The heroes of the old order are fighting men—Mowbray, the Crusaders, Edward III, the Black Prince (than whom "never lion rag'd more fierce"). Richard, with his ceremonial sorrow and public self-dramatization, is not one of them. We might make a distinction between the fundamentally ceremonial view of life that Gaunt and the other old warriors hold which controls and guides their energies, and the blurring, wandering ceremonies that the other characters, Richard especially, use in scene after scene where action is replaced with rhetoric. Some lines from *Julius Caesar* are easily adapted to describe these latter ceremonies: like love, when kingship "begins to sicken and decay, / It useth an enforced ceremony" (iv.ii.20–21).

I take it that a major effect of the heavy accent on ritual and pageant in the opening scenes is not, as is sometimes argued, to anticipate Gaunt's elegiac portrait of a dying order, but to make us impatient with a cloying ceremony which we later discover is simply a disguise for anarchy. We feel angry and frustrated when Richard stops the action at Coventry because ritual was finally about to be, dissolved into the world of decision, where Gaunt's heroes live and die.[11] The ceremony of the deposition scene is organized by Bolingbroke to legitimize his power; it fails because Richard instigates his own ceremonies of disrobing (iv.i.202–19), giving up the crown (181–89), and regarding his face in the mirror (276–91). There is little indication that either Bolingbroke's or Richard's ceremonies have anything to do with Gaunt's conception of kingship. As we will see, Richard's ceremonies here serve other important dramatic purposes, but their clotted, inturned, brooding tone is inconceivable in Gaunt or Carlisle.

On the Welsh coast and at Flint Castle Richard insists on performing interminable enforced ceremonies while his supporters plead for decisive action. His self-pitying gestures of defeat seek frequently to evade the facts of his situation rather than to confront them or change them. Apart from the helpless Gaunt's

---

11. The splendid speech by Mowbray's son in 2 *Henry IV* (iv.i.113–29) describing this scene supports this reading of Richard's action.

elaborate farewell to his son (i.iii.275–93)—perhaps even this
is not truly an exception—there is very little respect for ceremonies
as such anywhere in the play.

In tracing the contours of the play's ideal of kingship, it is of
course important to distinguish formality of language from ceremonial action. This difference is obvious in Gaunt's ceremoniously
formal descriptions of energetic ruling. The real test of this distinction comes with the garden scene, surely the most formal
scene poetically and imaginatively in the play.[12] If any scene
summarizes Gaunt's nostalgic vision of the nature of kingship,
both in content and form, it is the parable of the active gardener
who keeps his garden in good order as diligently as if he were
king of it.

Three men, whom we have not seen before and who are, by
their dress, of a social class we have not considered before, enter
to a space designated as "this garden" (iii.iv.1) where the Queen
has taken refuge unseen. One of the three, the head Gardener,
immediately issues commands, using similes that connect the
garden tasks with political events and the general social situation
("like an executioner," "like unruly children" 30–33). His "man,"
one of the two helpers, replies but drops the symbolic language
to make the connection between garden and state explicit.

> Why should we, in the compass of a pale,
> Keep law and form and due proportion,
> Showing, as in a model, our firm estate,
> When our sea-walled garden, the whole land,
> Is full of weeds, her fairest flowers chok'd up,
> Her fruit-trees all unprun'd, her hedges ruin'd,
> Her knots disordered, and her wholesome herbs
> Swarming with caterpillars?
>
> [iii.iv.40–47]

12. The recognizable formal elements in this scene are numerous. Besides the traditional metaphor of the garden filled with weeds representing
the threatened state, there are here elements of pastoral, allusions to
Christ's parables, hints of the emblem tradition, echoes of Genesis, and
even a few traces of the fifteenth-century pageants. These are all discussed
by Peter Ure in the Arden edition of *Richard II*, pp. li–lvii.

The echo in "sea-walled garden" of Gaunt's picture of England fortressed against Neptune's "envious siege" recalls that speech and marks the helper's words as an essentially negative view of Gaunt's positive. As such the scene loses its symbolic cast, becoming a literal comment on the condition of England at the present time. Indeed, until the very end of the scene, the underlying image of the garden as state is treated literally, as the gardeners and the Queen talk openly of affairs of state.

The strength of this scene, as I see it, comes from the fact that Shakespeare here combines two opposed metaphors. The central metaphor takes the garden as state and the state as garden, but to this is added a metaphor of weighing.

Queen. Thou, old Adam's likeness set to dress this garden,
How dares thy harsh rude tongue sound this unpleasing news?
What Eve, what serpent, hath suggested thee
To make a second fall of cursed man?

. . . .

Gardener. Pardon me, madam, little joy have I
To breathe this news, yet what I say is true.
King Richard he is in the mighty hold
Of Bolingbroke. Their fortunes both are weigh'd;
In your lord's scale is nothing but himself,
And some few vanities that make him light.
But in the balance of great Bolingbroke,
Besides himself, are all the English peers,
And with that odds he weighs King Richard down.

[iii.iv.73–89]

On the surface these images are not easily reconciled and the second may appear to cut away from the first, new realism replacing old biblical pastoralism. This would be in one sense appropriate, of course, since the whole scene is about the breakdown in the well-ordered garden of England. But only in one sense. For the metaphor of the king's being weighed in Fortune's scales in no way disposes of the earlier metaphor of the king as gardener (a failed and therefore fallen gardener, like Adam). On the contrary, the weighing joins itself to the gardening and the gardening

to the weighing in much the same way that the "teeming womb,"
in Gaunt's earlier speech, joins itself to and is joined by the idea
of "renowned . . . deeds," to open a larger perspective on the
royal office. In each case, something beyond the king's control
(birth and fortune) combines with something that should be well
within it (deeds and good gardening), and in each case, too, a
willed use, good or bad, is made of the bounty that God and
nature provide.

The weighing image is appropriate and necessary to the garden
image because it insists on the kind of realistic concern that has
put "in the balance of great Bolingbroke . . . all the English
peers," leaving in Richard's balance only himself, "And some few
vanities that make him light." A romantic preference for a more
optimistic view of nature and government must not blind us to
this scene's uncompromising image of all life as a struggle to
shape nature for her own good, preserve order for the benefit of
all, and increase growth through decisive pruning. To say of this
scene, as some do, that the pressure of imagination has fallen off,
and that Shakespeare propounds traditional remedies which are
too feeble requires us to assume that Shakespeare intended the
scene to point "the pattern and moral of the play." [13] But if on
the contrary we see the scene as embodying a particular view of
the world, and especially of kingship, that is in process of being
replaced by a new view with Bolingbroke, a view even more
fiercely energetic, none of these criticisms apply. The formality of
the language will then be seen not as a reflection of a ceremonial
conception of kingship on Shakespeare's part, but rather as a
highly characteristic dramaturgical device for alerting his audience
to the presence of choric materials, the obvious tenor of which is
the need for more vigorous action and fewer ceremonies of sorrow
like those we have just watched Richard perform (III.ii and III.iii).

At the very end of the scene a stylistic shift of equal importance
occurs. The Queen, saddened to anger by the Gardener's news of

13. Tillyard, *History Plays*, p. 250. Tillyard argues that the "pattern"
is the constant weighing of Richard and Bolingbroke, that the "moral" is
the consequence of deposition. This is certainly an important aspect of
the garden scene, but the moral must also have something to do with
the dire effects of failing to prune the weeds in the kingdom, as well as the
seriousness of rebellion.

Richard, curses him, "Pray God, the plants thou graft'st may never grow" (101)—on which the Gardener sorrowfully comments to his helpers:

> Poor queen, so that thy state might be no worse,
> I would my skill were subject to thy curse.
> Here did she fall a tear; here in this place
> I'll set a bank of rue, sour herb of grace.
> Rue, even for ruth, here shortly shall be seen,
> In the remembrance of a weeping queen.
>
> [iii.iv.102–07]

This quiet end to a scene that has stressed ruthless energy in both the good gardener and the good ruler contrasts dramatically with the Gardener's earlier lines. At the same time the Queen's word "graft'st" introduces a milder quality into the political-horticultural equation which began with references to cutting off heads and rooting away weeds. After the long discursive middle of the scene the style of the poetry now turns back toward the rhetorical contrivance displayed in the opening lines.

> Go, bind thou up young dangling apricocks,
> Which like unruly children make their sire
> Stoop with oppression of their prodigal weight,
> Give some supportance to the bending twigs.
> Go thou, and like an executioner
> Cut off the heads of too fast growing sprays,
> That look too lofty in our commonwealth:
> All must be even in our government.
> You thus employed, I will go root away
> The noisome weeds which without profit suck
> The soil's fertility from wholesome flowers.
>
> [iii.iv.29–39]

But there are two main differences now. First there is a change from the comparative impersonality of the Gardener's directions to his assistants, to the highly personal compassionate tone of "Poor Queen . . . Here did she fall a tear"—which matches in small the play's larger alternations between scenes of public action and scenes (usually involving one or two lonely and bewildered figures) of private anguish. Second, the Gardener now creates a symbolism of his own in the rue planted for the Queen's sorrow. This is a point of some importance. The effort, care, and skill that in the middle of the scene were shown to be necessary for controlling the garden and the state are now applied by the Gardener to the creation of symbols, artifacts of the human imagination. This shift should draw our attention to both the strength and limitation of the Gardener's position. Its strength is that his skill is *not* subject to the Queen's curse, just as his garden can and must be cultivated, even though the larger sea-walled garden of state is full of weeds and caterpillars. Therefore, despite the fact that Richard's "Dear earth" will not arise and smite the rebellious oppressor as he hopes (III.ii), the Gardener's skill can still make plants grow in memory of the Queen's sorrow. The essential cooperation between nature and the king that is part of Gaunt's vision of kingship survives at least in the Gardener's skill. But the weakness of the Gardener's position is, of course, that his power survives *only* within the garden. The flowers he plants will honor the sorrowing Queen only through the power of the human imagination. Though his skill is not subject to the Queen's curse, it has no power over the political events that elicited the curse in the first place.[14]

After two scenes in which we see Richard confront and then yield to the facts of a new world, and after many lines of advice

14. E. W. Tayler, in *Nature and Art in Renaissance Literature* (New York: Columbia University Press, 1964), traces the Renaissance interest in the relationship between nature and art, arguing that in gardening treatises and literary criticism of the period "by a familiar migration of metaphor, what one does in the garden becomes analogous to what one does in writing poetry" (p. 17). We are here watching the Gardener create a "living poem" out of the bank of rue which will memorialize the Queen's grief. The Renaissance was fascinated by the split and interplay between manageable, permanent art that is unreal, and unruly, transient nature that is, however, real. The Gardener's shift in this scene from the realm of natural suffering and national politics beyond his control to the realm of the closed garden which is in his control might possibly be seen in these terms. What he cannot accomplish in the political world he will attempt in his special world; where power is lacking, art and imagination may succeed. Nature supplies the material, but the Gardener must do all the rest to establish the kind of correspondence between rue and the Queen's sorrow that Richard consistently assumes exists between the world and his emotions.

on how the political garden must be governed by rigorous pruning and shaping, we come upon a moment when before our eyes the power and vision are compelled to retire within—to a tiny garden, like that of Marvell's Fairfax at Appleton House, to a personal symbolism that can interpret "rue even for ruth," and to a world lost, like Eden, that now exists mainly "in the remembrance." As we shall see, this movement parallels the change in Richard's career and emerges, particularly in stage performance, as a beautiful but delicate oasis of harmonious correspondence in a world of "civil and uncivil" warring between kings. The gentle pensiveness and imaginative creativity of the Gardener in this quiet moment marks a shift in the play from the affairs of history to increased emphasis on Richard's personal experience as king. But the new note lasts only a moment, for the stern garden management recommended earlier in the scene reasserts itself promptly as Bolingbroke enters with the words, "Call forth Bagot" (iv.i.i).

In short, as I understand it, Shakespeare's purposes in this scene are more complex than is usually supposed. The scene, taken as a whole, is neither an illusory dream nor an ideal manqué leaving "a fragrance which will outlive the futilities of history." [15] The Gardener's directions to his helpers are quite the equal of Bolingbroke's for active efficiency. The withdrawal into symbol at the end of the scene is not a repudiation of what has gone before but rather a recognition of another dimension of experience. It is not "ceremonious" but actively imaginative, as vigorous in its own way as the Gardener's binding of young apricocks. Though formal in its dramatic technique, the scene openly opposes ceremony for its own sake. The pity it acknowledges is pity that Richard failed to trim and dress his garden, not that he broke the old ceremonies of traditional kingship. Gaunt's and the Gardener's ceremonies are those of action; too frequently Richard's are the enforced ceremonies of delay and self-indulgence.

If John of Gaunt is the center of a dying conception of energetic Christian rulership which drew its authority from God,

15. John Palmer, *Political Characters of Shakespeare* (London: Macmillan and Co., 1945), p. 168.

pruned the garden at home, and performed noble deeds abroad,
Bolingbroke is the center of an order of expedient realism that,
at least initially, draws its authority from self-interest and efficiency, begins pruning the garden of state for its own benefit as
well as for the national welfare, and has altogether pragmatic
reasons for any noble deeds to be performed abroad: to wash
Richard's blood from Bolingbroke's guilty hands (v.vi.50) and,
if we may trust the new king's hindsight from a later play, "to
busy giddy minds / With foreign quarrels" (*2 Henry IV*, iv.v.214–
15). Gaunt's nostalgic view was narrow, imperialistic, even cruel,
but it was clear, assertive, and comprehensive. About the new
order of expedient realism very little is clear. Gaunt's motives were
perhaps naive and anachronistic, but he and we knew what they
were—above all, he wanted order to prevail and the glory and
strength of England to increase through the power of her active
kings. Bolingbroke's motives are never so clear. He and all around
him are essentially ambiguous while being effectively irresistible
as a political force.

Our first view of the new order occurs in the scene in which
Gaunt outlines his feelings about the old one. Dramatically, this
is appropriate, since it juxtaposes the two outlooks that frame the
action of the play. After Richard has stormed off to Ireland,
Northumberland, Ross, and Willoughby stay behind to talk. The
confused mixture of righteous anger, subtle plotting, and assertions
of loyalty to the king's body politic perfectly catches the pervasive
ambiguity that typifies the new expedient realism. As the scene
progresses, there are increasing hints that what appears initially to
be spontaneous conversation between friends, moving naturally
from Gaunt's death to his son's survival, may rather be a careful
scheme by Northumberland. This never becomes certain, but the
possibility is indicated in Northumberland's smooth direction of
the conversation from initial praise for Richard and blame for
his flatterers ("The king is not himself, but basely led" ii.i.241)
to the "Reproach and dissolution" (258) hanging over him, to a
final, blunt "most degenerate king!" (262). At this, he takes
occasion to hint that help against disaster may yet become available—only "I dare not say" (271). Forty lines earlier he had urged
on an equally reluctant Ross who chose not to speak; now he has
Ross urging him in turn. This remarkable reversal may or may not

suggest manipulation, but it does dramatically portray a complexity—perhaps duplicity—of motive and behavior that is unimaginable in Gaunt. As we noted, Gaunt's reasons for refusing to attack Richard were elaborate (i.ii.1–8), but they were set forth in striking clarity to the Duchess of Gloucester. There was none of the hedging and backing that dominates this intrigue.

The implications of this self-regarding parley between the king's barons, in which the name of God is never used except as a speech-intensifier, are clear enough, especially so soon after Gaunt's elaborate eloquence about a God-centered politics. For the view dramatically opposed to this in the play is, of course, his "God's is the quarrel," with its assumption that a man's destiny is finally in hands not his own and that man himself is only a link in a chain of correspondences which he by no means controls. Whether the barons here are right, whether human affairs can be isolated from the rest of the universe, as Ross seems to assume when he assures Northumberland that his words will be as private as thoughts (276) and that "We three are but thyself" (275), is a question on which the whole play will comment.[16]

In any case, our sense of possible manipulation in this scene deepens when Northumberland announces that Bolingbroke has already set sail for England. The play's editors have noticed that this is logically impossible. To make it possible, Bolingbroke would have had to set out for England before he was disinherited. In the theater, on the other hand, the breach of logic is effective, perhaps on two grounds. Bolingbroke's return *should* follow speedily on his father's death and his own disinheritance, as this enables it to do. Moreover, the logical confusion enhances the impressions of disjunction and ambiguity which the new world is making on our minds. To these impressions, Northumberland's final words add a further touch.

> If then we shall shake off our slavish yoke,
> Imp out our drooping country's broken wing,

16. A parallel statement by Northumberland later in the play makes the same confident claim and proves just as ambiguous: "My guilt be on my head, and there an end" (v.i.69). This is clearly opposed by Carlisle's view that guilt goes on and on: "The blood of English shall manure the ground, / And future ages groan for this foul act" (iv.i.137–38).

> Redeem from broking pawn the blemish'd crown,
> Wipe off the dust that hides our sceptre's gilt,
> And make high majesty look like itself,
> Away with me in post to Ravenspurgh.
>
> [II.i.291–96]

The piling up of images recalls the structure of Gaunt's speeches and the lines express a similar concern with the health of the nation. But whereas Gaunt stated so definitely that God alone could restore the national health, here Northumberland urges his colleagues to take matters into their own hands. Corruption cut so deep in Gaunt's view that it lay beyond his power to cure it by life or death (II.i.68); here it is seen as mere "dust" to be wiped away. Northumberland's presumably unconscious pun on "guilt" may hint at the same shallowness of perception.

But these plotting barons *are* ambiguous. Their plotting is punctuated with phrases like "if justice had her right" (227), "speak thy mind" (230), "a royal prince" (239) referring to Bolingbroke, and "The king is not himself" (241), which seem to reflect honest desires to do openly what is right. Even if, as I think likely in the theater, we are tempted to interpret such phrases as merely the gilded masks behind which these conspirators hide their motives, Northumberland's argument will weigh heavily with us if we have been at all attentive to the words of Gaunt.

> Wars hath not wasted it, for warr'd he hath not,
> But basely yielded upon compromise
> That which his ancestors achiev'd with blows—
>
> [II.i.252–54]

Conspirators as these furtive barons definitely are, they seem in some ways to be closer to Gaunt's ideals of vigorous rulership than is Richard. But when we learn that Bolingbroke is delaying his invasion until "The first departing of the king for Ireland" (290), our sympathy may swing back to Richard. If Northumberland's rousing lines (291–96, quoted above) echo Gaunt's vision of a glorious England, the fact that they imply the death of Richard— the action we have seen absolutely rejected by Gaunt—marks them as entering a new complicated realm of politics. It is one of the ultimate ironies of the play that *all* Bolingbroke's supporters seem quite prepared for the deposition of Richard fully two acts before Bolingbroke himself—as far as we can tell—reaches this point. And yet the language of diplomacy—as one euphemistically calls it—seems never to change, and even Northumberland's "Redeem from broking pawn the blemish'd crown" stops just short of legal clarity, leaving hidden what will have to be done to bring this "redemption" about.

The new forces dramatized in this scene are embodied in Bolingbroke. They range from hints of opportunism and craft to glimpses of magnanimity, and from refreshing pragmatism to suspicious myopia. Their key characteristic, as has been pointed out, is ambiguity, a reluctance to define themselves. Many have traced the ambiguity of Bolingbroke's progress toward the throne. Some think he acts out a calculated plan, others see him in the grip of fate or divine will.[17] The truth of the matter is that Shakespeare simply does not give us a certain answer. Is this a careless omission on his part? Or is it an aspect of his characterization of Bolingbroke, a way of telling us how Bolingbroke sees himself? Evidently the latter, if we may judge from the words he regularly puts in Bolingbroke's mouth, which, like his acts, are susceptible of more than one interpretation. His farewell to the king, for instance, flatters explicitly, claiming to take comfort in a sharing:

> this must my comfort be,
> That sun that warms you here, shall shine on me,
> And those his golden beams to you here lent
> Shall point on me and gild my banishment.
>
> [1.iii.144–47]

But it is possible to read this in such a way that the word *shine* is felt to be an improvement on *warms,* and the word *lent* a poor substitute for *point on* and *gild* (besides the hint it may contain of the king's transience as king or as mortal man). Again, Bolingbroke ceremoniously insists that Berkeley call him by his title, Lancaster

17. The most notable example of the former view is that of Coleridge (*Coleridge's Shakespearean Criticism,* ed. T. M. Raysor, 2 vols. [Cambridge, Mass.: Harvard University Press, 1930], 2:188–89). Dover Wilson argues the latter view in his edition of *Richard II* (Cambridge: Cambridge University Press, 1939), pp. xix–xxii.

(ii.iii.68–75), yet supports Northumberland when York chides the latter for leaving off Richard's title (iii.iii.5–17).

Bolingbroke speaks with an admirable warmth of friendship to friends ("My heart this covenant makes, my hand thus seals it" ii.iii.50), but he never fails to remind his supporters that they will be rewarded in material ways as well.[18] Though he graciously sends to the Queen his "kind commends" (iii.i.38) and commands that she be "fairly . . . intreated" (37), he later has no qualms about separating her, despite her obvious helplessness, from Richard. When he sends Northumberland to Richard at Flint Castle to show his "stooping duty" (iii.iii.48), he musters his army at the same time so that "from this castle's tottered battlements / Our fair appointments may be well perus'd" (52–53). He will play the "yielding water" (58) to Richard's fire in the intellectual world of elemental hierarchies, but the ambiguous image does not exclude the possibility that in the real world of everyday experience, his "rain" (59) may put the king's fire out.[19] Though he and his men mercilessly cut down all the members of Aumerle's conspiracy, he nevertheless shows some mercy to old Carlisle, merely banishing him to "some secret place" (v.vi.25). His sparing of Aumerle's life, merciful in one way of looking at it, is perhaps fully as much a gesture of favoritism as Richard's unequal punishment of the two disputants at the start of the play (i.iii). He rejects the lyric imagination with which Gaunt bids him gild his exile (i.iii.294–303), yet greets Carlisle's description of Mowbray's life and death with words that suggest sympathy and admiration for the style of his former enemy: "Sweet peace conduct his sweet soul to the bosom / Of good old Abraham!" (iv.i.103–04).[20] He can defeat Richard without raising his arm, but is unable to control his son (v.iii.1–12). He assures York he has returned only to claim his deserved inheritance, but at the same time vows "to weed and pluck away" (ii.iii.166) Bushy and Bagot, whom he describes as caterpillars. He wishfully repeats "Have I no friends

18. Cf. ii.iii.49, ii.iii.60, v.vi.12.

19. The possible pun—"reign"—would add to the sense of confusion and hidden meanings.

20. Cf. Richard's abrupt response to news of Gaunt's death: "So much for that" (ii.i.155).

will rid me of this living fear?" (referring to the imprisoned king), and yet appears genuinely sorry at Richard's death. His comment at that moment, "I hate the murtherer, love him murthered" (v.vi.40), is as ambiguous as everything else about his action and speech: does he love Richard who is dead or does he love him because he is dead? What is presumably, though ambiguously, the moment when Bolingbroke's progress turns from the way of his inheritance to the way of the throne is masterfully handled by Shakespeare to accentuate just the mixture of deceit, ambiguity, and effective political power which I have been describing.

> *Richard.* Set on towards London, cousin, is it so?
> *Bolingbroke.* Yea, my good lord.
>
> [iii.iii.208–09]

Buried somewhere in that half line—three parts grace, one part rebellion—is the death of the idea of the king as God's anointed representative. God's is the quarrel no more.

After the original conspiracy scene (ii.i), Northumberland is used by Shakespeare to portray the negative side of the new realism. The negative side and the assured side; for there are few ambiguities in Northumberland, few hesitations, unformed or even half-formed motives to be left in a comforting obscurity. He it is who hounds Richard mercilessly to read a confession of his crimes in the deposition scene, and he it is who leaves off the title "King" when speaking of Richard (iii.iii.6). To York's protest at this omission, Northumberland answers, "only to be brief / Left I his title out" (iii.iii.10–11), a claim that would be more believable had he not recently answered Bolingbroke's brisk one-line question, "How far is it, my lord, to Berkeley now?" (ii.iii.1), with seventeen lines of flattery and gracious tribute (2–18). It is also he who answers Carlisle's soaring prophecy of what will happen to England if Richard is deposed with the brutal summary:

> Well have you argued, sir, and, for your pains,
> Of capital treason we arrest you here.
>
> [iv.i.150–51]

The contrast between the play's two views of kingship stands out at this point most dramatically. Carlisle's speech is fierce, strong, confident, and angry. He shares the sense that a whole scheme of things supports the king, and he threatens terrible consequences. Northumberland's answer is flat, but leaves no doubt as to where, in his opinion, lie the powers that count. As a later warrior once said, "How many divisions has the Pope?"

What is striking about Shakespeare's management of these two "new" men is that Bolingbroke's acts, though surrounded by ambiguities of motive, are marked by the same undeviating direction as Northumberland's words. In a sense, he quietly *performs* the brutality that Northumberland merely *speaks,* moving with an unswerving progression (which may equally be stratagem or simple opportunism) from his landing at Ravenspurgh to the throne. From the moment we first see him in the court of royal inquiry at Windsor, he is decisive, aggressive, even irresistible, though for a time Richard imagines otherwise.

Confronted in the Aumerle episode with a threat of immense complexity, Bolingbroke cuts through the almost ridiculous dilemma of a father pleading for his son's death with a refreshing balance, control, and compassion. He is forced, partly by his role as king and partly by his own self-interest, to some rather pompous rhetoric, as in:

> O heinous, strong, and bold conspiracy!
> O loyal father of a treacherous son!
> Thou sheer, immaculate and silver fountain,
> From whence this stream, through muddy passages,
> Hath held his current and defil'd himself,
> Thy overflow of good converts to bad.
>
> [v.iii.57–62]

But, in general, he displays a remarkable flexibility and sense of humor ("Our scene is alt'red from a serious thing" 77) that enables him to satisfy fairly well all three kneeling petitioners. It is essential to give Bolingbroke his due—as Shakespeare scrupulously does—so that his clash with Richard will be rich with complexity. And while emphasizing Bolingbroke's ambiguities of motive and protean flexibility of action, we must not overlook those occasional moments when he looks remarkably the way we might imagine a young Gaunt in the days of full power. One such moment:

> Thanks, gentle uncle. Come, lords, away,
> To fight with Glendor and his complices:
> A while to work, and after holiday.
>
> [III.i.42–44]

This sounds like the perfect blend of Hotspur's naive love of battle and Gaunt's vigorous order: fight today, holy day tomorrow. But, significantly, we do *not* see him fighting "Glendor" where we could cheer him on wholeheartedly. Rather, we see him with his own "complices" threatening his king, a most unholy day. Nevertheless, in the theater, the contrast between the Richard of act III and the Bolingbroke of the same act is always stunning and the latter's virtues—decisive strength and vigor—contrast radically with Richard's inturned wanderings.

Of course, the clearest example of Bolingbroke's admirable balance and grasp on reality occurs when he answers directly his father's advice on how to improve exile with cheerful thoughts.

> *Gaunt.* Suppose the singing birds musicians,
>   The grass whereon thou tread'st the presence strew'd,
>   The flowers fair ladies, and thy steps no more
>   Than a delightful measure or a dance;
>   For gnarling sorrow hath less power to bite
>   The man that mocks at it and sets it light.
> *Bolingbroke.* O, who can hold a fire in his hand
>   By thinking on the frosty Caucasus?
>   Or cloy the hungry edge of appetite
>   By bare imagination of a feast?
>   Or wallow naked in December snow
>   By thinking on fantastic summer's heat?
>   O no, the apprehension of the good
>   Gives but the greater feeling to the worse.
>
> [I.iii.288–301]

This passage has importance beyond its role in this scene, for later, when Richard will try what Gaunt here recommends, the special strength of Bolingbroke's view will appear. But when Bolingbroke totally disregards the role of the imagination (e.g., IV.i.292–93), we feel there is something missing in him that, in their different ways, both Gaunt and Richard have.

But whatever he lacks in imagination is balanced with a magnetic popular appeal. Support races to him as rapidly as it deserts Richard; his words become facts, his muttered thoughts become murder. In all this, Bolingbroke obviously provides the main skeletal framework of the play. On his forward movement, as later on Hal's in *1* and *2 Henry IV*, Shakespeare hangs all the qualifying episodes and experiences on which Bolingbroke's success is a comment and which comment on his success. In *Richard II*, most of these elements have to do with the failure and sufferings of the king.

In the two conceptions of kingship we have been defining, two kinds of power are opposed. Gaunt's cosmic order has been challenged by Bolingbroke's effective "management." Unyielding clarity has been replaced by effective ambiguity. This seat of Mars has been filled by Proteus. This is, however, less a description of the action of *Richard II* than of its ambience. In terms of the plot Bolingbroke clearly has, or soon comes to have, all the effective power, yet the stalking and killing of Richard takes place in a more complicated realm. For Gaunt, Richard's fall would have been the story of a royal throne unkinged; for Bolingbroke, it is simply the story of an inheritance seized and of a king abdicating or deposed. For the whole play, it is something different from either of these views, something unique and significant.

Holinshed, Shakespeare's major source, says comparatively little about Richard's personal qualities as he describes the events of his reign. But what he does say is interesting in its apparent concern to have things both ways, divided between praise and blame. For example, he describes the king as one "given to follow evill counsell, [who] used such inconvenient waies and meanes, through insolent misgovernance and youthfull outrage, though otherwise a right noble and woorthie prince." [21] One might assume that the "otherwise" refers to Richard's private, personal virtues, but in the next paragraph Holinshed calls Richard "prodigall, ambitious, and much given to the pleasure of the bodie," and describes England as rife "with abhominable adulterie, specially

21. *Holinshed's Chronicles*, 2:868. I have modernized the *u* and *v* of the original throughout.

in the king." [22] Later, having commented on the "fowle enormities wherewith his life was defamed," Holinshed adds his own opinion: "what I thinke: he was a prince the most unthankfully used of his subjects, of anyone of whom ye shall lightlie read [Holinshed here restates all Richard's faults] yet in no kings daies were the commons in greater wealth, if they could have perceived their happie state: neither in any other time were the nobles and gentlemen more cherished, nor churchmen lesse wronged. But such was their ingratitude towards their bountifull and loving sovereigne, that those whome he had cheeflie advanced, were readiest to controll him." [23]

Obviously the details here have little relevance to Shakespeare's Richard. The general charge of following evil counsel is picked up as a background element by Shakespeare, though we only hear about it: we *see* Richard making his own mistakes. The mention of adultery may be behind Bolingbroke's surprising charge against Bushy and Greene (III.i.11–15), but again this is something we hear about only; all the evidence indicates a loving and loyal relationship between king and queen. "Fowle enormities" might apply to either the ambiguous death of Woodstock or the confiscation of Gaunt's property, but we never see much ambition in Richard nor is he noticeably given to pleasures of the body. Likewise there is no indication in Shakespeare's play that the commons are well off (blank charters suggest otherwise), or that nobles are cherished (Gaunt is viciously abused before our eyes). Certainly Bolingbroke, who returns to "controll" Richard, is not one "cheeflie advanced" by the king.

The one element in Holinshed that does reappear in Shakespeare's play is the ambivalent attitude toward Richard.[24] Shakespeare as usual complicates what he finds in his source, combining sustained ambivalence with a dramatic shift in attitude. We are aware of Richard as both villain and suffering hero throughout,

22. Ibid.

23. Ibid., p. 869.

24. Michael Manheim, in "The Weak King History Play of the Early 1590's," *Renaissance Drama*, n.s. 2(1969) : 71–80, has formulated a class of plays which have as their common characteristic a movement from criticism of the king to sympathy. Obviously *Richard II* would belong to such a group.

but we also come increasingly to sympathize with him rather than with the rebels as the play progresses. The change is not surprising since it mirrors the way the public in general responds to leaders: "While these monarchs reign secure, we groan at their inadequacies; when they are at bay, suddenly they are martyrs." [25] Holinshed tells us Richard was a bad, misled king who was nonetheless bountiful and loving and unthankfully used; Shakespeare takes us beyond this contradiction toward understanding.

In act I, all our views of Richard leave us in doubt as to what we are to make of him. The ambiguity surrounding Woodstock's death in the opening scene is effective because it allows us, or rather obliges us, to watch his actions and reactions without any special knowledge. And our first view is by no means unfavorable. He pays tribute to Gaunt (who was a national hero in Elizabeth's time), and tries to check into the importance of the charges he must rule on.

> Tell me, moreover, hast thou sounded him,
> If he appeal the Duke on ancient malice,
> Or worthily as a good subject should
> On some known ground of treachery in him?
>   [I.i.8–11]

He speedily takes charge: "Then call them to our presence; face to face" (15). He seems properly shrewd when he says to Bolingbroke and Mowbray, "We thank you both, yet one but flatters us" (25), impressively fair when he assures Mowbray, "impartial are our eyes and ears" (115). There is nothing particularly damning in his failure to get the accusers to take up their gages—Bolingbroke will fail similarly in act IV—nor is there anything very obviously wrong in his desire to avoid bloodshed. We may perhaps sense a certain weakness when his assertion of his power in terms of the natural hierarchy—"lions make leopards tame" (174)—is answered by Mowbray with an appeal to an even more basic aspect of the natural order: "Yea, but not change his spots" (175). But his failure to stop the quarrel adds, I think, less

25. Ibid., p. 80.

to our sense of weakness in him than to our recognition of the quarrel's importance.

Even the second scene, with its revelation of Richard's guilt for Woodstock's death, does not wholly darken our image, for equally impressive is Gaunt's determined loyalty *despite* the murder.

> Let heaven revenge, for I may never lift
> An angry arm against His minister.
>
> [1.ii.40–41]

We may here sense what will become the major complexity in Shakespeare's conception of Richard's character: he is king as well as ordinary man. And at least one wise old counselor would rather be loyal to the king than revenged upon the man.

In the scene at Coventry, Richard's willfulness begins to show. We have already noted the dramatic letdown when he stops the fray just when speeches are about to be replaced with deeds, and he bears the blame for this. Furthermore, even though they were determined in council, the uneven periods of exile are his responsibility. But even here the picture of Richard is not simple. He reduces Bolingbroke's short sentence after telling Mowbray "After our sentence plaining comes too late" (1.iii.175)—a sign of weakness, perhaps—but he does so out of pity for an old man's sorrow, hardly a disgraceful motive: "Thy sad aspect / Hath from the number of his banish'd years / Pluck'd four away" (209–11). Furthermore, before taking charge decisively—"Six years we banish him and he shall go" (248)—he reasons fairly and patiently with old Gaunt.

> Thy son is banish'd upon good advice,
> Whereto thy tongue a party-verdict gave:
> Why at our justice seem'st thou then to lour?
>
> [1.iii.233–35]

We see here moments of some weakness, and others of willfulness and favoritism, and we know he has been involved in a murder, but we also see a king faced publicly with a very difficult situation which he does not let master him even if he does not completely master it.

The last scene of the opening act shows us the private man. Though the sarcastic jesting at "high Herford" (1.iv.2) is not admirable, the scene hardly offers the prodigal voluptuary among effeminate favorites painted by Holinshed. In fact, Richard again displays refreshing shrewdness as he sees through Bolingbroke's "craft of smiles" (28). Aumerle's and his plainspeaking comes almost as relief after the long scenes of public self-righteousness on all sides. But this complicated tone goes sour when news of Gaunt's illness arrives. The king leaves Ely with the nastiest lines in the play:

> Now put it, God, in the physician's mind
> To help him to his grave immediately!
>
> [1.iv.59–60]

It is as if the mere mention of Gaunt—even a dying Gaunt— sufficed to make Richard's gray look black.

Having shown us these aspects of character and laid the groundwork for his plot, Shakespeare prepares the conflict. Woodstock's murder and even the confiscation of Gaunt's goods are merely the efficient causes of this. The deeper sources are set forth in the long scene at Ely House that opens act II. Here Shakespeare shapes the scene to show two opposed conceptions of kingship— Gaunt's and Northumberland's—and then sandwiches Richard, at his least kingly, in the middle.[26] Following the sixty-five lines of Gaunt's retrospective vision, Richard enters only to exemplify the extent to which it is threatened from within. There is no trace now of the Richard we caught glimpses of in the first act. Instead, he is sarcastic, and when Gaunt refuses to be put off, adjusting his own style to suit the king's bitter wit ("I see thee ill, / Ill in myself to see, and in thee, seeing ill" 11.i.93–94), the sarcasm turns to anger and insult: "A lunatic lean-witted fool, / Presuming on an ague's privilege" (115–16). Ironically, Richard most insists on his royalty (118–20) when his uncontrolled abusive

26. Norman Rabkin, *Shakespeare and the Common Understanding* (New York: Free Press, 1967), treats the play from a similar dualistic perspective. Though I see a more dynamic relationship than Mr. Rabkin's "complementarity," I have found his book both stimulating and informative.

anger shows him to be least royal. That Gaunt should die after this attack, after this travesty of fitting royal conduct, is symbolically appropriate. And with him dies one conception of kingship as an active possibility.

The alternative conception of kingship, Bolingbroke's, is also apparent in this scene, symbolized by Northumberland. Richard's seizure of Gaunt's goods departs not only from Gaunt's code, in which everything is shaped by powerful tradition, but also from Bolingbroke's practical ways, which would never allow so blatant and unpopular a crime. Likewise, Richard's Irish wars may be presumed to be unworthy of the king from Gaunt's view, since they destroy the economy and public order at home, and from Bolingbroke's, since they are wasteful and ineffective.[27] That Richard's behavior is unacceptable to either of these framing standards is dramatized in his response to York's pleas. York here clearly represents that part of each nation—each man—which will turn wherever a clear authority can be established; he is a public order man. He argues against the seizure of Gaunt's property both for pragmatic reasons and for reasons of a more philosophical sort.

> If you do wrongfully seize Herford's rights,
> Call in the letters patents that he hath
> By his attorneys-general to sue
> His livery, and deny his off'red homage,
> You pluck a thousand dangers on your head.
> [II.i.201–05]

> Take Herford's rights away, and take from time
> His charters, and his customary rights.
> [II.i.195–96]

He also echoes Gaunt's sense (II.i.124–31) of the noblesse—and here, the noblesse oblige—of Edward's royal line:

27. That it is not any particular act but rather the timing and style of the act that is important is suggested by the different attitudes taken toward different foreign adventures. Richard's is seen as politically and economically foolish; Bolingbroke's proposed trip in act v is not criticized practically but questioned morally; Henry V's foreign adventure in the later play passes largely uncriticized as did the adventures of the "royal kings" we have heard Gaunt extol (II.i.51–56).

I am the last of noble Edward's sons,
Of whom thy father, Prince of Wales, was first.
[II.i.171–72]

York thus touches on the two conceptions of kingship—those of
pragmatic ruler and God's chosen deputy—that Richard is ignoring. But Richard responds to all of York's eloquent arguments
with contempt:

Think what you will, we seize into our hands
His plate, his goods, his money and his lands.
[II.i.209–10]

If it is appropriate that Gaunt should die in the face of the
fierce, narrow-minded, unkingly conduct of Richard, it is equally
appropriate that Bolingbroke should spring into renewed life after
such a display of willful arrogance and foolish inexpediency. As
we have seen, this is precisely what happens when Northumberland announces, at this symbolic moment, his "intelligence" of
Bolingbroke's return.

The first scene of act II succeeds, then, in showing us a king
who is unfit to be one. For Gaunt's world, this means death; for
Bolingbroke's, remedial action; for York's, dilemma as he seeks a
real king. What it means for Richard, no one is yet ready to see,
and Shakespeare begins now to explore the problem. The plot,
of course, simply shows us Richard's progressive replacement by
Bolingbroke; but the action as a whole brings to the surface more
complex problems than simple political revolution, as it uncovers
aspects and levels of experience which come close to dominating
the political conflict by the play's end.

The method of this discovery is, at least through act III, an
ever-widening emphasis on the gulf between body politic and
body natural, man and king. After the scene at Ely (II.i), this
disjunction is dramatized in four scenes in which Richard is not
present, so that when he reappears (III.ii) we are partly prepared
for the changed king which we see.

Effectively juxtaposed to Northumberland's plotting at Ely is
the quiet scene at Windsor Castle (II.ii), showing the Queen
among Richard's favorites. This combination—the king's personal

supporters in a private situation without him—alerts us to aspects
of Richard different from those we saw in the preceding public
scene. When the Queen appeared at Ely House before, she spoke
but one line, "How fares our noble uncle, Lancaster?" (II.i.71).
But the difference between this greeting and Richard's brusque
"What comfort, man?" (72), together with her silent presence
throughout Richard's abuse of Gaunt, were perhaps intended to
remind us of the existence of gentler days and ways.[28] Now, at
any rate, her answers to Bushy's questions tend to rehabilitate
Richard by showing how much he is loved.[29]

> I know no cause
> Why I should welcome such a guest as grief,
> Save bidding farewell to so sweet a guest
> As my sweet Richard.
>
> [II.ii.6–9]

Much of her sorrow is expressed in terms heavy with conceits:

> So, Greene, thou art the midwife to my woe,
> And Bolingbroke my sorrow's dismal heir;
> Now hath my soul brought forth her prodigy,
> And I, a gasping new-deliver'd mother,
> Have woe to woe, sorrow to sorrow join'd.
>
> [II.ii.62–66]

But one suspects that the lapse is Shakespeare's, not the Queen's,
as he is still experimenting in this play with ritualized grief
(cf. v.i.79–102). In any case, there is genuine affection here for
Richard that balances the unsympathetic picture from the preceding scene.

The scene does more, however, than merely restore some luster
to Richard's character. There is conceited talk as well about substance and shadows:

28. This is an occasion on which staging will make all the difference:
the Queen's position and action during the scene can either mark her
as part of Richard's attack, or (as I think preferable) show her to be
essentially sympathetic with Gaunt.
29. This happens each time the Queen appears. Cf. III.iv and v.i.

> Each substance of a grief hath twenty shadows,
> Which shows like grief itself, but is not so.
> For sorrow's eye, glazed with blinding tears,
> Divides one thing entire to many objects,
> Like perspectives, which, rightly gaz'd upon,
> Show nothing but confusion; ey'd awry,
> Distinguish form. So your sweet Majesty,
> Looking awry upon your lord's departure,
> Find shapes of grief more than himself to wail,
> Which, look'd on as it is, is nought but shadows
> Of what it is not.
>
> [II.ii.14–24]

This passage gives specific terms to a question that is pervasive throughout the play: who is the shadow king, who is the real; who has more substance as a man, Richard, Gaunt, Bolingbroke? When the Queen insists on the substantial reality of her grief ("conceit is still deriv'd / From some forefather grief; mine is not so" 34–35), she effectively insists on the reality of her love and Richard as a man capable of being loved. At the same time the very distinction between substance and shadow contributes to our increasing awareness of duality in the conception of kingship. Bushy's comparison with the "perspectives" does nothing, of course, to resolve the complexity since "perspectives" are *intended* ("rightly") to be viewed from the side ("ey'd awry"), suggesting that the Queen's perception of sorrow is not mistaken. This speech seems thus to assert realities implicitly while laboring to deny them formally.[30]

When Greene and York enter with news of Bolingbroke's return, the tone of the scene shifts from personal praise of Richard to his political failure as king. Whatever his substantial virtues as a person, he is now merely the shadow of a monarch, represented at home by a weak old man. York, the royal surrogate, is still loyal to the body politic under Richard but has no illusions about his own physical or political strength:

---

30. Bushy's comparison offers an interesting example of the complex didactic quality of fictional artifice—*la voie oblique* turns out to be the straight way.

> Here am I left to underprop his land,
> Who weak with age cannot support myself.
>
> [II.ii.82–83]

York further sees in his responsibilities a precarious balance:

> Both are my kinsmen:
> Th' one is my sovereign, whom both my oath
> And duty bids defend; th' other again
> Is my kinsman, whom the king hath wrong'd,
> Whom conscience and my kindred bids to right.
>
> [II.ii.111–15]

Oath and duty clash with conscience and wronged kindred. The way this balance will tip in practice is foreshadowed, after York leaves the stage, in the discussion between Bushy, Greene, and Bagot. Bagot plans to join Richard in Ireland, but the others "will for refuge straight to Bristow castle" (134). The first third of the scene has shown personal devotion to Richard despite his failure as king; the middle third has reminded us of his political failure and has shown York wavering between loyalties; now the last third shows two of Richard's personal friends deserting him, only one going to his aid.[31] The disparity between Richard the man, to whom the Queen remains loyal, and Richard the king, from whom the rats are beginning to flee ("our nearness to the king in love / Is near the hate of those [who] love not the king" 126–27), grows obvious.[32]

Bolingbroke's return offers further evidence of Richard's weakening control of the crown and the body politic. First, Northumberland and his son join Bolingbroke; next, Ross and Willoughby arrive with more support. Then York enters, and though he

31. This is, I suggest, the effect at this point. Later, of course, Bushy and Greene will die loyal to Richard (III.i), while Bagot will accuse Aumerle of disloyalty to Bolingbroke (IV.i). As the Arden editor, Peter Ure, notes (at III.ii.122), there is some ambiguity here, especially surrounding the identity of Bagot.

32. The neat parallel between the three parts of this scene and the three parts of the preceding one should be noticed. Complexity, rather than simplicity, seems to be Shakespeare's goal at the start of this play.

valiantly advances all the reasons against rebellion (ii.iii.89–146)
and claims to remain politically "neuter" (158), in fewer than a
hundred lines he has effectively allied himself with his nephew.

This shift of power is summarized in the next scene, on the
Welsh coast, when the Captain tells Salisbury that his army has
dispersed. Not only the army, in fact, but the elements themselves
appear to have abandoned Richard.

> The bay-trees in our country are all wither'd,
> And meteors fright the fixed stars of heaven,
> The pale-fac'd moon looks bloody on the earth,
> And lean-look'd prophets whisper fearful change,
>
> . . . .
>
> These signs forerun the death or fall of kings.
>
> [ii.iv.8–15]

Salisbury's reply also calls attention to what is happening, but
in a more subtle way. On entering, he says to the Captain, "The
king reposeth all his confidence in thee" (6); but when he hears
of the army's dispersal, he murmurs, "Ah, Richard!" (18). The
shift from "king" to "Richard" expresses admirably the disparity
between the king's two bodies, whether Salisbury is conscious of
it or not.

The last scene before Richard's reappearance adds to and clarifies
all the earlier indications. Bolingbroke reveals in his manner of
handling Bushy and Greene that he is stronger than Richard, and
not merely because of his armies. Without hesitation he wields
the power of life and death as if he were already crowned. When
we see York efficiently serving him, we sense that he has won,
before the confrontation with Richard ever takes place.

By the time we see Richard on the coast of Wales, then, we
are effectively convinced that he has lost his throne. Furthermore,
we have been shown external evidence of the division between
the man and the king. Shakespeare's technique here, external and
indirect dramatization of a change in a character while that character is offstage, is typical (see both *Hamlet* and *Macbeth*) and
prepares us for the changed personality at the same time that
other plot lines are being developed. From ii.ii to iii.ii, we have
seen Bolingbroke's power grow in every respect (military, political,

legal,[33] and personal). At the same time we have been given hints about the causes and meanings of this attack on the throne. When Richard reappears, our attention can focus on his response to events we already know about.

On the Welsh coast, Richard is forced to live through a scene where everything is exactly contrary to what happened to Boling-broke when he landed. There Bolingbroke opened the scene by asking, "How far is it, my lord, to Berkeley now?" (II.iii.1); here Richard's opening lacks comparable assurance: "Barkloughly castle call they this at hand?" (III.ii.1). Whereas three groups of friends crowded onto the stage bringing support to Bolingbroke's invasion, two friends arrive singly and unsupported to tell Richard bad news about lost aid.

Richard opens with two splendid—if somewhat hysterical—speeches filled with images of his kingly glory and all the power—natural and supernatural—that he wields. Carlisle's practical suggestion for action is swamped in images of stones becoming armed soldiers and the searching eye of heaven making rebels tremble. Salisbury's news about the Welsh army punctures this airy fantasy and suddenly Richard shrinks before our eyes.

> Have I not reason to look pale and dead?
> All souls that will be safe, fly from my side.
>
> [III.ii.79–80]

But Richard's shift here, from the style of the grandiose body politic to the pain of the feeble body natural, does not last long. Just one line from Aumerle stimulates him to more rich and extreme images of the body politic.

> I had forgot myself, am I not king?
> Awake, thou coward majesty! thou sleepest.
> Is not the king's name twenty thousand names?
> Arm, arm, my name!
>
> [III.ii.83–86]

But this is followed again, on Scroope's bad news, by a re-assertion of mortal weakness: "and death will have his day" (103).

33. York's allegiance lends a certain de facto legality to Bolingbroke's claims.

The gap between the two bodies has so widened that king and man now look like two different, even contradictory, realities.

> I live with bread like you, feel want,
> Taste grief, need friends—subjected thus,
> How can you say to me, I am a king?
>   [III.ii.175–77]

Meantime, our own response to Richard is also double. When he exclaims "Our lands, our lives, and all, are Bolingbroke's, / And nothing can we call our own but death (III.ii.151–52), we recognize the truth in what he says, and feel that he is waking to his situation. At the same time, we have been so steeped in images of royal power asserted—from Gaunt to Aumerle—that we agree with Carlisle that "wise men ne'er sit and wail their woes" (178), and wish that Richard would act. Thus far Shakespeare has taken care to ensure an ironic and detached view: when it was time to pause and consider, Richard acted impetuously; now that it is time to act clearly, he pauses to consider. What before he might have seen as a danger to be avoided he now accepts as fate. His whole long speech about graves, "the death of kings," "the hollow crown," and vain "ceremonious duty" (145–77) is touched with the irony that surrounds the right thought (however wildly expressed), at the wrong time.

Probably the most important aspect of this scene of elaborate rhetorical artificiality is one we notice instinctively in the theater but find difficult to describe in the study. At the start, King Richard is struggling to maintain the traditional meanings of his title as head of the body politic. But about half way through the scene (see lines 129ff., especially 144ff.) an abrupt shift occurs that marks the way for the rest of the play. Richard's attention swings primarily to his status as suffering man—"the mortal temples of a king" (161). The interest lies in the way he takes to his description of those who "live with bread . . . feel want, / Taste grief, need friends"; he uses the same rhetoric that just previously supported the idea of the inseparability of body politic and body natural. The same baroque and exaggerated version of Gaunt's cosmic harmony that before pictured stones rising against Bolingbroke now depicts in gothic extravagance the frailty of the mortal condition. What before supported the royal throne now is used to detail—and glamorize?—its ruin. The sacred balm which wrote "king" on a mortal man finds its match in the human tears which "Write sorrow on the bosom of the earth" (147). Something strange is happening before our eyes as a history play begins to lose its central interest in history and to focus increasingly on the mind and heart of its unkingly king.

The following scene at Flint Castle recapitulates the fluctuations from king to man that we have learned on the Welsh coast will be the marks of Shakespeare's characterization of Richard from now on.[34] Never in the play does Richard sound more royal than when he addresses Northumberland.

> We are amaz'd, and thus long have we stood
> To watch the fearful bending of thy knee,
> Because we thought ourself thy lawful king;
> And if we be, how dare thy joints forget
> To pay their awful duty to our presence?
> If we be not, show us the hand of God
> That hath dismiss'd us from our stewardship;
> For well we know no hand of blood and bone
> Can gripe the sacred handle of our sceptre,
> Unless he do profane, steal, or usurp.
>
> [III.iii.72–81]

But Northumberland's response, humble and cautious, cannot hide the hard reality of the "glittering arms" (116) which now control the situation, and Richard's illusion of power crumbles: "all the number of his fair demands / Shall be accomplish'd without contradiction" (123–24). Richard sees precisely what has happened and what must be:

> O that I were as great
> As is my grief, or lesser than my name!
> Or that I could forget what I have been!
> Or not remember what I must be now!
>
> [III.iii.136–39]

34. For a very thorough analysis of this scene and IV.i from a more historical point of view, see Ernest W. Talbert, *The Problem of Order* (Chapel Hill: University of North Carolina Press, 1962), pp. 146–200.

The body politic is only a name, no longer linked essentially to the mortal body of Richard. The simple fact of Bolingbroke's power —unused—proves this. The king who could compare his power to the searching eye of heaven must now descend into the base court, "where kings grow base" (180). Boasting at the start of the scene that "God omnipotent, / Is mustering in his clouds, on our behalf, / Armies of pestilence" (85–87), Richard, by the end, has had to accept a completely different metaphysic of kingship, in which God is replaced with physical power: "They well deserve to have / That know the strong'st and surest way to get" (200–01).

The king's lines on receiving his first piece of bad news on the Welsh coast call our attention to a second feature that will henceforth mark Shakespeare's characterization of him.

> But now the blood of twenty thousand men
> Did triumph in my face, and they are fled;
> And till so much blood thither come again,
> Have I not reason to look pale and dead?
>
> [III.ii.76–79]

In these lines Richard turns fact into metaphor; he transmutes an army into a personal physical attribute. Two effects here are worth noting. First of all, Richard's speeches usually remind us, as here, of all the connections that traditionally exist between a king, his people, and his realm. This will be increasingly important, as his claim to the throne dissolves, in keeping before us a developed image of what he is allowing to be destroyed. The technique of restoring to a hero through language what is being taken away from him in the action is typical of Shakespeare and helps account for the rich ambiguity of his plays. Second, the metaphorizing tendency that Shakespeare shows us here transforming an army into the king's blood catches in little the whole cast of Richard's mind. Sometimes hysterically, sometimes quietly and perceptively, he interiorizes all experience (in this respect, as in some others, he foreshadows Hamlet).[35] Of each new situation he

35. He may also at this point anticipate the Gardener with his bank of rue. Both men interiorize—is the closed garden wholly unlike the garden of the mind?—what they cannot control in the larger world of political facts.

makes a little drama, a scene to play. The hysterical vein is obvious in comparisons of himself to Christ, as when he exclaims, "Three Judases, each one thrice worse than Judas!" (III.ii.132), and in the tears which he will drop "still upon one place, / Till they have fretted us a pair of graves" (III.iii.166–67). The quieter, more probing vein surfaces in his thoughts on the realities of the crown:

> for within the hollow crown
> That rounds the mortal temples of a king
> Keeps Death his court, and there the antic sits,
> Scoffing his state and grinning at his pomp.
>
> [III.ii.160–63]

A powerful example of a middle style in which both layerings participate may be seen in the following:

> What must the king do now? Must he submit?
> The king shall do it. Must he be depos'd?
> The king shall be contented. Must he lose
> The name of king? a God's name, let it go.
> I'll give my jewels for a set of beads;
> My gorgeous palace for a hermitage;
> My gay apparel for an almsman's gown.
>
> [III.iii.143–49]

Here are visible both Richard's slightly frantic love of self-dramatization and his clearest realization of the split that has developed between his body politic and his body natural.[36] As he goes on, his tone becomes more and more hysterical.

> Or I'll be buried in the king's highway,
> Some way of common trade, where subjects' feet
> May hourly trample on their sovereign's head;
> For on my heart they tread now whilst I live:
> And buried once, why not upon my head?
>
> [III.iii.155–59]

But the grotesqueness of the picture of his grave should not blind us to the aptness with which he perceives his situation. The set

---

36. Richard speaks here of himself in the third person for four lines. The shift (line 147) from royal objectivity to the suffering "I" is telling.

of mind that can turn the soil of Wales into an army of supporters of the king is the *same* as that which turns tears into an erosive force capable of hollowing out a grave for a man; and it is this set of mind which distinguishes Richard from all the other characters and allows Shakespeare to transform his history play into tragedy—or, at least, as Polonius might put it, into something "tragical-historical."

The scene at Flint Castle brings home both to Richard and to the audience the radical duality that is inseparable from the nature of kingship, brings it home as clearly as is possible short of the actual murder of the body natural. This final action is still two acts away. The interim is filled with significantly new developments that further shift history toward tragedy and give special meaning to the regicide when it occurs.

Following the emblematic garden scene summarizing and explaining Richard's failure as king, the play seems to start over again in act IV with accusations of treason in open court, like those we heard in act I. This makes it plain that Bolingbroke, though demonstrating better control than Richard could in act I, is himself unable to roll away the past. More important, it establishes a cyclical historical rhythm in the play—new king, new accusations—on top of which Richard's more personal tragic rhythm may be imposed. His linear fate and fortune are to be seen against the circular procession of history. This is a structural characteristic in all of Shakespeare's tragedies, perhaps in all tragedy.

Richard's face-to-face meeting with Bolingbroke at Westminster is immediately preceded by Carlisle's great defense of the sacramental attitude toward kingship, last gasp of an order that is about to be officially destroyed. Though there has been no question as to the outcome of the official confrontation of king and rebel since it was first announced, Shakespeare manages to build a kind of suspense through his complex orchestration of various themes. Though we know Bolingbroke has won, we see him here unable to halt the challenges; and though we know Richard has lost, we are reminded through Carlisle how much depends on the beaten king still. This is the deposition of a weak ruler, yet we watch him take over the stage and for one hundred and fifty lines dominate a court filled solely with his enemies. Shakespeare enables him to do this primarily in two ways: through his usual flair for self-dramatization, and, much more importantly, through the increasing depth of his awareness as he continues to interiorize and imaginatively transform everything around him.

The episode with the crown is an obvious example. Eager to justify and dramatize himself, Richard creates a little parable:

> two buckets, filling one another,
> The emptier ever dancing in the air,
> The other down, unseen, and full of water.
>
> [IV.i.185–87]

There is something too pat about this; as usual, he has created a self-pitying and self-justifying tableau:

> That bucket down and full of tears am I,
> Drinking my griefs, whilst you mount up on high.
>
> [IV.i.188–89]

Yet, there is also something new and perceptive here. Richard plays essentially with the image of Fortune's wheel,[37] but he has added something special and moving to the traditional image, a sense of the deep personal suffering of those involved in Fortune's turns; he has taken a cliché and reinterpreted it. Richard *is* the lower bucket—filled with sorrow and self-pity, but also with some insight. Though infinitely self-centered, he does see and feel to a degree that Bolingbroke does not, as far as this play shows. This is partly why he is so much more interesting as a character; it may be the reason, too, why Bolingbroke will make the better king.

Though the posturing and "conceiting" is thick indeed—especially when Richard plays on "care" nine times in four lines (195–98)—the voracious interiorizing capacity constantly gropes through to new realizations.

> My crown I am [willing to resign], but still my griefs
> are mine.

37. The bucket image is traditionally related to Fortune's wheel. See Howard Patch, *The Goddess Fortuna in Mediaeval Literature* (Cambridge, Mass.: Harvard University Press, 1927), pp. 52–57.

> You may my glories and my state depose,
> But not my griefs; still am I king of those.
>
> [IV.i.191–93]

We sense that something of great moment is being said about the
relation between the king and the man. His act of self-divestiture,
a kind of de-coronation, dramatizes vividly how much more than
simple humanity is being expelled from the throne in this scene,
though it is simple humanity that must grieve for the loss.

> I give this heavy weight from off my head,
> And this unwieldy sceptre from my hand,
> The pride of kingly sway from out my heart.
>
> [IV.i.204–06]

"The pride of kingly sway": in its fullest sense, this is something
which Bolingbroke will never really come to know even in the
Henry IV plays. And Richard adds:

> With mine own tongue [I] deny my sacred state,
> With mine own breath release all duteous oaths;
> All pomp and majesty I do forswear.
>
> [IV.i.209–11]

Thus he underscores what is happening to kingship as well as to
himself. Even his solemn injunction to Bolingbroke, "Long may'st
thou live in Richard's seat to sit" (218), reminds us that the seat
is his, however much he has abused its rights. As Tillyard has
pointed out,[38] a sense is communicated in the play that no king
will ever fully repossess the *pride* of kingly sway or sit in *sacred*
state once Richard is deposed. This deposition is as final as the
Fall, indeed has already been referred to as "a second fall of
cursed man" (III.iv.76).

Still clearer proof of the way Richard's interiorizing disposition
leads to insight as well as self-dramatization comes when he for
the first time applies his critical awareness to himself as well as to
his enemies.

> Mine eyes are full of tears, I cannot see.
> And yet salt water blinds them not so much

---

38. Tillyard, *History Plays*, pp. 261–63.

> But they can see a sort of traitors here.
> Nay, if I turn mine eyes upon myself,
> I find myself a traitor with the rest.
> For I have given here my soul's consent
> T'undeck the pompous body of a king;
> Made glory base, and sovereignty a slave;
> Proud majesty a subject, state a peasant.
>
> [ιν.i.244–52]

This is perhaps the first time in the play that any character has blamed himself for anything. The only one who has come near such self-criticism heretofore is York, who lamented his palsied weakness (ιι.iii.98–104). Otherwise, from the opening accusations on, this has been a world in which each character has found himself blameless, the others guilty. Richard's lines express a stunning ability to see himself as *both* king and rebel, both traitor and betrayed. He has achieved the profound internal awareness that the king's two bodies are at open civil war.

With the famous episode of the mirror, Richard, I think, comes to his most complex awareness of his own situation and of the human condition in general. Traditionally, the mirror has been representative both of truth (thanks to Plato's *Republic*[39]) and of vanity. Shakespeare may draw here on both traditions, but dramatically he uses the mirror as a touchstone to distinguish his two kings. Richard comments on what he sees:

> No deeper wrinkles yet? hath sorrow struck
> So many blows upon this face of mine
> And made no deeper wounds? O flatt'ring glass,
> Like to my followers in prosperity,
> Thou dost beguile me.
>
> [ιν.i.277–81]

Always there is that note of self-pity ("Like to my followers . . ."), but there is more. The man who up to this point has come painfully to learn that there is no necessary connection between his

---

39. See Peter Ure, "The Looking-Glass of *Richard II*," *Philological Quarterly* 44(1955):219–44.

fallible self and the sacred role of king now has to learn that even
his body natural is essentially impervious to his deepest personal
suffering. Not only has the universe failed his expectations of a
massive "sympathy of nature" (iii.ii.1–81), but his face too betrays him, showing no wounds. Richard has been stripped of his
kingship and is now in effect stripped of support from his natural
body. His only essential self, he now realizes, lies in his internal
pain and awareness.

It is this internal pain that expresses itself in throwing down
the mirror to create a symbol of shattered glory that the face has
failed to supply. In this action Shakespeare lets Richard show us
the partiality and irrelevance of the truth that the literal mirror—
in some sense a surrogate perhaps for Bolingbroke's kind of factual
awareness—has to tell. Its images are clear, but superficial, like
Bolingbroke's comments in the scene: "I thought you had been
willing to resign" (190), "Part of your cares you give me with
your crown" (194), "Go some of you, and fetch a looking-glass"
(268), "Urge it no more, my Lord Northumberland" (271).
Bolingbroke is in charge—decent and confident. But Richard,
driven by his suffering, imagination, and conceit, seems to be
living now on a different imaginative level than Bolingbroke, a
level that makes him unfit to be king but that makes the play
his. When the mirror tells him Bolingbroke's "truth" about his
face, he shatters it to create a truth of a different kind, a symbol of
his inner ruin.[40] The gesture, though melodramatic, is again deeply
probing. Bolingbroke ignores it. He completely misses the point of
Richard's gesture.

> The shadow of your sorrow hath destroy'd
> The shadow of your face.
>
>   [iv.i.292–93]

To Bolingbroke the mirror is merely vanity, as are Richard's
meditations.

The lines just quoted may well remind us that we have already
seen a confrontation of attitudes like this one, carefully set back

---

40. Again the similarity with the bank of rue in iii.iv—the victory
in art or metaphor that cannot be had in the real world of nature—
should need no laboring.

in act II, when Bushy tries to convince the Queen that her grief
at Richard's departure "look'd on as it is, is nought but shadows /
Of what it is not" (II.ii.23–24). That the Queen's brief is later
proved to have sound basis even in Bushy's kind of "fact" should
alert us to the importance of shadows despite Bolingbroke's dis-
dain. As we later see, Richard's "shadows" too have a solid reality
that even Bolingbroke will have to recognize.

The volatile mixture of conceit and insight, shadow and substance that we have been tracing is yet more obvious during
Richard's parting from his Queen. We see still the tendency toward self-dramatization which seems in Richard to be part of
the process of self-awareness.[41]

> A king of beasts, indeed—if aught but beasts,
> I had been still a happy king of men.
>
> [v.i.35–36]

And his picture of his Queen's future years in France reveals
his usual indulgent self-pity combined with a feverish imagination.

> In winter's tedious nights sit by the fire
> With good old folks, and let them tell thee tales
> Of woeful ages long ago betid;
> And ere thou bid good night, to quite their griefs
> Tell thou the lamentable tale of me,
> And send the hearers weeping to their beds;
> For why, the senseless brands will sympathize
> The heavy accent of thy moving tongue,
> And in compassion weep the fire out,
> And some will mourn in ashes, some coal-black,
> For the deposing of a rightful king.
>
> [v.i.40–50]

Yet, extreme as it is, Richard's image of the fire sympathizing
with his fall reminds us of the cosmic support which was so real

41. W. B. C. Watkins, in *Shakespeare and Spenser* (Princeton: Princeton University Press, 1950), mentions the complex relationship between
self-pity and self-dramatization (pp. 101, 107) but fails to pursue what to
me is the more interesting question of the relationship between self-
dramatization and self- or internal-awareness. See below, chap. 4.

a fact to Gaunt. Clearly, this is not the place or the time for winter's tales—there will be a place and time for Shakespeare, if not for Richard—but the words that come from the stage are nonetheless moving. Indeed, part of their effect stems from the fact that neither in Bolingbroke's political realm nor in his realm of discourse will there ever be room for winter's tales or weeping brands or mourning ashes. For better and worse, such visions will die with Richard.

Shakespeare also gives Richard in this scene a new, quiet control. He seems to have awakened from his dream of power without responsibility and to have recognized that "our profane hours here have thrown [us] down" (25). This is a marked extension of his awareness of himself as traitor in the deposition scene and is especially effective coming as a voluntary confession to his most loyal and personal supporter, his wife. Her presence reminds us— like Ophelia's in *Hamlet*—of the meaning of king killing for the little people who are drawn into the ring of suffering despite their desires and their innocence. Richard's warning to Northumberland displays a political insight that he has too thoroughly lacked before.[42]

> Northumberland, thou ladder wherewithal
> The mounting Bolingbroke ascends my throne,
>
> . . . .
> The love of wicked men converts to fear,
> That fear to hate, and hate turns one or both
> To worthy danger and deserved death.
>
> [v.i.55–68]

Now, when it is too late, Richard sounds indeed like a king, is lovingly reunited with his wife, and shows himself shrewdly aware of Bolingbroke's nature.

But Richard has lost the crown, and political insight is now of secondary importance. For this reason, I think, Shakespeare

42. These lines are "remembered" by Bolingbroke in 2 *Henry IV* (iii.i.70–71) as examples of Richard's awareness and foresight. If, as the Quartos have it, Richard speaks the line "That were some love, but little policy" (84), this will come as further evidence of a new perceptiveness and balance in Richard.

uses all of Richard's long scene in Pomfret Castle to explore other kinds of awareness and to dramatize other values. No one would wish to argue that Richard leaves behind, on entering prison, the set of mind that interiorizes everything and dramatizes the self above all. Quite the contrary: he is very much the old Richard, but he is now (as I read the last act) unmistakably growing.

In his mental "hammerings" he examines in turn the traditional relations that a man may have with the world. First, in the religious realm, where he discovers no satisfaction:

> thoughts of things divine, are intermix'd
> With scruples, and do set the word itself
> Against the word,
> As thus: "Come, little ones"; and then again,
> "It is as hard to come as for a camel
> To thread the postern of a small needle's eye."
>
> [v.v.12–17]

Next in the realm of power, which only teaches him his helplessness:

> Thoughts tending to ambition, they do plot
> Unlikely wonders: how these vain weak nails
> May tear a passage thorough the flinty ribs
> Of this hard world, my ragged prison walls;
> And for they cannot, die in their own pride.
>
> [v.v.18–22]

And, finally, in the personal realm:

> Thoughts tending to content flatter themselves
> That they are not the first of fortune's slaves,
> Nor shall not be the last—like silly beggars
> Who, sitting in the stocks, refuge their shame,
> That many have and others must sit there;
> And in this thought they find a kind of ease,
> Bearing their own misfortunes on the back
> Of such as have before indur'd the like.
>
> [v.v.23–30]

But here too the offered solutions fail. Richard sees through the
self's rationalizations, the attempts to numb personal anguish by
universalizing it, by unpacking the heart with words. The failure
of comfort here is particularly poignant since Richard is now explicitly rejecting his own chief recourse, the very habit he has
indulged from the start. Self-pity is no more than self-pity after
all.

From all this, Richard's conclusion follows naturally.

> Thus play I in one person many people,
> And none contented. Sometimes am I king,
> Then treasons make me wish myself a beggar,
> And so I am. Then crushing penury
> Persuades me I was better when a king;
> Then am I king'd again, and by and by
> Think that I am unking'd by Bolingbroke,
> And straight am nothing. But whate'er I be,
> Nor I, nor any man that but man is,
> With nothing shall be pleas'd, till be be eas'd
> With being nothing.
>
> [v.v.31–41]

Critics have too often overlooked the context of this statement in
supposing that it shows a still-frivolous Richard playing when he
should be acting, a man who has learned nothing.[43] But this is
not what the play says; the play's Richard remains in "none contented" for the very reason that he has examined the escapes and
found them all inadequate. What I take Richard to be focusing on
here is the idea that reality lies at last in the individual consciousness and only there; the profound effects of the individual human
susceptibility to suffering become the final test that all ideas and
ideals of human grandeur must pass. Gaunt's ideal of kingship

43. Most insistent on this interpretation is James Winny, *The Player
King* (London: Chatto & Windus, 1968), pp. 48–85. Arthur Colby
Sprague, in *Shakespeare's Histories* (London: The Society for Theatre
Research, 1964), p. 31, quotes a review of Kean's Richard II in 1815
showing that this actor at least saw the king growing in act v: "a vigorous
and elevated mind, struggling indeed against necessity, but struggling like
a king . . . greater beyond comparison in his dungeon than Bolingbroke
on his throne!" (*The New Monthly Magazine*, 1 June 1815).

has little room for personal satisfactions; everything is subordinate to the overarching ideal of vigorous Christian service. Bolingbroke, as always in *this* play, is distant and ambiguous, so that we never know whether he counts on human weakness or simply never sees it. Richard alone takes up the three major modes of individual fulfillment—spiritual, political, psychological—and finds each wanting.

The rest of this final scene seems to be constructed to give a special dramatic stature to Richard even in his hour of passion. Everything now reminds him of his failure as king and of the reasons for that failure. When music mysteriously plays, then breaks its tempo—"how sour sweet music is / When time is broke and no proportion kept!" (42–43)—he grasps its implications for his own case at once, "So is it in the music of men's lives" (44). Just possibly he grasps more, if we believe Gaunt's assessment of the counsel he meant to give Richard in act II. His words were to have a compelling music in them: they would "Inforce attention like deep harmony" (II.i.6); they would be memorable because final—like "The setting sun, and music at the close" (12). Richard was impervious to *that* music, but circumstances have made him more sensitive, and whatever the source of what he now hears, it brings to him, at any rate, the counsel Gaunt had so desired to convey.

> And here have I the daintiness of ear
> To check time broke in a disordered string;
> But for the concord of my state and time,
> Had not an ear to hear my true time broke:
> I wasted time, and now doth time waste me.
> [v.v.45–49]

The Groom who enters at this point reminds us of traditional loyalties to the king, which one man has shattered, and also prepares us for Richard's death. As Richard's punning on their respective worth implies ("The cheapest of us is ten groats too dear" 68), there are senses in which a faithful groom is more than a failed king. The man who is untorn by any internal division has a kind of simple integrity unmatched by the man who has failed to reconcile the king's two bodies. The Groom's last line, "What my tongue dares not, that my heart shall say" (97), adds,

however, an interesting development to the play's imagery of the
relation between meaning and gesture.[44] His view, that lack
of public gesture need not reflect lack of private intention and
value, may reflect on Richard, whom we have been watching
develop internally in the very place that his opportunity for external gesture of any sort is most limited. It certainly stands out
as a reversal of facts in a play filled with external gestures (hands,
knees) which hide the internal intention (heart), a reversal exploring the possibility of the very correspondence between different parts of the world which Richard has watched disintegrate
under his own and Bolingbroke's abuses and attacks. For most of
the play, we have seen Richard as a sham collection of words, ceremonies, and willful whims underneath which lay the quivering
mortal who lived on bread like other men. The Groom's words
may be seen as raising the possibility that, just as the Groom is
unable to express his deep, internal love in external words, so
inside the quivering, helpless, mortal Richard, there might be the
core of a real king unable to express himself in effective actions.

This possibility is reinforced almost immediately, when Exton
enters with the murderers. Richard, the king whose most energetic
actions thus far have been sitting, descending, kneeling, and
throwing down a warder and a mirror, speaks one line and kills
one attacker, then one more line as he dispatches a second. The
dramatic effect is electrifying. It is becoming a critical commonplace to reject these actions as meaningless reflexes,[45] and there
can be no question that the irony of "too little too late" hangs
over the whole scene. But just as, regardless of political wisdom,
Richard's interruption of the combat in act I came as a dramatic

44. Every reader since Van Doren, *Shakespeare* (New York: Henry
Holt and Co., 1939), pp. 85–88, has noticed how often "tongue" appears
in the play, and "heart" appears nearly as often. But especially common
are pairs of terms like the Groom's here with one term of external gesture
and one of internal meaning. A few among dozens of instances are:
"Show me thy humble heart, and not thy knee" (II.iii.83), "My heart
this covenant makes, my hand thus seals it" (II.iii.50), and "you debase
your princely knee . . . Me rather had my heart might feel your love"
(III.iii.190–92).

45. Three recent critics who do this are Winny, *Player King*; Sanders,
Received Idea; and M. M. Reese, *The Cease of Majesty* (London: Arnold,
1961).

letdown, so here, regardless of its ultimate futility, Richard's sudden galvanic explosion satisfies a dramatic longing for some clear action in this murky world of hidden motives and excessive rhetoric. Too little and too late, Richard finally grows in dramatic stature to fill the traditional public role which he has been playing so badly.

At first the effects of Richard's action are visible only in the walled garden of death, the prison, as Richard asserts with a new credibility the connection between his death and the health of the land:

> Exton, thy fierce hand
> Hath with the king's blood stain'd the king's own land.
> [v.v.109–10]

But the effects can be seen rapidly spreading in Exton's "O, would the deed were good!" (114) which suggests the general inadequacy of Bolingbroke's new morality of power that does not look ahead. Even the murderer senses—immediately after he has killed the king—that he deserved to live despite the political inexpediency of leaving an old king alive. In these last moments there is no longer any clear distinction between the two bodies of the king. We cannot tell whether Exton is moved by a sense of Richard's kingliness or by simple human pity. But suddenly it does not matter. Exton comments that Richard was "as full of valor as of royal blood" (113). In death, Richard has become a king by Gaunt's strictest definition. Exton has destroyed both the body natural and the body politic. A man has been murdered and politics has been irrevocably changed, cut off from tradition and religion.

The effects of the king's murder spread into Bolingbroke's court when Exton enters, bringing Bolingbroke his "buried fear" (v.vi.31). The new king has just been acting on the simple assumption that the dead rebels of Aumerle's plot are fears buried, but Richard's corpse, especially after his final demonstration of a certain innate kingly heroism, undercuts this, adding to Exton's line the irony that Richard, buried, may now be Henry IV's fear. Bolingbroke's fierce but effective clarity of action now is clouded with blood that both nourishes and taints, both secures and threatens. Bolingbroke's troubled response to Richard's death—for which

he is at least indirectly responsible—is set both against his own
response to Mowbray's death, which excites the only lyric lines
he speaks, and against Gaunt's response to Woodstock's murder.
Here the new king is troubled and ambiguous but plans to try
to right matters with a crusade. The image of Gaunt's deeply
principled refusal to seek revenge for murder offers a standard by
which we can judge Bolingbroke's revenge for being deprived of
his patrimony which has ended in regicide. It is not so much that
one is right, the other wrong; they are totally different—in terms
of morality, legality, and *monarchy*. *Richard II* has dramatized
the birth of this difference.

Initially, Northumberland claimed the rebel forces intended
only to "Wipe off the dust that hides our country's gilt," but the
dust has become blood, the gilt, guilt. When Bolingbroke com-
plained that Richard had left him as emblem of his nobility "no
sign, / Save men's opinions and my living blood" (III.i.25–26), he
had no idea how thoroughly blood would come to mark the
new age of which he was to become king.[46] In the last scene, he
protests "That blood should sprinkle me to make me grow"
(v.vi.46), but there is nothing he can do about it. He is as frozen
into his role as king with its responsibilities as Richard was before
him. The man who represented the effective, flexible body natural,
putting little stock in royal traditions, rituals, and laws, is now
weighed down with the customary, and sometimes mysterious, responsibilities of the body politic.

The new king's last lines show how thoroughly he is now caught
in a net of new responsibilities.

> I'll make a voyage to the Holy Land,
> To wash this blood off from my guilty hand.
>
> [v.vi.49–50]

He now feels he must at least pay tribute to the old conception
of Christian service which Richard abused and he destroyed by
attacking his king. But, just as dust has turned to blood, so the
ambiguity that used to surround Bolingbroke's actions and motives
has now become irony that the audience perceives at the new

---

46. The word "blood" appears more in *Richard II* than in any other
of Shakespeare's plays except *King John*.

king's expense. The proposed voyage to the Holy Land invokes all the images and allusions that he is least able to support. The comparison of this foreign adventure with Gaunt's "Christian service and true chivalry . . . in stubborn Jewry" or Mowbray's "Streaming the ensign of the Christian cross / Against black Pagans, Turks, and Saracens" (iv.i.94–95) is highly unfavorable to Bolingbroke, especially as his motive appears to be not England's protection or Christ's greater glory so much as "to wash this blood off from my guilty hand." [47]

By this point in the play, the image of washing has acquired a rich flavor of connotations, all of which add to our ironic distance from Bolingbroke at the end. He himself offered reasons for Bushy's and Greene's deaths "To wash your blood / From off my hands" (iii.i.5–6) but, in the light of Richard's warning at his desposition, Bolingbroke's easy confidence that a little voyage will clear him of his deed seems hollow indeed. [48]

> Though some of you, with Pilate, wash your hands,
> Showing an outward pity—yet you Pilates
> Have here deliver'd me to my sour cross,
> And water cannot wash away your sin.
>
> [iv.i.239–42]

And, although Bolingbroke emerges in the *Henry IV* plays as a significantly older and deeper character, the irony of this planned voyage haunts him to his death, which—lest we miss the point—is expressly announced as occurring in the Jerusalem Chamber. It is a bitter irony indeed, but one central to Shakespeare's plan in his tetralogy, that the effective, swift-moving, popular power that sweeps to its revenge in *Richard II* never succeeds in busying giddy minds after killing the king, and therefore never crusades closer to the Holy Land than the neighbor room.

47. The unconscious metonymy ("guilty hand") merely reinforces the sense of unexpected and inescapable consequences.

48. The washing image has occurred elsewhere, enriching its meaning. We have already noted Richard's claim that "Not all the water in the rough rude sea/Can wash the balm off from an anointed king." Later he claims, "With mine own tears I wash away my balm" (iv.i.207). The Queen hopes to "wash [Richard] fresh again with true-love tears" (v.i.10). Paradoxically every use of the image in this play is in fact part of some contrived attempt to *avoid* seeing the clean, clear truth.

In effect, the final scene of *Richard II* serves as much to demonstrate what has been lost in Richard as to interest us in the new king's effective rule. Bolingbroke, firmly in charge of the kingdom, is, we now see more clearly than ever, imaginatively shallow. Richard has lost in the plot, but the contrast in depth between his last scene and Bolingbroke's makes him victor in the poetry. It is his play. The cycle of kingship continues with its ceremonies, foreign adventures, and domestic rebellions; but Richard's linear progression stops, and with it stops the play's real fascination. Though Richard is easily killed, the play seems to show that legitimacy, hierarchy, Christian service, and the ideal unity of the king's two bodies are conceptions at least as deeply rooted in man's nature, as necessary to rule and life, as the new political pragmatism. Richard is unable to reconcile the two bodies of the king in fact. That was where the Elizabethan lawyers were naively optimistic—the two bodies proved tragically irreconcilable as well as fatally inseparable.[49] But he has reconciled them imaginatively or, at least, brought them together in his imagination, as Bolingbroke could not.

At Richard's death there is a strong man on the throne who intends to perform vigorous service. But with Richard, much of the royalty of that throne dies and with it Gaunt's overriding ideal of vigorous Christian service and jewel-like universal unity. In the *Henry IV* plays there are many goods and many evils, strengths and weaknesses, truths and lies—but they are all inextricably entwined. Henry, Hal, Falstaff, Hotspur: all are fascinating, lively, human. But they are diverse, opposed, and mixed—good and evil growing together almost inseparably. It is said of the new King Henry:

> His foes are so enrooted with his friends
> That plucking to unfix an enemy
> He doth unfasten so and shake a friend.
> [2 *Henry IV*, iv.i.207–09]

The world of the *Henry IV* plays is a richer and fuller world,

---

49. Cf. Brutus's comment in *Julius Caesar*—the epitome of a certain tragic awareness of the inseparability of the two bodies: "O, that we then could come by Caesar's spirit,/And not dismember Caesar! But, alas,/Caesar must bleed for it" (ii.i.169–71).

possibly even a better world, but it is definitely a world in which Gaunt's powerful vision of divine correspondences and Christian service is merely an echo from the past or an act of policy for the present. And in place of Richard's reluctant, painful, internal awareness of the paradox of human kingship, there is Hal's shrewd, confident manipulation and exploitation of the variety and ambiguity of life.

Gaunt believed in, and Richard talked of, a world united in harmonious cooperation between heaven and earth, king and people. Henry V actually does bring unity out of the human fact of diversity. The French, Irish, Welsh, Scottish, and English are all brought, through skillful leadership, to support England's king. The appealing Falstaff and, in due course, his small-scale imitations are cut away as unreformable, and dangerous traitors are quickly and effectively uncovered. Whereas, previously, Falstaff (and a younger Henry) had masqueraded as the king (*1 Henry IV*, II.IV.371–474), in *Henry V* the king himself gives up the privilege of his rank in an effort to cheer his men ("A little touch of Harry in the night" IV. Prologue. 47) and, disguised as an ordinary soldier, debates as an equal with Williams and Bates. The battle at Agincourt is fierce and bloody, but Henry is successful in, and generous after, the fighting. He restores the ordered garden of England as no other Shakespearean king can. But ironies and problems gnaw at the edges of the ideal portrait: at the start of the play "England's rightful claims" in France are, at best, somewhat ambiguous, and our dissatisfaction with the Archbishop of Canterbury's arguments is at best clouded, not removed, by the Dauphin's insult of the tennis balls; at the end of the play Burgundy's famous speech picturing the fertile garden of France (*Henry V*, v.ii.38–67) emphasizes as much the present ruin as the future harvest; Henry's threats at Harfleur (III.iii.1 –43) are successful but incredibly brutal, detailing every imaginable horror of a victorious English army gone wild; and, as Norman Rabkin reminds us, the ensuing disaster of *Henry VI*— already familiar to Shakespeare's audience through his own plays —may hang ominously over the picture of restoration and victory at the end of the play.[50]

50. Rabkin, *Common Understanding*, p. 98.

But we need not in any way deny the remarkable picture of a glorious king to recognize that Henry V's way, however admirable in intention and result, is not the way of Gaunt, or, if our glimpses let us judge, of Edward III and the Black Prince. Henry V's is the order of a king who outwits his enemies in court and in the field, and who unites his supporters with his quicker, keener knowledge of human frailty, weakness, and flexibility. The measure of the difference—and of what dies with Gaunt and Richard— can be seen by placing Gaunt's vain hope that his "prophet's" voice will "Inforce attention like deep harmony" against Henry's words at the start of his career, "I know you all" (*1 Henry IV*, 1.ii.190). Between these is no difference in vigor—or rather the difference is in Henry's favor—but the difference is in the view of the world in which, and the means with which, vigor operates. The shift is from religion to politics. Proteus makes a glorious king but his throne is further from God. Most important, the extravagant, brooding, internalizing Richard has vanished to reappear as Hamlet.

✿ 2 ✿

The Name of Action

Richard II and *Hamlet* are both plays about king killing. While the history play, however, leads steadily toward the death of the king, the tragedy moves steadily away from the death of one king and haltingly toward the death of another. *Richard II* reveals the conflict that leads to regicide; *Hamlet* uncovers layer by layer the effects of having killed the king and simultaneously shows the uneven path toward a new, different act of regicide under the label of revenge.

Hamlet, as we might expect, is uniformly more complex than *Richard II.* In place of one dead king, *Hamlet* shows two—old Hamlet and eventually Claudius—besides a dead prince. The opening confusion of conflicting, fiercely held, clearly articulated political claims in *Richard II* gives way in *Hamlet* to the more mysterious uneasiness of frightened guards confronted with a Ghost. Instead of a massive collision in the form of ritual challenges, we hear uncertain voices challenging each other from the dark: "Who's there?" "Nay, answer me; stand and unfold yourself." "Long live the king!" (i.i.1–3). The remarkable thing about this exchange—which sounds a note recurrent in the play—is that neither voice actually answers the other.

In the second scene of *Richard II* we are informed plainly of certain political facts; in the same scene of *Hamlet* we watch Claudius's virtuoso solo performance which accomplishes much business but as a whole only enhances our uncertainties concerning the Ghost. Instead of an emblematic garden scene summarizing the ideals underlying the confused race of historical events, *Hamlet* presents a troupe of players from England—actors acting —who for the most part only add to the pervading ambiguity despite Hamlet's confidence that a "play" is "the thing" to cut through his problem. The single prison soliloquy at Pomfret becomes in *Hamlet* four soliloquies and a long encounter in the graveyard. Richard's prison seems to symbolize the closing in on him of the forces of history, and perhaps also his solipsism, the imprisonment in his own image-making theatrical ego that has characterized him from the start. The graveyard in *Hamlet*, with its references to Caesar and Alexander and all sorts of ages and professions, may also intend this, but it makes us more conscious as well of the broader forces of mortality closing in, and at the same time of the omnipresence of Claudius as he and his court literally invade Denmark's boneyard.

Even to the extent that it shares elements of structure with *Richard II*—as in the close, where in both cases we have movement from meditation to violent death to continuing activities of state— *Hamlet* is more complicated, confused, and subtle. *Richard II* is a play enacted in the main against a background of clear political standards and ideals which cast a certain glow of irony on both the usurper and the king. *Hamlet* is a play of intricate tragic ironies where the background is never clear but where prince and king, especially the former, are granted moments of clairvoyance. Here, too, however, there is a middle ground of resemblance. In both plays, what clarity there is has to do with two opposing sorts of life-style: one that is simpler, infinitely appealing, but no longer viable, especially in the area of kingship; the other complicated, shrewd, and ambiguous. In both plays, the hero manages a peculiar and limited reconciliation of the two—untidy, contingent, but splendid—through a painful growth of insight. But whereas much of the imaginative energy in the history play stems from what I have called a nostalgic vision of an English monarchy supported by the whole host of heaven and responding with Christian service and true chivalry, in *Hamlet,* although the Ghost's command ostensibly moves the plot, the imaginative center lies in the realm that in the preceding play is given to Bolingbroke, the mixed realm of "the indifferent children of the earth" (II.ii.233). The immense variety of an "unweeded garden" now replaces, as the focus of attention, the order of "this other Eden, demi-paradise."

After four scenes of mystery, debate, public ceremony, and private questioning, the Ghost of old Hamlet appears for the second time and speaks to his son. From his first words—"Mark me" (I.v.2)—we feel we are in a climate that contrasts with all the carefully constructed ambiguities of the preceding scenes. The

Ghost knows exactly what he is about, and when his words elicit pity from Hamlet, he counters with "Pity me not, but lend thy serious hearing / To what I shall unfold" (5-6). Hamlet's response underscores a growing consciousness of purpose—"Speak; I am bound to hear" (6)—on which the Ghost then builds: "So art thou [bound] to revenge, when thou shalt hear" (7). With this, we are launched into the short, tense scene that (ostensibly) establishes the motive-power of the plot for the rest of the play. In the first five lines the Ghost has cut through all the uncertainty, pretense, and hysterical passion ("O God! a beast, that wants discourse of reason, / Would have mourn'd longer" i.ii.150–51) of the previous scenes and has turned a play of mystery into a story of revenge. Into an Elsinore of bewildering confusion and deceit comes a clarion call for *action*, pure and simple.

This does not come as a complete surprise, however, since from the opening scene everything we have heard about old Hamlet has emphasized his direct, clear, forceful nature and personality. He comes in armour; his form is "fair and warlike" (i.i.47); he "stalks away" (50) as only a man of physical grandeur can do. He is capable of the "frown" that belongs to monarchs and men accustomed to command, and his military prowess is apparently already legendary.

> Such was the very armour he had on
> When he the ambitious Norway combated;
> So frown'd he once, when, in an angry parle,
> He smote the sledded Polacks on the ice.
>
> [i.i.60–63]

He was known as "valiant," Horatio tells us, to this whole "side of our known world" (84–85).

Against this background, the encounter between old Hamlet and the older Fortinbras that Horatio goes on to describe takes shape in our imaginations as an example of a chivalric form of statecraft that we shall soon learn (from i.ii) is forever past. The two mighty combatants met face to face "in an angry parle" (i.i.62), drew up "a seal'd compact / Well ratified by law and heraldry" (86–87) as to what the winner would take as prize, boldly risked their royal lands on the wager, and then fought openly to the death. Since Hamlet won, he received Fortinbras's

land, and that, by the code of these warriors, should have been
the end of the matter. Old Fortinbras's son, however, evidently
not content with individual trial by battle, plans to try to regain
"by strong hand / And terms compulsative" (102–03)—and with
an army of "lawless resolutes" (98)—the land his father lost. This
attempt reveals a new code wherein power takes precedence over
honor, as the contrast of "compulsative" and "well ratified by
law" suggests. Horatio, who we are later told is "e'en as just
a man / As e'er . . . conversation coped withal" (iii.ii.62–63),
seems to intend a certain difference between father and son when
he describes the way the two Fortinbrases behave: the father
"prick'd on by a most emulate pride, / Dared [old Hamlet] to
the combat" (i.i.83–84); the son—"Of unimproved mettle hot and
full" (96)—has "Shark'd up a list of lawless resolutes" (98). A
certain uncomplicated directness in the individual action and responsibility has given way, one gathers, to more ambiguous initiatives (Denmark has had to *infer* his hostile aims), lawless ruffians,
and mercenary recruitment. All of these details serve to set apart a
world of chivalry whose leading representatives, we now know,
are both dead.

Further reports brought to us by later scenes confirm, while
they also enlarge and civilize, the image we have begun to form
of the elder Hamlet. Horatio calls him, in his conversation with
the prince about the Ghost, "a goodly king," a phrase that seems
to have more in it than simply a glance at physical beauty; and
Hamlet caps this with:

> He was a man, take him for all in all,
> I shall not look upon his like again.
>
> [i.ii.187–88]

In Hamlet's words there sounds again the note of something
precious lost. Earlier, in the first soliloquy, two comparisons have
been made which similarly tend to smooth and humanize one
who might otherwise be seen as simply a roughhewn tribal chief:

> So excellent a king; that was, to this,
> Hyperion to a satyr.
>
> [i.ii.139–40]

> My father's brother, but no more like my father
> Than I to Hercules.
>
> [I.ii.152–53]

Throughout the play, Hercules will reappear as an image in Hamlet's language, underlining how far the world has fallen since the days of heroes.[1] The comparison with Hyperion will recur later in the play too, as Hamlet tries to make Gertrude share his sense of falling off.

> See what a grace was seated on this brow;
> Hyperion's curls, the front of Jove himself,
> An eye like Mars, to threaten and command;
> A station like the herald Mercury
> New-lighted on a heaven-kissing hill;
> A combination and a form indeed,
> Where every god did seem to set his seal
> To give the world assurance of a man.
>
> [III.iv.55–62]

No doubt this passage tells us as much about young Hamlet as about his father, but it represents also a superlative picture of the old king, invoking the whole weight of the classical tradition to support the image of a paragon of men—embodiment of beauty, power, and harmonious variety. The conjunction of Hyperion with Jove, Mars with Mercury, makes old Hamlet a true Renaissance ideal, displaying a perfect balance of virtues—and indeed the seal of every god. Here the style of Hercules is apparently reconciled to the style of Proteus, Mars to Mercury, nor is it forgotten that the reconciliation of strength to grace applies only to men who have, in the manner of Pico's *Oration on the Dignity of Man,* and in the manner of Prince Hamlet's own one-time thoughts of man's action ("how like an angel") and apprehension ("how like a god"), successfully chosen "to be reborn into the higher forms which are divine."[2] The earlier comparison of

---

1. I.iv.83, II.ii.382, v.i.313.

2. Quoted in *The Renaissance Philosophy of Man,* ed. Ernst Cassirer, P. O. Kristeller, and J. H. Randall (Chicago: University of Chicago Press, 1948), p. 226.

Hyperion and a satyr seems likewise to have the upward and down-
ward capacities of man in mind.

Here, at any rate, is an image of superlative humanity that
emerges from reports of the elder Hamlet. Does it conform really
with "this thing" (1.i.21) that appears upon the battlements of
Elsinore? Quite clearly not, or at least not completely. The Ghost,
as we see him, lacks the grace and fullness of being that old
Hamlet is remembered for. He is harsh, even angry, when he
talks with his son. And this difference is only proper, for, as
he himself says to Hamlet, "I am thy father's spirit" (1.v.9) come
back from a prison house of fire to demand vengeance. Furthermore, this Ghost mentions foul crimes done in his "days of nature"
(12) and protests having been "sent to my account / With all
my imperfections on my head" (78–79). In the theater, of course,
the fact that we hear of these crimes only from old Hamlet himself is likely to impress us far more with his own conscience than
his guilt. But they also add to our sense of present confusion
and complexity, however simple the past may have been. The
remembered old Hamlet, the being on whom every god had set
his seal, is forever gone; the days of giants in the earth are past.
Though memory—often idealized—still informs his son's imagination and though his command can still ring loud in the court of
Claudius, the actual human embodiment of so much grace, harmony, and clear virtue has been irrevocably destroyed—if he ever
was as great as memory (and not only Hamlet's) makes him. The
only other great relic of heroic days, old Norway, is himself
"impotent and bed-rid" (1.ii.29). The brontosauruses are doomed.
What we and Hamlet see on the battlements perhaps, in one
way of looking at it, is the last struggling effort of a past or passing
realm to make an impression on the present; and the interest in
the play then comes, as we all know, from the tensions caused by
the old realm's demand for vengeance in a new realm where
ambiguities, masks, and human frailties dominate.

As noted a moment ago, the Ghost's addresses to Hamlet have
a drive and confidence that has been lacking in the language of
the play before. He quickly reveals his demand—"Revenge his
foul and most unnatural murder" (1.v.25)—tells the story of his
death, and vanishes with the instruction: "remember me" (91).

Within the space of ninety lines, he has not only supplied the facts that have been so confusingly missing to this point, but has revealed his personality and values, besides adding (simply by his status as one returned from the dead) a mythic dimension to the meaning of the old king's death. Predictably, from Horatio's description in the first scene of the kind of man he was in life, the Ghost's views are extremely clear and firm. He expresses himself characteristically in superlatives or at least in language of great intensity: his murder was "most foul, strange, and unnatural" (28); his son would be a "fat weed" (32) if he were not "apt" to his father's request; his brother is "that incestuous, that adulterate beast" (42). He knows without hesitation or qualifications that his love for his queen was

> of that dignity
> That it went hand in hand even with the vow
> I made to her in marriage.
>
> [I.v.48–50]

Here his unquestioning confidence in a one-to-one relation of gesture and meaning is striking, especially after Hamlet's earlier words about "seeming" (I.ii.76–86) and after Polonius's advice that Laertes not give his thoughts a tongue or an act (I.iii.59–60).[3] In the same absolute terms—virtue is unshakable and lust unredeemable—he sees his queen's falling off.

> But virtue, as it never will be moved,
> Though lewdness court it in a shape of heaven,
> So lust, though to a radiant angel link'd,
> Will sate itself in a celestial bed,
> And prey on garbage.
>
> [I.v.53–57]

Further, he has a mind evidently used to making direct and rather unqualified projections from interior self to exterior reality. Thus he easily takes for granted in talking to his son that he is "thy dear father" (in this assessment he is right), and satisfies himself with a generalization, as we have just seen, that shrinks everyone involved in his story to a morality figure: Gertrude is equated

---

3. For us it may be especially surprising after the exploitation of the gulf between hand and heart which we noted in *Richard II*.

with lust, Claudius with garbage, and the injured husband with "a radiant angel" (in at least the first of these simplifications he is wrong, as his own concern for Gertrude indicates).

To all this Shakespeare adds, in a decisive touch, that old Hamlet was murdered during his daily rest, "my custom always in the afternoon" (60). The effect of all these little touches is again to enhance our sense of simple forthright "accustomed" ways, a "tradition-oriented" life-style as a modern sociologist might call it, that has been destroyed by Claudius's act of murder.

The murder is given additional mythic dimension, of course, by the vague but suggestive analogy with the Eden story which seems to be available in such allusions as those to the "serpent" in the "orchard." Though we are not, of course, to take this literally, the idea of a serpent in Denmark's garden adds a coloring from Christian sources to the classical references that mark old Hamlet's death as a momentous break, the end of an era, and we perhaps glimpse in his queen's infidelity a more than ordinary "falling-off" (I.v.47). Later images confirm the biblical echo and with it our impression that we look back in some sense upon a lost kingdom. Claudius sees his murder as paralleling Cain's—"It hath the primal eldest curse upon't" (III.iii.37). Hamlet refers to "our old stock" (III.i.119), whose corruption still "relishes" in the fruit it bears, and to Claudius as "this canker of our nature" (v.ii.69), as if the king in some special way epitomized the ineradicable capacity to sin inherited from Eden. Throughout the play, the idea of Denmark as a possible type of the fallen garden is kept before us. The comparison brings a delicately elegiac note to the situation as a whole.

To be sure, Shakespeare balances against these classical and biblical allusions that magnify the image of old Hamlet and his kingdom certain intimately humane concerns that keep the play from becoming either a morality story of a paradise lost or a Senecan story with the Ghost as allegorical Revenge. The Ghost, for example, appears at first to have formulized his narrative as a revenge plot.

> If thou hast nature in thee, bear it not;
> Let not the royal bed of Denmark be
> A couch for luxury and damned incest.
>
> [I.v.81–83]

But he suddenly shifts his tone and commands Hamlet not to turn against Gertrude, the frail woman he has just obliquely characterized as "lust." "Leave her to heaven," he says, sounding like Gaunt to the widowed Duchess, but then, pointing the new, internal direction of this play, adds "And to those thorns that in her bosom lodge" (86–87). Moreover, when he reappears in Gertrude's chamber (iii.iv.110–15), four of his six lines are devoted to protecting her from Hamlet's intensity. Settled, confident, and direct though he may be, in short, he is not as narrowly single-minded as he at first appears, and as his predecessors on the English stage had generally been. On the other hand, the Ghost's first lines upon his reappearance—"Do not forget: this visitation / Is but to whet thy almost blunted purpose" (iii.iv.110–11)—rekindle vividly what must be considered after all the main effect of the play's references to King Hamlet: our sense, and the prince's sense, of a unity of being in which word and deed correspond fully one to the other.

Since the elder Hamlet represents a world in which the boundaries of things—moral, psychological, and philosophical—are settled and rather clearly drawn, its similarities to Gaunt's world are obvious. Its major difference from his is, however, more important for our present purposes. In *Richard II* the stress falls on the idea of a king who is active in Christ's service and, as corollary to that, in the service of the nation; in *Hamlet* it falls on the philosophical or even psychological integration that causes and inspires wholesome action, rather than on the political acts and disciplines in themselves. Though it is a mistake, I think, to see *Hamlet* as merely a personal tragedy,[4] the many critics who do so are right in arguing that the play focuses on peculiarly personal and psychic aspects of problems that Shakespeare elsewhere considers in other terms. In *Richard II*, moreover, the garden offers in an emblematic picture a summary of the ideal: natural growth cultivated and pruned with skill and especially with vigor. In *Hamlet*, no such single emblem exists, but rather a collection of glimpses of an age—of an imagined age—when a man was *integer vitae*. Furthermore, much of the idealization of time past in *Hamlet* has no clear existence outside of the prince's idealizing memory,

4. Among others, John Danby says that king killing in *Hamlet* is "purely private"; see *Shakespeare's Doctrine*, p. 150.

whereas Edward and the Black Prince are historical persons, and we all see Gaunt and the Gardener.

Nevertheless, in *Hamlet* an image of direct action, embodied primarily in the dead king and his dead and dying colleagues, does inform the play with a happy contrast to the muddled present. The overtones from medieval chivalry and from the classical Pantheon contrast with the "weary, stale, flat, and unprofitable" (I.ii.133) quality of the present times under a "satyr" king; and the Edenic overtones of a period before time, or of a period when at least one could count on his "secure hour" (I.v.61), contrast with the unweeded Elsinore of the play, where "Time qualifies" not only the spark and fire of love (IV.vii.114) but everything.[5]

To these contrasts Shakespeare has added one more that deeply humanizes the whole question of direct action—the contrast of father and son. The impact of this special emphasis is obvious from the proliferation in this century of psychoanalytic criticism. Though one suspects this new trend in criticism does not so much explain the special fascination of *Hamlet* as pay it tribute, the psychoanalysts do at least point to a profound reservoir of meanings and implications in the play's images of action as they involve the personal relationship between father and son. *Hamlet* is not lacking in complexity on this matter either: the two Hamlets, the two Fortinbrases, and Polonius and Laertes offer three varieties of father-son relation. Furthermore, scenes in which an older person advises a younger (as if father to son) include, besides those in which the above take part, the scenes in which Claudius tries to advise Hamlet, Norway's advice to Fortinbras is reported, Polonius instructs Reynaldo, and Claudius solicits Laertes. Two of these have a very considerable bearing on the theme of direct action: old Hamlet's instruction to young Hamlet and Norway's to Fortinbras, as reported by Volitimand in act II:

> [Norway] sends out arrests
> On Fortinbras; which he, in brief, obeys,
> Receives rebuke from Norway, and, in fine,

5. All is affected; even the shipwrights do "not divide the Sunday from the week" (I.i.76) any longer.

> Makes vow before his uncle never more
> To give the assay of arms against your majesty.

[II.ii.67-71]

Though some of the brevity comes undoubtedly from the fact that an ambassador is reporting, still an impression of clear and simple acting and reacting is prominent again. Even though "old Norway," as Voltimand refers to him, is "impotent and bed-rid," he is far from helpless and still acts with a directness unmatched in Elsinore under Claudius.

As in *Richard II,* Shakespeare keeps certain limited aspects of this idea of direct action before us throughout the play. One vehicle of the idea is of course young Fortinbras. As we have seen, he is introduced to us framed by Horatio's criticism in the first scene. He is not, we infer from that scene, the man his father was. On the other hand, if he is no respecter of formalities and heraldries, he nevertheless keeps some of his father's zeal for action since he plans to seize back—"by strong hand" (I.i.102)—the lands his father lost. Elsewhere he is shown displaying an equal vigor. He accepts old Norway's rule but not without obtaining his permission to invade Poland. When, eventually, we see him (IV.iv), his low-key businesslike tones may remind us of Bolingbroke's on his way to Flint Castle:

> Go, captain, from me greet the Danish king;
> Tell him that, by his license, Fortinbras
> Claims the conveyance of a promised march
> Over his kingdom.

[IV.iv.1-4]

And he is again like Bolingbroke in being efficient, terse, careful to maintain the forms of ceremony, while at the same time making his case as strong as possible—his "license" and "promised," for example, are clearly calculated to evoke from Claudius a respect for past agreements.

The remainder of this transit scene brings the "direct" world and the "mixed" one together in such a way that they raise some searching questions about each other. Hamlet, ever susceptible in imagination to the appeal of action that is *not* sicklied o'er with thought, and perhaps especially to any action that allows him to expiate his failure to act in self-reproaches, is disposed to glorify the Polish enterprise.

> How all occasions do inform against me,
> And spur my dull revenge! What is a man,
> If his chief good and market of his time
> Be but to sleep and feed?
>
> [iv.iv.32–35]

>   Now, whether it be
> Bestial oblivion, or some craven scruple
> Of thinking too precisely on the event,—
> A thought which, quarter'd, hath but one part wisdom
> And ever three parts coward,—I do not know
> Why yet I live to say "This thing's to do."
>
> [iv.iv.39–44]

>   How stand I then,
> That have a father kill'd, a mother stain'd,
> Excitements of my reason and my blood,
> And let all sleep, while, to my shame, I see
> The imminent death of twenty thousand men,
> That, for a fantasy and trick of fame,
> Go to their graves like beds, fight for a plot
> Whereon the numbers cannot try the cause,
> Which is not tomb enough and continent
> To hide the slain?
>
> [iv.iv.56–65]

Yet he knows at the same time, from the mouth of Fortinbras's captain, that the ground they go to fight for is worthless and that the opposing side, with equal folly, intends to defend it, and this knowledge keeps breaking through.

>   Examples, gross as earth, exhort me;
> Witness this army, of such mass and charge,
> Led by a delicate and tender prince,
> Whose spirit with divine ambition puff'd
> Makes mouths at the invisible event;
> Exposing what is mortal and unsure
> To all that fortune, death and danger dare,

> Even for an egg-shell. Rightly to be great
> Is not to stir without great argument,
> But greatly to find quarrel in a straw
> When honour's at the stake.
>
> [iv.iv.46–56]

Though this paragraph is panegyrical, there is a current flowing the other way in terms like "gross," which quite clearly means more than just "outstanding," and in the implication of something very gay but childish, or perhaps even overweening, in "puff'd" and in "making mouths" and in doing all this "for an egg-shell." Similar currents of opposition move elsewhere in the speech. The first passage quoted is *not* followed, as one might anticipate, by praise of a life of executive decisiveness, but by praise of reason, looking before and after.

> Sure he that made us with such large discourse,
> Looking before and after, gave us not
> That capability and god-like reason
> To fust in us unused.
>
> [iv.iv.36–39]

The second passage deprecating scruple and all worry about outcomes is nevertheless obliged to acknowledge that one time in four there might be wisdom in these inhibitions, an acknowledgement we are likelier to applaud because having scruples and thinking too precisely about the event seems to be established by the context as the unavoidable fate of human kind, in distinction from the "bestial oblivion" of the animals. The countercurrents in the third passage are strongest of all and need no laboring.

What Shakespeare gives us here, I take it, is a confrontation calculated to stir in us something like the same sense of paralysis among unanswered and unanswerable questions that Hamlet seems to experience in himself. How far, we wonder, does Fortinbras represent an active resolution that we must admire? how far an unreflecting egoism that we must deplore? Does he show us a deterioration that has occurred in the old martial virtues in the new world? or simply how the old martial virtues look when viewed from another perspective than their own? Is this honor or merely "the imposthume of much wealth and peace, / That inward breaks" (27–28)? Perhaps there is an ultimate question raised by this troubling passage that goes deeper still. Does it not ask, through its vigorous and dramatic counterpoint of soldiers marching and lonely meditative analysis, whether competing life-styles can ever, in fact, be reconciled, whether action does not by its very finality, always prejudice thought, and thought action? And if this is so, what becomes of all those harmonies of being that we have seen attributed in earlier plays to Henry V and Brutus and in this play to the elder Hamlet, who bears the seal of every god? What becomes of the Renaissance dream of reconciling contraries in the thrilling unison of apprehension and act that Hamlet describes to Rosencrantz and Guildenstern (but even there elegiacally) if the contraries, in fact, tear us apart?

" 'Twere to consider too curiously, to consider so," Horatio would certainly tell us at this point, and possibly he would be right. Yet in the role of Horatio himself the question seems to recur. As many critics have pointed out, he and Fortinbras together make up a "frame" for the prince, one critic choosing to see in them also the basic opposition of the play—thought versus action.[6] It seems to me doubtful, however, that a persuasive case can be made for associating Horatio primarily with "thought" (from the material which the play provides, no gesture could possibly convey this association), and I believe Shakespeare intends them instead as two variant but equally significant embodiments of what I have been outlining here as the image of direct action: centered in old Hamlet, dying but still powerful in Norway, persisting but much modified in Horatio and Fortinbras.

Both these characters stand curiously outside the main action of the play. This seems dramatically appropriate since they are (among other things) subjects whose kings—old Hamlet and old Fortinbras—have been killed. They are, however, distinguished in kind from characters like the Gravedigger, who similarly stands outside the action. Unlike Fortinbras and Horatio, the Gravedigger appears only once and clearly represents certain grim facts that underlie—and undercut—any conception of order or action, reality or appearance. Fortinbras and Horatio have as little to do

6. Holland, *The Shakespearean Imagination,* pp. 163–65.

in spirit with the Gravedigger as they have to do in fact with Claudius. They are also distinguished from the Players, structurally again by their continued role throughout the play, thematically in that they have, apart from other differences such as higher social status, an altogether contrary dramatic function. While the Players enter in the middle of the play and, through their performance and in fact their very presence, complicate the ambiguities of the court, Fortinbras and Horatio throughout remain aloof from the confusion in an apparent simplicity of purpose that challenges it.

This clarifying and contrasting function is perhaps more obvious in Horatio than in Fortinbras. In the very first scene he is called upon by Marcellus to speak to the Ghost because he is "a scholar" (i.i.42), and there is a quiet finality that persuades us in his evaluation of Marcellus's view of the effect of Christmastide on ghosts, "So have I heard and do in part believe it" (165). It is he who explains the recent events that have upset Denmark, and he who takes responsibility for bringing news of the Ghost to Hamlet. I would not suggest on any of these accounts that Horatio is another Fortinbras, a man of action. During most of the play he is content to stand silently beside Hamlet, occasionally helping his greater friend (i.ii.189–242 and iii.ii.95–97), sometimes warning him of danger (i.iv.69–78 and v.ii.226–28). Of his very few lines, most are spoken in the opening and closing scenes, when none of the major characters is able to hear, and before the central conflict has begun or else after it has ended. But perhaps the more for this very reason, he comes through to us strongly as a man whose personality and few actions extend to the new generation something like the simplicity and directness of the elder Hamlet.[7] He therefore serves dramatically as a kind of touchstone, helping to distinguish gold from lead in the surrounding characters and actions.

His touchstone quality is clearly suggested in the tribute Hamlet pays him just before the play within the play:

7. Horatio's concluding line of i.iv ("Heaven will direct it") resembles Gaunt's, "God's is the quarrel." But just as Gaunt was balanced by the Duchess, Horatio is answered by a realist, Marcellus: "Nay, let's follow him."

> Nay, do not think I flatter;
> For what advancement may I hope from thee,
> That no revenue hast but thy good spirits,
> To feed and clothe thee? Why should the poor be flatter'd?
> No, let the candied tongue lick absurd pomp,
> And crook the pregnant hinges of the knee
> Where thrift may follow fawning. Dost thou hear?
> Since my dear soul was mistress of her choice,
> And could of men distinguish, her election
> Hath seal'd thee for herself; for thou hast been
> As one, in suffering all, that suffers nothing;
> A man that fortune's buffets and rewards
> Hath ta'en with equal thanks.
>
> [III.ii.64–76]

What in the "actor" like himself is a moment of achievement—

> use all gently; for in the very torrent, tempest, and, as I may
> say, the whirlwind of passion, you must acquire and beget a
> temperance that may give it smoothness [III.ii.6–10]—

is in Horatio a settled condition that seems to Hamlet supremely
to be desired, like the harmonious unison he will soon attribute
(in his mother's bedroom) to his father. In some respects we must
of course agree. There is an appealing sober realism in all the
glimpses we have of Horatio. Reminded of the speed of the
Queen's remarriage after her husband's death, he agrees, but
with the air of one who has already assessed the matter for himself: "Indeed, my lord, it follow'd hard upon" (I.ii.179). Put off
by Hamlet's pretense that the Ghost only told him "There's ne'er
a villain dwelling in all Denmark / But he's an arrant knave"
(I.v.123–24), he quietly explodes it: "There needs no ghost, my
lord, come from the grave / To tell us this" (125–26). In the
conclusion of Hamlet's jingle after the play scene, where the word
intended to match "was" and characterize Claudius should have
been "ass," he wryly points the joke, "You might have rhymed"
(III.ii.299). His comment on Osric is characteristically shrewd:
"This lapwing runs away with the shell on his head" (V.ii.190).
Throughout, he displays a quiet judiciousness and rational fancy
that distinguish him from Hamlet, whose imagination leads him
alike to ridiculous conclusions and to profound insights.

On the other hand, the very moderation which is the keynote of Horatio's character emphasizes his limitations. He is not on stage when the Players arrive (II.ii.446) or after the murder of Polonius, when Hamlet most needs support and when his antic disposition most resembles genuine madness (IV.i–iv). Is this accident? or is there something in him that might not be able— dramatically—to cope with the questioning of action and identity that occurs when the Players arrive? Shakespeare brings Rosencrantz and Guildenstern and Polonius up against the undercutting nature of the Players' presence, but he spares Horatio. Likewise, when murder has been committed and the noble prince is looking his least noble, Horatio again disappears until after Hamlet has left for England.[8] Shakespeare had of course no use for Horatio in these scenes, since Hamlet serves as his own interlocutor. Would it be fair to add that his presence might also have emphasized the inadequacy of self-sufficiency when faced with Hamlet's dilemma?

In act V, at any rate, Shakespeare certainly uses Horatio's fine sobrieties and balance to convey to us just how much more deeply Hamlet sees into the complexities of his situation than does Horatio. For apart from his little jests at Osric, Horatio's lines in the last act consist almost wholly of "Ay, my lord" and "E'en so, my lord." Of some thirty speeches before Hamlet's death, Horatio has only two lines of any substance, each indicating simultaneously the strength and weakness of his kind of address to the world.

> 'Twere to consider too curiously, to consider so.
>
> [v.i.227]

---

8. According to both the Folio and Quartos, Horatio appears just once before act V, in IV.v with the Queen. In the Folio he has no lines to speak, in the Quartos just two ("'Twere good she were spoken with . . ." 14–15), which the Folio gives to the Queen and which many editors since have given to the Gentleman. Either of these solutions is preferable to the Quarto version, since the lines are scheming and unlike Horatio elsewhere but appropriate to the Queen. Also these lines would spoil the pattern of Horatio having *nothing* to do with the ruling powers of Denmark. The textual evidence is inconclusive but suggests that Horatio's appearance may stem in the first place from an attempt to eliminate the need for the Gentleman.

If your mind dislike any thing, obey it.

[v.ii.226]

At two of the most significant moments in the play—two "epiphanies" with respect to Hamlet's character and development—Horatio can only put the case for common sense. He is not Prince Hamlet, nor was meant to be.

This does not, to be sure, make his simple loyalty less impressive, and, though far outshone in flexibility and understanding, he fearlessly allies himself with his friend in the final duel and would follow him even to death. Both his loyalty and his special quality of stoic moderation ("for thou hast . . . fortune's buffets and rewards . . . ta'en with equal thanks") receive their appropriate recognition in his role of the saving remnant who can endure to draw his breath in pain to try to tell the truth of Hamlet's story. This is a man, obviously, to be worn at the heart's core, like all "Whose blood and judgment are so well commingled / That they are not a pipe for fortune's finger / To sound what stop she please" (iii.ii.77–79). But is he not also one who shows us how high a price this well commingling exacts? As before with Fortinbras, do we not wonder whether he is Shakespeare's wistful epitaph on the Renaissance dream of the man who is *integer vitae,* instead of his hardheaded exemplum of it?

However this may be, the two main survivors at the play's end, Fortinbras and Horatio, are men who have avoided poisons—the former by remaining at a physical distance, the latter by remaining at a moral distance. One may cite, perhaps, as an indication of his special status, the fact that Horatio is the only Dane whom Claudius neither attempts to lure nor succeeds in luring into his web of ambiguities. Even the Priest (v.i) has been influenced by the King to enlarge Ophelia's "obsequies . . . as far . . . as we have warrantise" (v.i.248–49), and the Gravedigger, oldest and most stable of all professionals, has been compelled to break custom and church law (29). Horatio alone, protected apparently by the very self-sufficiency that makes Hamlet admire him, escapes the Claudian touch.

There is then in *Hamlet* a group of characters—old Fortinbras, old Hamlet, old Norway, Fortinbras, and Horatio—who keep alive in their different ways a clear image of an uncomplicated simplicity and sensibility that none of the other characters, Hamlet included, can imitate.

I have mentioned that in every respect *Hamlet* is immensely more complex than *Richard II*. Nowhere is this clearer than in its vast array of "indifferent children of the earth" who fill the role that was assigned in *Richard II* primarily to Bolingbroke and Northumberland. In *Hamlet* the attitudes of Bolingbroke and Northumberland, treated in the earlier play within the limited frame of politics and especially kingship, leaf out to become a whole world of people, relationships, and actions that are as old as Adam and as new as Osric's fashionable modernisms, as socially exalted as the king and as lowly as the Gravedigger, as active as Hamlet (for by the lights of this world, Hamlet *is* active; it would never have occurred to Claudius to reproach Hamlet with delay!) and as passive as Ophelia.

On the imaginative level, *Hamlet* also shows a certain kinship with *Richard II* in the pattern of its action. The earlier play moves almost literally from the order of Gaunt's "other Eden" to "this new world" (iv.i.78) of power under Bolingbroke. In *Hamlet,* this same pattern seems to be implied in the image of the garden that was once secure but is now invaded by a serpent and turned into an unweeded tangle by fratricide—timeless perfection shattered by an act causing death (like Cain's act, to which Claudius refers) and hence the beginning of time. In this sense—a sense that is illuminating and yet so tenuous that even to mention it is almost to warp it—the serpent Claudius has effected a paradigm of the Fall, and even the presence of the Gravedigger, who tells us that he holds up "Adam's profession," becomes a function of Claudius's act. This mythic scheme, suggested in the imagery, hangs like a semitransparent curtain between us and the ordinary political and domestic action of the play. But its effect is not, as in *Richard II*, to mark the change from a sacramental politics to a secular one but to separate a monist world from a pluralist one. *Hamlet* does not focus so much on the *origin* and history of a new conception of kingship as on a *constant* lifelike variety of confused conceptions—not simply of kingship and politics, but of man, nature, God, art, action, life, death, and many more.

Not only does the portrayal of multiplicity and variety replace

what in *Richard II* was essentially a confrontation of an old and
a new kind of power, but the killing of the king and his murderer's
succession to his power is used as a means of exploring in detail
aspects of life that have nothing to do with kingship. It is as if
Bolingbroke the ambiguous politician opposing a king has been
split into numerous little ambiguities in every walk of life, and
a clear rebellion against abused authority has been translated into
terms so complex and sophisticated that rebellion has almost lost
its meaning. For the motto of everyone in this new world, as I
suggested earlier, is that time modifies all intentions and changes
all values and realities. Only Fortinbras and Horatio manage to
escape it, and even the Ghost registers its reality—"O Hamlet,
what a falling-off was there!" (i.v.47)—though he, of course, opposes his own binding command "remember me" (91) to this
tendency toward degeneration and change.

Prominent among those for whom time qualifies all things are
Rosencrantz and Guildenstern, contrasted with Horatio as Hamlet's schoolmates.[9] His joy at first seeing them is obviously genuine
—"My excellent good friends!" (ii.ii.230)—but he quickly senses
that they, unlike Horatio, have changed with time. After this, he
treats them as the tools they have become. Shakespeare's touch
was sure in the creation of this pair. Their names (which vary
a good deal in the early editions, as if no one could keep them
straight, or cared to) perfectly suit the idea of busy little agents
going cheerfully and ineffectively about the business of betrayal.[10]
Their lack of differentiation, to which Gertrude draws attention
(ii.ii.34), renders their shallow frivolity unforgettable. It would
be wrong to see them as villains. They are merely (in their own
Broadway idiom) Fortune's "privates" (240)—witty, shallow, corrupt, and irrelevant. Having betrayed a friend, in time they are in
turn betrayed—the pattern is a little demonstration of the complex
ways in which time qualifies all in Denmark.

9. Appropriately, Richard II's friends split two to one against him
in ii.ii as do Hamlet's. So with Lear and his daughters and with Alonzo
and his companions in *The Tempest*. This seems to be roughly the
dramatic ratio of evil to good in much of Shakespeare's world.
10. The names in the 1603 Quarto—Rosencraft and Guilderstone—are
the most suggestive, though implying some psychological differentiation
not supported by the text.

The creation of the Polonius family was another stroke of genius. Here the family relationship expresses ideally the similarity that exists underneath all variety among the indifferent children of the earth; their total annihilation exemplifies the fierceness of the struggle begun by old Hamlet's murder; and the father-child relationships within the family reverberate, as we have seen, throughout the play against other parent-child relations. Through the three members of the Polonius family, Shakespeare develops with care and variety the theme of Claudius's world, showing in several new ways how time qualifies all. At the same time, especially in the two men, another theme is introduced and developed: the question of what an action is in a world whose layers of deception and self-delusion make it unresponsive to actions either resolute or reckless.

Polonius sets the tone for the family, offering perhaps the clearest opposition that the play contains to old Hamlet's unwavering command to action.[11] He is "assays of bias" (ii.i.65) personified, a windy "windlass" big with confused devotion, old-fashioned wit, honest concern, and expedient corruption. It is not, I think, by chance that Hamlet's encounter with the Ghost on the battlements is framed by scenes of Polonius in action (i.iii and ii.i.), for if ever there was a sensibility antithetical to the Ghost's it is Polonius's. His advice to Laertes, just before the scene on the battlements ("give thy thoughts no tongue . . ." i.iii.59–80), is well known for its disturbing mixture of wisdom and hypocrisy. Cautious, shallow, traditional, and yet sound in its worldly sententious way, it passes over as solved all the crucial problems—such as what the self is to which one must be true.

11. Logically, of course, Polonius must have served old Hamlet too, and we should probably read his character as some indication that all was not so well or clear under the dead king as Hamlet's idealizing and simplifying memories would indicate. But imaginatively it is, I believe, fair to say that Shakespeare manages to convey the impression that he has somehow sprung full-armed ("full of wise saws and modern instances") from the head of Claudius after the crime—a prime example of the new world, or new mode of address to the world, that the crime has generated. In the one temporal clue offered—"Hath there been such a time, I'd fain know that, / That I have positively said ' 'tis so,' / When it proved otherwise?"—"Not that I know" (ii.ii.153–55)—Shakespeare allows Polonius to speak as if he has been in Claudius's employ indefinitely.

We are left wondering where, if a young man masters only these surface graces and manners, the inner man that "apparel oft proclaims" (i.iii.72) will be found. Polonius's advice to Ophelia, warning her against Hamlet with a cloud of references to finance ("pay," "sterling," "tender," "lends," "rate," "brokers," "investments," "suits," 106–29), is a good deal darker in tone and expands our awareness of the principle of appetite and fear of appetite that reigns in this court.[12] The scene after that on the battlements is yet more revealing, for here Polonius, checking on his son through Reynaldo, reveals what an empty ritual he actually suspects his counsel to his son was: a facade like all the other facades that he is about to arrange. Death through an arras, a direction by indirection found, is entirely appropriate.

It is also appropriate that Polonius drops out of the action in the middle of the play. By then, he has served his many functions, first and foremost among them the function of dramatizing for us what it is like to become, in his own phrase, "a thing a little soil'd i' th' working" (ii.i.40), as everyone in Claudius's world must. With him die too the bumbling humor and itch to please which, along with more sinister qualities, characterize him. As the tragedy progresses and the lines of conflict harden, it is as if Polonius's malleable, shifting, profoundly human weakness can no longer find room to breathe, or an arras to hide behind.

Ophelia—a servant of Claudius in a different, more passive way than her father—dramatizes the way time qualifies everything, first in the abstraction of which Shakespeare makes her the mouthpiece, "Lord, we know what we are, but know not what we may be" (iv.v.41–42), and then in her observation of time's effect on Hamlet, "Oh, what a noble mind is here o'erthrown! . . ." (iii.i.158–69). Her fate helps define the ambiguities of action and responsibility in a world of masks, antic dispositions, and ghosts. In love with Hamlet but loyal to her father, she is beset by the circumstance of opposed duties which besets Hamlet more variously and deeply. Her simple retreat into

12. Old Hamlet—at least as pictured by his son—was no stranger to natural desires, since Gertrude "would hang on him / As if increase of appetite had grown / By what it fed on" (i.ii.143–45). There is nothing puritanical in our picture of old Hamlet, just strong natural appetites and energies properly cultivated and controlled.

obedience to one single, paternal command contrasts radically with Hamlet's extended vacillation between demands. Similarly, her role parallels Gertrude's betrayal of the elder Hamlet. Both the play's women "fail" their men, displaying the same mixture of innocence and guilt that saturates all action in Elsinore. But whereas the emphasis on Gertrude's character underlines the play's theme—it is almost a principle—that obedience to one demand does not absolve a person from responsibility for ignoring another, Ophelia is used differently by Shakespeare to sound an elegiac note of lost innocence that underlines the sinister realities of Claudius's rule.

For despite her acceptance of the role of decoy in Polonius's attempts to pluck out Hamlet's mystery, Ophelia brings into the play a different kind of dramatic existence from that of anyone else. She alone is associated with music, songs, prayers, flowers, naive innocence, love-madness—all elements of a lyric, or even a "ballad," tradition that we watch crushed by the ironic and dramatic realities of court life. She reminds us of Barbara in *Othello*, whose Willow Song Desdemona sings shortly before her death. Like her, Ophelia "was in love, and he she loved . . . did forsake her. . . . And she died singing" (*Othello*, iv.iii.26–33). Her gay wit as she warns her brother to follow his own advice (i.iii.46–51) contrasts sharply with Polonius's sending Reynaldo to spy on Laertes; her honest humility answers Hamlet's ruthless "I loved you not" with the simple "I was the more deceived" (iii.i.120–21). She brings us a reminder of the prince that Hamlet was before his father's murder in her collection of love tokens and awkward little poems, and in her elegy to a fallen lyric ideal.

> The courtier's, soldier's, scholar's, eye, tongue, sword;
> The expectancy and rose of the fair state,
> The glass of fashion, and the mould of form,
> The observed of all observers, quite, quite down!
>
> [iii.i.159–62]

Hamlet has had to put all this away, or has had it driven out of him by experience, like the lovely innocent childhood in which she remains. In some ways, her presence continues in the play another aspect of the lost garden world of innocence focused in old Hamlet.

But that world is lost, and Ophelia's lyric life-style is out of
touch with the new Denmark. Her lovely songs are also dirges,
or else are undercut with sexual connotations. In her madness—
as so often in Shakespeare—she touches on many of the play's
themes: sorrow, cruelty, loss, sexuality, mutability, and death.
Her own death is richly prepared for and described, distinguishing
her from Polonius, who dies without a word; Rosencrantz and
Guildenstern, who are cut down offstage; and Laertes, who has
time only to warn Hamlet and beg forgiveness. It would appear
that Shakespeare intended her madness and death to lend dramatic weight to the cost of being corruptible, as well as to the
meaning of being caught between mighty opposites. Like Richard's
Queen, though not so innocent, she shows us the weakness, waste,
and suffering that involves and then uses up little people in a
tragic world.

The description of her death perfectly marks the end of a
way of life for which there is no longer nourishment in Elsinore.

> There is a willow grows aslant a brook,
> That shows his hoar leaves in the glassy stream;
> There with fantastic garlands did she come,
> Of crow-flowers, nettles, daisies, and long purples,
> That liberal shepherds give a grosser name,
> But our cold maids do dead men's fingers call them;
> There, on the pendent boughs her coronet weeds
> Clambering to hang, an envious sliver broke;
> When down her weedy trophies and herself
> Fell in the weeping brook. Her clothes spread wide,
> And, mermaid-like, awhile they bore her up;
> Which time she chanted snatches of old tunes,
> As one incapable of her own distress,
> Or like a creature native and indued
> Unto that element; but long it could not be
> Till that her garments, heavy with their drink,
> Pull'd the poor wretch from her melodious lay
> To muddy death.
>
>   [IV.vii.168–85]

The innocent nymph of the flowers, "native and indued / Unto
that element" of nature, drowns in "the weeping brook"—the

metonymy supports the picture of nature's sympathy. Only the "envious sliver" was hostile. The purity has already been destroyed, however, in that "grosser name" one of her flowers has, and in the sexual obsession madness has released in her in an earlier scene (iv.v.23–65). Her drowning is the perfect emblem of the symbolic value that seems to enfold her: at first her clothes, trappings of the court, hold her up, like her obedience to Polonius, but before long the same courtly trappings pull her to her death. Like a wild bird caged, she flourishes at first, but then is destroyed by the tragic realities of a dramatic—as opposed to a lyric—world.

Polonius is killed in act iii, Ophelia dies in act iv, and Laertes, the last member of the family, is destroyed in act v. In many ways the least interesting of the three, and by far the least seen, Laertes plays nonetheless an important role, especially in presenting further variations on the confused and debilitated nature of action in Claudius's court. Perhaps the most interesting thing about him is the remarkable split in his character between his two appearances. In his advice to Ophelia in act i he sounds like his father—cautious, wise, appropriately cynical. He warns Ophelia that indeed time qualifies all—even though Hamlet "loves you now" (i.iii.14) his love will change with time, for "his will is not his own" (17). Here is yet another occurrence of what Ophelia says when mad about the nature of action in a world dominated by time and change. Laertes, speaking here for all the true servants of Claudius, in effect defines man as something far less autonomous and heroic than old Hamlet's conception of himself as one "whose love was of that dignity / That it went hand in hand even with the vow." In Laertes's view, since a man's will is not his own, his nature must be ever the product of time, place, status, and appetite.

Remarkably, however, when Laertes returns from France (iv.v) he appears changed. The cause of the change is his father's death and this contrasts, or clearly is meant to, with Hamlet's failure to fulfill his vow to "sweep to my revenge" (i.v.31). Laertes now sounds more like the Ghost than like his father: "That drop of blood that's calm proclaims me bastard" (iv.v.116), "I'll be revenged" (134), "O heat, dry up my brains!" (153), and again:

> It warms the very sickness in my heart,
> That I shall live and tell him to his teeth,
> "Thus didest thou."
>
> [IV.vii.56–58]

There is a directness, passion, simple clarity, and confidence here that we have not heard since the scene on the battlements. The Gentleman's description of Laertes's return reminds us of the kind of power that Horatio paid tribute to in his description of old Hamlet on the ice.

> The ocean, overpeering of his list,
> Eats not the flats with more impetuous haste
> Than young Laertes . . .
>
> [IV.v.98–100]

Yet there is a word—"impetuous"—that marks a difference from old Hamlet and an excess that will lead to Laertes's own inglorious death. Another difference is that old Hamlet's first act solemnity and deep religious concern have given way to blasphemy:

> Cut off even in the blossoms of my sin,
> Unhousel'd, disappointed, unaneled;
> No reckoning made, but sent to my account
> With all my imperfections on my head.
>
> [I.v.76–79]

> To hell, allegiance! vows, to the blackest devil!
> Conscience and grace, to the profoundest pit!
> I dare damnation.
>
> [IV.v.130–32]

A little later Laertes declares his willingness "To cut [Hamlet's] throat i' the church" (IV.vii.127). The only other lines remotely similar are Hamlet's in the prayer scene:

> Up, sword, and know thou a more horrid hent;
> When he is drunk asleep, or in his rage,
> Or in the incestuous pleasure of his bed,
> At gaming, swearing, or about some act
> That has no relish of salvation in't;
> Then trip him, that his heels may kick at heaven

> And that his soul may be as damn'd and black
> As hell, whereto it goes.
>
> [III.iii.88–95]

Such extreme language points in both men more toward hysteria than toward action. Intoxicated with fantasies of drinking "hot blood," Hamlet immediately passes up a chance to kill Claudius while he is trying, but not managing, to pray (III.iii). Ready for "bitter business," he mistakenly slaughters an irrelevant Polonius—bitter business indeed. The irony of the two mistakes, coming hard upon his uncompromising assertions of preparedness, underscores the weakness in this kind of narrow, intense passion. It also, of course, adds further evidence of the complexity and ambiguity in the performance of any action at all, apart from "accidental judgments, casual slaughters," among the arrases of Elsinore. Likewise with Laertes: his blind blasphemous ferocity leads to no clear revenge but simply allows him to become a tool in Claudius's plot. Within thirty lines of his stormy entrance, he has dwindled from the revenger he would be to the tricky villain Claudius will use. The change is enormous and in the theater electric. To use Hamlet's terms, it becomes evident that not only from "thinking too precisely on the event" (IV.iv.41) can "enterprizes of great pitch and moment . . . lose the name of action" (III.i.86–88) but also from feeling too passionately. The result is always the same in Elsinore: the contraries of mind and feeling are not reconciled in some ineffable unison of being, but pulled apart, and the action planned becomes blurred, ambiguous, confused.

This is pitilessly detailed in the rest of Laertes's short career. The man who dared damnation is soon plotting to cheat at games, and adds a horrid poison in case his dueling skill should fail him. The man who stormed alone into the royal presence ordering his supporters to remain outside (IV.v.111) soon allows Claudius to back up his poisoned sword with a poisoned drink. The man who demanded straight answers, crying, "I'll not be juggled with" (IV.v.129), learns to make niggling distinctions so that his plot of stealthy murder may succeed.

> I am satisfied in nature,
> Whose motive, in this case, should stir me most

> To my revenge; but in my terms of honour
> I stand aloof.
>
> [v.ii.255–58]

And he meets the courteous apologies of his victim with a lie:
"I do receive your offer'd love like love, / And will not wrong it"
(v.ii.262–63). Time has qualified another action, turning justifi-
able anger into treachery.

Buried in the middle of the long, dark scene in which Laertes
and Claudius plot Hamlet's death is a short passage that contrasts
with what surrounds it and by comparison makes the process of
Laertes's seduction yet more sinister. As background for his plot,
Claudius recalls the visit to Elsinore of a certain Lamord, and for
no very obvious reason, describes his horsemanship at length.

> I have seen myself, and served against, the French,
> And they can well on horseback; but this gallant
> Had witchcraft in't; he grew unto his seat,
> And to such wondrous doing brought his horse
> As he had been incorpsed and demi-natured
> With the brave beast; so far he topp'd my thought,
> That I, in forgery of shapes and tricks,
> Come short of what he did.
>
> [iv.vii.84–91]

The passage is remarkable for its evident irrelevance to Claudius's
plan, which has nothing to do with horsemanship, and also for its
superlatives. The picture it offers of Lamord and his mount, control and power ideally fused, contrasts totally with the deep divisions, psychic as well as sacred, that we have seen in Elsinore. The
passage might well recall Carlisle's description of Mowbray's foreign exploits in *Richard II* (iv.i.91–100), a lyric glimpse of lost
simplicity and vigor that likewise appeared in the middle of a
scene of plotting, though this in *Hamlet* is the more stunning since
here Claudius, the plotting villain, pays tribute to a unity that is
beyond even his power to imitate, expert though he is "in forgery
of shapes and tricks." It is as if Shakespeare were bent on keeping
the possibility of "integrity" before us even while we watch it
swamped by confusion and duplicity. In Elsinore, control and
power, thought and feeling, charioteer and chariot are never at
one.

The Polonius family is, of course, matched by the "family" of Players who dominate three crucial scenes in the center of the play. For clarity's sake, I will postpone consideration of their infinite variety until later when they can be viewed together with Hamlet—with whom they become so essentially allied. Here we need only note that, as is appropriate to representatives of Shakespeare's own profession, these Players refuse to be classified in any simple way. They embody a cheerful memory out of Hamlet's happy past at school, yet they slide immediately into his present complex and devious intrigue. Their travels are a product of the hard times, and yet their art recalls great and timeless memories. They are competent and efficient in action, and yet their actions are essentially the feigned actings of the stage. In other words, like the chameleon or that favorite Renaissance figure Proteus,[13] they change their color and shape depending on where they are and how we see them. And, as we will see, Elsinore's view (or views) of the Players may be significantly different from our own.

In the last act, three new characters are added to the play, as if to replace some of the variety lost through the actors' departure and the deaths of Polonius and Ophelia. The Gravedigger (and helper) and Osric, low and high, outdoor and indoor, blunt and devious, serve to make inescapable the qualifyings of time and the ambiguities that have been developed throughout the first four acts. But a new dimension to the picture of Claudius's "children" is added with these characters, or rather is clarified through them: the relationship between word and act.

Osric is one of the most bizzare and daring of Shakespeare's creations. In the very last scene of the play a character never before seen bursts onto the stage, interrupting Hamlet's conversation with Horatio to announce the wager of the king. But he does not just interrupt. He stays and talks for over one hundred lines, so that when he finally leaves there are only two hundred lines left in the play. In one respect, his entrance resembles Exton's in *Richard II*, for he too is a death-bringer, yet the very mention of this com-

13. For a wonderfully complete and suggestive discussion of the figure of Proteus in the Renaissance see A. Bartlett Giamatti, "Proteus Unbound: Some Versions of the Sea God in the Renaissance," in *The Disciplines of Criticism*, ed. Peter Demetz, Thomas Greene, and Lowry Nelson, Jr. (New Haven: Yale University Press, 1968), pp. 437–75.

parison reminds us again how much more indirect and various *Hamlet* is than the earlier play. In ten lines Exton can contemplate, perform, and reflect on Richard's murder, while it takes Osric ten times that long merely to issue an invitation to a match in which murder will occur. There is a brutally tight connection in suiting the action to the word in Exton, whereas in Osric the word completely overwhelms action apart from the waving about of a hat.

Osric is the quintessence of air. He renews our sense of the protean ambiguity of court language as he makes his unconscious puns and double entendres ("weapon," "carriages," "imponed," "answer"). He renews our sense too of protean pliability in the courtier personality as he echoes Polonius's discussion of cloud shapes (iii.ii.395–401), seeking to humor Hamlet's contradictory views. But whereas Polonius at least sought directions by his indirections, Osric flows in whatever way Hamlet leads him; and whereas Polonius can be run through with cold steel, mistakenly but fatally, because he is engaged with his world not only as "actor" but also in his own oblique ways as one who acts, Osric (one likes to imagine) could not. He is utterly the tool, so completely unsubstantial that he would be safe even between the fell incensed points of these mighty opposites (as indeed he is in the final duel). We are never even told whether he is aware that one sword is poisoned. In Claudius's world, which is of course also ours, the surfaces have become so persuasive that the messenger of death may not even know the meaning of his message, the carrier of poison may be ignorant of what he carries.

Superficially, the Gravedigger and his helper appear to be the opposites of Osric. Osric waves his hat, they dig; he represents the court, they represent the country; he flatters Hamlet, they answer his questions bluntly while keeping to their work. But these obvious differences are far outweighed by essential similarities in the roles they play and the themes they help develop. Like Osric, they dramatize the extremes of confusion and ambiguity, the overwhelming complications of action, words, and time's changes.

To consider action first, the Gravedigger has no trouble at all with a kind of complexity that we have watched other characters wrestle with in so many ways: "an act hath three branches, it is, to act, to do, and to perform" (v.i.11–13). However, as so often in

Elsinore, this neat summary with its clear, tidy distinction, does not hold up,[14] and the Gravedigger is soon considering whether the water acted in drowning Ophelia, or she in entering the water: "Here lies the water; good: here stands the man; good: if the man go to this water, and drown himself, it is, will he nill he, he goes; mark you that: but if the water come to him, and drown him, he drowns not himself: argal, he that is not guilty of his own death shortens not his own life" (15–22). His earlier conclusion, "argal, she drowned herself wittingly" (13), is obviously at variance with Gertrude's description in the preceding scene of Ophelia's madness and the envy of the "sliver."[15] Action has already been distorted and confused by someone's story. Rejecting the puzzling possibility that "she drowned herself in her own defense" (6–7), he and his helper are soon talking as if an action had nothing to do with Ophelia's burial, taking for granted that even in the graveyard an action is, to adapt Hamlet's words on the subject, only one part wisdom and ever three parts social manipulation: "If this had not been a gentlewoman, she should have been buried out o' Christian burial" (25–27).

That the whole passage (v.i.1–31) apparently has roots in an actual law case of the day may have pointed up its humor for the

14. All simple summaries—like Polonius's "it must follow, as the night the day, / Thou canst not then be false to any man" (i.iii.79–80), the Ghost's "So art thou [bound] to revenge, when thou shalt hear" (i.v.7), Claudius's "And where the offence is let the great axe fall" (iv.v.217), and Hamlet's "My thoughts be bloody, or be nothing worth!" (iv.iv.66)—all these and many more are shown to be inadequate or impossible in the complex life of Elsinore.

15. Memory of that "envious sliver" may keep the gravediggers' discussion of whether the water came to Ophelia from degenerating into merely crude wit—there may be unconscious method in their madness, just as there was in Richard's hope that his horse would stumble under its new rider. The possibility of a genuine sympathy (Richard's horse) or conspiracy (Ophelia's water) of nature remains alive throughout Shakespeare, even when it is exiled to the very edges of his world, as here. The special quality of scenes like these, or the Gardener's with rue in *Richard II* and Ophelia's with the same flower in this play (iv.v.180–82), keeps open the possibility—however faint—that flowers can really participate in the emotions their names symbolize, that nature can match and surpass art. This of course becomes a central concern in the last plays, especially *The Winter's Tale*.

original audience.[16] But simply in terms of the preceding scenes, the purpose of this pseudotheological debate is clear. Along with the rest of the gravediggers' speeches, it shows that they have no less trouble with language than the other characters. Osric is merely an extreme case of a contagious disease in which words become treacherous, either as masks to hide false meanings, or as levers that enable meanings to be shoved around at will. Claudius's opening monologue, to be considered shortly, clearly relies on the capacity of words to make clear meanings evaporate. Polonius can make the simple revelation of Hamlet's love poem take eighty lines (ɪɪ.ii.86–167). In Hamlet's speech, too, the sense always has to struggle with an excess of words. That this is often the result of uncontrollable passion (ɪ.ii.129–59) or part of an antic disposition (ɪɪ.ii.172–223) does not lessen the effect on the audience of hearing language repeatedly disintegrate into a verbal puzzle or game.

There is, however, an important difference in the gravediggers' verbal games. Osric abuses language through his desire to impress, and he constantly forces and misapplies words so as to make them strut. Hamlet parodies this tendency brilliantly: "But, in the verity of extolment, I take him to be a soul of great article, and his infusion of such dearth and rareness, as, to make true diction of him, his semblable is his mirror, and who else would trace him, his umbrage, nothing more" (v.ii.118–23). The gravediggers' problems are different. They do not use words to impress, but in a literal way that creates ambiguity: "The crowner hath sat on her, and finds it Christian burial." Heraldry, weaponry, and anatomy become all entangled when the Gravedigger describes Adam as "the first that ever bore arms" (36). Indeed, their use of words is so often ambiguous that it is hard to tell when they are punning consciously, as here, and when unconscious meanings undercut their intention, as in the "crowner" who "hath sat on" Ophelia. When Hamlet asks whose grave is being dug, the Gravedigger delights in the extended confusion he can create by answering the question with words used in their most basic senses.

> *Hamlet.* Whose grave's this, sirrah?
> *Gravedigger.* Mine, sir. . . .

16. *Hales* v. *Petit.* See Introduction, n. 26.

Hamlet. I think it be thine, indeed, for thou liest in 't.

Gravedigger. You lie out on't, sir, and therefore 'tis not yours; for my part, I do not lie in 't, and yet it is mine.

Hamlet. Thou dost lie in 't, to be in 't, and say it is thine; 'tis for the dead, not for the quick; therefore thou liest.

Gravedigger. 'Tis a quick lie, sir; 'twill away again, from me to you.

Hamlet. What man dost thou dig it for?

Gravedigger. For no man, sir.

Hamlet. What woman, then?

Gravedigger. For none, neither.

Hamlet. Who is to be buried in 't?

Gravedigger. One that was a woman, sir; but rest her soul, she's dead.

[v.i.128–47]

Hamlet's comment, "How absolute the knave is! we must speak by the card, or equivocation will undo us" (148–49), draws attention both to the peculiar, reductive nature of the Gravedigger's wordplay and to the essential similarity, though at a different language level, between this equivocation and that of Claudius and Polonius. As in court, so here; meaning gets suffocated in surfaces, and people pay less attention to the meanings than to those surfaces with which tricks—fashionable (as by Osric) or absolute (as by the Gravedigger)—can be played.

The whirligig of time is the one clear, predictable reality for the gravediggers. This it is that makes them "ancient gentlemen" along with gardeners and ditchers (32), except that *their* work will last till doomsday" (66).[17] A man will last "some eight year or nine year," assuming that "a' be not rotten before a' die,—as we have many pocky corpses now-a-days, that will scarce hold the laying in" (179–82). What little moral optimism lies in the hint that a man need not be rotten before he dies is taken away in the rude hierarchy of the graveyard: here the tanner is king, because "his hide is so tanned with his trade that a' will keep out water a great while" (185–87). And the Gravedigger's reference to "pocky corpses" certainly seems to indicate that they are becoming more

17. This reference completes the chronological pattern from Eden to the end, the biblical pattern from Genesis to Revelation.

numerous "now-a-days"—another case of degeneration from the past. Time qualifies all—even Yorick's skull is moved in thirty years. The cycle is relentless:

> *In youth, when I did love, did love,*
> *Methought it was very sweet,*
> *To contract, Oh! the time, for, Ah! my behove,*
> *Oh! methought there was nothing meet.*
>
> *But age, with his stealing steps,*
> *Hath claw'd me in his clutch,*
> *And hath shipp'd me intil the land,*
> *As if I had never been such.*[18]

[v.i.68–81]

Sooner or later, everything ends up here: *"Enter Priests, etc. in procession; the Corpse of* Ophelia, Laertes *and Mourners following;* King, Queen, *their Trains, etc."*

Claudius, while clearly not the cause or creator of all the indifferent children of the earth, is appropriately their king—their best and worst. Murderer of the old king, he is the epitome and the dynamic center of all the ambiguities, changes, and masks that now fill Elsinore. With him, the medieval dream of the prince who is a mirror of all knighthood has darkened into Machiavelli's prince who is a master of treasons, stratagems, and spoils: he has become the manipulator, the mask wearer, the stage manager. Polonius displays traces of this function but is too old, awkward, bumbling, and too much pleased with his own sagacity to be effective at it. Neither of his little plays managed from behind curtains (iii.i and iii.iv) turns out successfully. All the other characters we have considered lack the necessary depth and self-awareness to be villains in their own right—they are useful only as actors in Claudius's complicated plot to hide his murder and secure his throne.

In fact, Claudius himself is not so much an indifferent child of

---

18. Time even qualifies the Gravedigger's song as his exertion interrupts the rhythm of the first stanza. It was time the musicians in *Richard II* could not keep either.

the earth like the others as he is (drawing on the same nonbiblical tradition Milton was to popularize) a fallen angel, who, though darkened, yet shines. His main characteristic is ambiguity. It is an ambiguity of which he is fully conscious, and in this respect he is unlike Bolingbroke. It is also an active ambiguity, and in this he differs from his victims. Ophelia and Laertes collaborate in ambiguous situations, but they do not make them. Claudius does. He is "creatively" ambiguous. Before the final duel at one moment—and only one—he sounds like a traditional uncomplicated villain.

> And, England, if my love thou hold'st at aught,—
> . . . .
>   thou may'st not coldly set
> Our sovereign process; which imports at full,
> By letters conjuring to that effect,
> The present death of Hamlet. Do it, England;
> For like the hectic in my blood he rages,
> And thou must cure me.
>   [IV.iii.61–70]

But only when under extreme pressure from Hamlet, as here, does Claudius appear like the kind of man we would expect to have murdered old Hamlet. At other times, he sounds precisely like a proper king, in the vein of Gaunt, Richard, or his own older brother:

>   do not fear our person;
> There's such divinity doth hedge a king,
> That treason can but peep to what it would,
> Acts little of his will.
>   [IV.v.121–24]

This is undercut, of course, by irony. No one knows better than Claudius just how inadequate "divinity" was to "hedge" the previous king. The same irony (in Claudius's mind and ours) pervades the comment of Rosencrantz and Guildenstern when they take up the king's view that Hamlet has become a personal danger to him.

>   The cease of majesty
> Dies not alone, but like a gulf doth draw

> What's near it with it; it is a massy wheel,
> Fix'd on the summit of the highest mount,
> To whose huge spokes ten thousand lesser things
> Are mortised and adjoin'd; which, when it falls,
> Each small annexment, petty consequence,
> Attends the boisterous ruin. Never alone
> Did the king sigh, but with a general groan.
>
> > [III.iii.15–23]

And here the irony is sharpened by our suspicion that they speak only what they know Claudius wants to hear. Nevertheless, these traditional reverberations have the effect of adding to Claudius's dignity because he is in fact a king, and, in the course of the play, all the characters except Hamlet (and Horatio and Fortinbras, of course) do in some way come to "serve" him. When he toasts Hamlet in the last scene, we know that he is cunningly misapplying the ancient rituals and correspondences.

> And let the kettle to the trumpet speak,
> The trumpet to the cannoneer without,
> The cannons to the heavens, the heaven to earth,
> "Now the king drinks to Hamlet!"
>
> > [v.ii.286–89]

Yet we can still kindle to the image of the whole universe in unison with the true king, even as we recognize that Claudius is not such a king.

If at one moment Claudius sounds like a villain, at another like a king, at still other moments he sounds like a wise observer with a broad awareness of the human condition.

> Not that I think you did not love your father,
> But that I know love is begun by time,
> And that I see, in passages of proof,
> Time qualifies the spark and fire of it.
> There lives within the very flame of love
> A kind of wick or snuff that will abate it;
> And nothing is at a like goodness still,
> For goodness, growing to a plurisy,
> Dies in his own too-much; that we would do
> We should do when we would; for this "would" changes,

And hath abatements and delays as many
As there are tongues, are hands, are accidents;
And then this "should" is like a spendthrift sigh,
That hurts by easing.

[IV.vii.111–24]

This is a remarkable passage. It offers an approach to life that could conceivably explain Claudius's earlier act of murder ("that we would do / We should do when we would") and it is also part of Claudius's seduction of Laertes. But there is more here. The idea that the "wick" or "snuff" in the very flame of love must kill it is an even bleaker image of human limitation than the Gravedigger's view of the "many pocky corpses" rotten before they die. For Claudius's image claims that time qualifies not from without but from within, from some internal dynamic or divisiveness inside love itself. These are hardly the typical views of a king-killing "over-reacher." The notion that goodness "Dies in his own too-much" might even be used to raise questions about Hamlet and old Hamlet, if, as appears, it may be stretched to imply that murder is not a moral outrage, since goodness destroys itself if it is not destroyed by something else.[19]

This speech alone establishes Claudius's view of the world as fascinating and frightening. What he says about love has certainly been shown to be true in a play of hasty remarriage, betrayal of friends and loved ones, deceit, confusion, madness, death. Yet at the same time there is considerable evidence of his continuing affection for Gertrude even in this very scene.

She's so conjunctive to my life and soul,
That, as the star moves not but in his sphere,
I could not but by her.

[IV.vii.14–16]

His star-imagery evokes the full weight of the traditional correspondences between man and the hierarchical universe to emphasize the quality and permanence of his love. Are we to suppose that there are more things in heaven and earth than are dreamt

19. Cf. Hamlet's comment on wealth and peace festering (IV.iv.27–29) which is thematically related to Claudius's here.

of in Claudius's conscious philosophy? or are we to assume that all this is put on for the benefit of Laertes?

The first time that we see the king—and first impressions count for a great deal in drama—we see a man who is completely in charge. It is frequently observed that Shakespeare brings us off the windy battlements into the close, corrupt court, Hamlet's "unweeded garden"; but it is equally true that he brings us from the cold and dark into the warm society of the court under Claudius's efficient hand. In either case, Shakespeare has clearly structured the scene to dramatize a ruler who deals efficiently with his predecessor's death, his marriage, a possible threat to his throne from Fortinbras, and the journey of Laertes, all in fifty lines.

Just as surely, on the other hand, Shakespeare has given to Claudius in this same first scene a language that becomes more and more enigmatic as we reflect on it. Consider, for example, his first sentence:

> Though yet of Hamlet our dear brother's death
> The memory be green, and that it us befitted
> To bear our hearts in grief and our whole kingdom
> To be contracted in one brow of woe,
> Yet so far hath discretion fought with nature
> That we with wisest sorrow think on him,
> Together with remembrance of ourselves.
>
> [1.ii.1–7]

This is an extraordinary opening, winding through five lines of qualification before the thing qualified is revealed! It is a skillfully constructed sentence of exceptional inversions and unusual metrical regularity, all of which enhance the formal and formulaic quality of Claudius's thought. Our introduction to the king is to a man who is taking his time, picking his words, qualifying his qualifications.

And the second sentence is like the first:

> Therefore our sometime sister, now our queen,
> The imperial jointress of this warlike state,
> Have we, as 'twere with a defeated joy,—
> With one auspicious and one dropping eye,
> With mirth in funeral and with dirge in marriage,

> In equal scale weighing delight and dole,—
> Taken to wife: nor have we herein barr'd
> Your better wisdoms, which have freely gone
> With this affair along: for all, our thanks.
>
> [I.ii.8–16]

Seven lines are used to say essentially eight words: therefore our sister have we taken to wife. The sentence positively groans with carefully matched antitheses: "sometime sister, now our Queen," "defeated joy," "one auspicious and one dropping eye," "mirth in funeral," "dirge in marriage," "delight and dole." Here surely is judicious balance growing to a pleurisy, dying of its own too-much. Claudius reminds those gathered that he consulted them, perhaps to thank them, perhaps to forestall all chance of protest now. Both possibilities make themselves felt.

When the king confronts Hamlet, the ironies become clearer, as everyone will recall: "But now, my cousin Hamlet, and my son—" (64). Claudius tries here to win over Hamlet, to insinuate that from being merely cousin, marriage has made him son, to envelop him in the smooth, public show that he is putting on. But Hamlet, on his side, demurs. He sees the point of Claudius's crescendo from cousin to son, but will not go along: "A little more than kin, and less than kind" (65). Though the king presumably does not hear the aside, he senses the rebuff, and his tone becomes more pointed: "How is it that the clouds still hang on you?" (66).

He now lets Gertrude attempt to mollify her son before making what must be one of the play's most curious speeches.

> 'Tis sweet and commendable in your nature, Hamlet,
> To give these mourning duties to your father:
> But, you must know, your father lost a father. . . .
>
> [I.ii.87–89]

Basically, this introduces sound advice on the need for "mourning duties" and for accepting death. But, carried away by his own rhetoric perhaps, the king rises to an intensity that seems to go beyond the requirements of the occasion.

> Fie! 'tis a fault to heaven,
> A fault against the dead, a fault to nature,

> To reason most absurd, whose common theme
> Is death of fathers, and who still hath cried,
> From the first corse till he that died to-day,
> "This must be so."
>
>   [I.ii.101–06]

As the play develops, Denmark's theme will indeed become the death of fathers—and wives, mothers, friends, and princes. But here as a general speech of consolation to reassure a moody grief-struck youth, the king's words seem to protest too much. To behave as Hamlet is behaving is "obstinate," "impious," "unmanly," "peevish"; he shows "a will most incorrect," "a heart unfortified," "a mind impatient," "an understanding simple and unschool'd" (93–97)! For a moment—though only for a moment—the sense of ease so expertly created by Claudius in his earlier speech staggers; traditional wisdom becomes a weapon. The very mask of reassuring words betrays that it is a mask.

In Claudius's first scene, then, Shakespeare introduces us both to management of words and to something in the man that threatens to break through the mask. During most of the play, we see only the managing Claudius, manipulating his creatures in a whole series of defensive little plays aimed at creating stability in the new state: Fortinbras is diverted to Poland, Rosencrantz and Guildenstern set to spying, Ophelia "loosed" to her lover, Hamlet shipped for England, Laertes seduced into Claudius's plot, the fatal duel arranged. These devices are not, however, uniformly successful. For one thing, Hamlet is also skillful at deceit and manipulation and this enables him to control Claudius's pawns. To use his own terms, he delves one yard below Claudius's mines, beats the king at his own game of masks. For another thing —and this is what I believe Shakespeare already hints at in Claudius's opening speech—there is something that makes for failure in the man himself, something he calls conscience:

> How smart a lash that speech doth give my conscience!
> The harlot's cheek, beautied with plastering art,
> Is not more ugly to the thing that helps it
> Than is my deed to my most painted word.
>
>   [III.i.50–53]

This is a moment of what in the preceding chapter I have called internal awareness. In *Richard II*, such moments usually involve an awareness of the disparity as well as the connection between the two bodies of the king and between gesture and meaning. Here, likewise, the moment of awareness is expressed in terms like "plastering art" and the distinction between "deed" and "painted word." For an instant, we are given a glimpse of both the mask of the king and the man who has murdered, both the painted word and the ugly deed behind it. Predictably, however, in this play, the demands of the moment—the qualifying effects of time —require reassumption of the mask as Hamlet enters and Claudius steps behind the arras, preferring the practical safety of stage-managing to the precarious nobility of complex internal awareness, choosing intrigue in place of insight.

In the prayer scene, we again see Claudius torn by his double awareness of the nature of his deed and the standards he has ignored. I have already noted the connection between his words in this scene ("It hath the primal eldest curse upon't, / A brother's murder!" III.iii.37–38) and the Fall imagery of the Ghost's speeches in act I. But themes more central to the play are developed further too. The constant problem of action and its ambiguous relationship to will reappears.

> Pray can I not,
> Though inclination be as sharp as will:
> My stronger guilt defeats my strong intent,
> And, like a man to double business bound,
> I stand in pause where I shall first begin,
> And both neglect.
>
> [III.iii.38–43]

The mention of "double business" may just possibly recall the biblical warning that no man can serve two masters, but the main emphasis still is on the theme of action ending in inaction, which is also to prove to be the experience of the hero. Claudius's comments on the same problem link the two opposite characters in a common experience.

In this condition of confusion, Claudius longs for a simplicity that the other indifferent children of Elsinore (excepting Ophelia) never seem to miss:

> Is not there rain enough in the sweet heavens
> To wash [this cursed hand] white as snow?
>
> [III.iii.45–46]

This recalls the washing imagery of *Richard II*, especially the Queen's vain hope that tears will wash away all stains and Richard's assertion that "water cannot wash away [the rebels'] sin." Claudius discovers here what Richard II and Henry IV both have to learn in their different ways: that though there are gaps between man and king, face and mask, deed and word, action and intention, there are also connections—subtle, strong connections that demand consideration and impose responsibility. One cannot kill a king and merely wash away the guilt with a crusade (Bolingbroke) or a marriage and the assertion that nothing has really changed (Claudius). Responsibility will make itself felt both externally (Richard at Flint, Bolingbroke in *1* and *2 Henry IV*, Claudius in act v) and internally (Richard in Pomfret, Bolingbroke with Hal in *2 Henry IV*, Claudius here).

Claudius also discovers that being a king involves more than merely killing a king and imitating a royal style. This may suffice for a while in Elsinore, but there is a bigger world:

> In the corrupted currents of this world
> Offence's gilded hand may shove by justice,
> And oft 'tis seen the wicked prize itself
> Buys out the law; but 'tis not so above;
> There, is no shuffling; there, the action lies
> In his true nature. . . .
>
> [III.iii.57–62]

Pervasively a religious play, though in nontheological terms, *Hamlet* constantly expands, as here, the private story of Denmark's royal family to include all Denmark, all Europe, all this world, and adumbrations of another. The particular terms, however, in which Claudius puts his conception of a realm of clarity and directness opposed to the "gilded" ambiguity of this world are revealing, for once again the difference is seen in terms of action: "there, the action lies / In his true nature." Throughout the play, this intuition of direct action beckons elusively in the middle of all the acting, lies, masks, confusion, and change.

As usual, however, time qualifies. Claudius is soon back to playing the efficient king and loving uncle, grieved by Hamlet's rashness in killing Polonius. Indeed, after this scene in act III, he never again evinces this kind of dramatic internal awareness, but becomes increasingly villainous and crafty—if also increasingly weary—until the very end. His only moment of dramatic complexity in the last acts comes at the close when he warns his wife, "Gertrude, do not drink!" (v.ii.301). This moment will depend largely on staging for its effect. In the text, it is not clear whether Claudius could have done more to stop Gertrude or whether, as he says, "it is too late!" (303). Having lost, or sacrificed, Gertrude, Claudius dies the villain, thinking only of his own defense ("Oh, yet defend me, friends; I am but hurt" 335), still trying to hide fatal realities under a mask of calming words.

It is in such a world—corrupt, wordy, changing, ambiguous— that Hamlet is ordered by the Ghost to "revenge his foul and most unnatural murder" (i.v.25) by killing the king.[20] Though Elsinore is still informed with faint recollections of direct action in the reported talk of a character like Fortinbras, and in brief glimpses of a simpler, clearer world like Norway's (i.i.60–63) and Lamord's —nonetheless, the Ghost's command stands apart as if it were some timeless norm in an essentially time-bound atmosphere.

Hamlet, like Richard II, is caught between two opposed value systems, but his problem from the start is much more an internal, even psychic, one than Richard's. The emphasis has shifted inward, and now the problems are not armies, allies, finances, crusades, and castles so much as will, insight, guilt, self-control, and intention.

Hamlet's development through the play is characterized by fluctuations between brief glimpses of clarity and long periods of confusion. When he confronts Claudius in the council scene, he is keenly aware but resigned. He sees all the disparity between word and deed, intention and action, appearance and reality that life in Elsinore reveals, but he is unable to do anything about it.

20. I owe here, and in general in this chapter, a debt to Maynard Mack's "The World of *Hamlet*," *Yale Review* 41 (1952):502–23.

He is reduced to defending himself with the double meanings of words ("kin," "kind," "common," "seems"), which Claudius seems rightly to see as a threat: anyone who can play with words clearly threatens the king's house of words.

In the midst of such frustration and confusion, the Ghost shows Hamlet a way to clear action. Told of his father's murder, he enthusiastically embraces revenge. He vows, in effect, to give over his torturing awareness of the disparity between ideal and real in favor of a simpler view.

> And thy commandment all alone shall live
> Within the book and volume of my brain,
> Unmix'd with baser matter.
>
> [I.v.102–04]

The last line seems to reflect the same desire for clarity and simplicity that Claudius shows in act III. Hamlet here is at the apex of uncomplicated response.

> Haste me to know't, that I, with wings as swift
> As meditation or the thoughts of love,
> May sweep to my revenge.
>
> [I.v.29–31]

This is rousing language, of course, and promises an exciting inter-view between angry revenger and crafty murderer, but it is so far only thought and words, not action (this is not the last time Hamlet will couch his determination to act in images of *thought*, see IV.iv.66), and even this much clarity of will does not last long in Elsinore. By the end of the scene Hamlet's enthusiasm for his task has lessened, as his awareness of what is involved has in-creased.

> The time is out of joint;—O cursed spite,
> That ever I was born to set it right!
>
> [I.v.189–90]

This tone of sorrowful acceptance, not the exultant rage of his scene with the Ghost, marks most of Hamlet's speeches through the middle of the play. He is a man who feels he could be bounded in a nutshell but that he has bad dreams: Shakespeare is showing us a man who cannot escape from his own sensitivity.

When Rosencrantz calls ambition "the shadow of a dream" (II. ii.266–67), Hamlet's answer, "Then are our beggars bodies, and our monarchs and outstretched heroes the beggars' shadows" (271–73), shows that nevertheless such "shadows" are what distinguish the king from the beggar. He here appears to accept both the essential frivolity and the effective reality of the difference between them. He is starting where Richard left off.

Likewise, Hamlet can sing out man's glory—"What a piece of work is a man! how noble in reason! how infinite in faculty! in form and moving how express and admirable! in action how like an angel! in apprehension how like a god! the beauty of the world! the paragon of animals"—and still conclude, "And yet, to me, what is this quintessence of dust?" (318–24). This famous speech builds on a version of the two bodies idea that we should expect in Hamlet: not the king's, but man's two bodies, demigod or dust. Pico's range of choice echoes here, but his optimism has vanished. Here again, in the midst of his ironic yet balanced awareness of both the highest and lowest aspects of man, there seems to intrude a reminiscence of clarity of action that contrasts with the muddled confusion of Elsinore in general and within Hamlet in particular—"in action how like an angel." Hamlet's gloom is all the more impressive for recognizing such a human possibility only to reject it. The tone of this scene with his former friends shows how far disillusionment has displaced his manic enthusiasm for revenge on the battlements. His new theme, "there is nothing either good or bad, but thinking makes it so" (257–59), reveals just how much he has changed from the absoluteness of his "O villain, villain, smiling, damned villain" (I.v.106) after the Ghost's revelation of Claudius's guilt.

At precisely this moment, the mood is changed by the arrival of the Players. Hamlet greets news of their arrival with the curious line "He that plays the king shall be welcome; his majesty shall have tribute of me" (II.ii.336–37). Some vague comparison of the Player and Claudius is implicit here, which can be surfaced if "his" is stressed: *his* majesty, not Claudius, shall have tribute of Hamlet. In any case, Hamlet seems immediately to sense that in a world of masks and roles, the Players' presence can only have a cleansing effect. As fire can often be fought best with fire, so indirection with indirection. Hamlet's spirits rise suddenly.

Immediately he begins to use the Players as a touchstone of
authenticity, and through them unconsciously summarizes, meta-
phorically, what has been happening in Denmark: "Do the boys
carry it away?"—"Ay, that they do, my lord" (381–82). This is
little more than a repetition in a new key of his theme about the
satyr who has replaced Hyperion. But the rest of Rosencrantz's
answer, "Ay, that they do, my lord; Hercules and his load too"
(382–83), with its probable reference to the Globe theater's sign,
adds a new note by collapsing all the levels of reality and illusion
together: mythical, political, Danish, English, and theatrical. All
are here simultaneously invoked in a single pattern of the old
and the genuine being replaced by the new and the false. Hamlet
picks up this conflation of levels and uses it to moralize on his
favorite pair of opposed realities, his father and his stepfather:
"It is not very strange; for my uncle is King of Denmark, and
those, that would make mows at him while my father lived, give
twenty, forty, fifty, an hundred ducats a-piece, for his picture in
little" (384–88). Before, Hamlet had turned to myth (Hyperion,
Niobe, and so on) to cast light on the recent events in Elsinore;
now he uses those same events to explain theatrical developments
in London: that the boys carry "it" away is not strange because
Hamlet's uncle has carried away Denmark. Though an audience
may well not notice this neat switch as it passes, it will notice
the way Hamlet uses Danish experience to gloss English theatrical
problems, while at the same time adding another image of dissolution in Elsinore.

The famous passage surrounding the Pyrrhus speech further
develops the importance of the Players to Hamlet's development.
Attempts to explain away Hamlet's apparent taste for bad poetry
are mistaken and unnecessary.[21] The poetry is certainly no worse
than the verse he enclosed in his letter to Ophelia, and its function, clearly, is to set up a more artificial rhetoric than that of the
play itself. Partly, of course, in order to enhance the realism of the

21. I do not want to enter the lists with critics who have fought for
so long over this passage. But S. L. Bethell's interpretation, in *Shakespeare
and the Popular Dramatic Tradition* (London: Staples Press, 1944), pp.
146–56, whereby we are to assume that the characters hear a different
speech from the one we hear, is a clear example of what "multi-consciousness" *cannot* do.

play's normal mode. But partly, too, I think, to convey a different world from that of the rest of the play. Here, intention and external appearance are united ("arms, / Black as his purpose" 483–84); inanimate objects become threatening ("ominous horse" 485) and seem to have minds of their own ("his antique sword, / Rebellious to his arm, lies where it falls, / Repugnant to command" 500–02). "Senseless Ilium" (505) seems to feel Pyrrhus's blow; a "hideous crash / Takes prisoner Pyrrhus's ear" (507–08) as if it had body and substance; a killing sword sticks in the air before Pyrrhus can force it to its task, and after a momentary pause Pyrrhus is described as abruptly setting himself "new a-work" (519). Clearly, this is not Hamlet's world, where sullied flesh will not melt in response to internal corruption, where "one may smile, and smile, and be a villain" (I.v.108), and where a sword stuck in the air never does get set "new a-work" (III.iii. 75–87). Nor is this Claudius's world in which one can easily murder a sleeping king and win his wife. If anything, this is closer to old Hamlet's direct conception of things in which consequences follow clearly and unrelentingly on actions. It is, however, as if such unity and clarity of passion and action can nowadays only be recalled in the artifice of a dramatic speech. Polonius's pedestrian comments (like, "my lord, well spoken" 497), drawing attention to the speech as fiction, keep us mindful of this, as does a quality of the language itself—the heavy use of simile: "like th' Hyrcanian beast," "as his purpose," "like carbuncles," "as a painted tyrant," "like a neutral," "as hush as death," "as low as to the fiends" (481–528).

After the Players have left Hamlet alone, he reflects on the status of the dramatic fiction, the *image* of action: drama is "But . . . a fiction . . . a dream of passion" (588). Yet Hamlet wonders at the actor's powers at the same time that he belittles acting in comparison with the business of revenge ("What would he do / Had he the motive . . . That I have?" 596–98). He admires the Player's ability to "force his soul so to his own conceit" (589), to make "his whole function [suit] / With forms to his conceit" (592–93). Hamlet (like many audiences) seems to see in the drama a possibility of achieving that unity and clarity which are lost always in the indirections of the world. Later he will urge the Players to "suit the action to the word, the word to the action"

(III.ii.20) in what looks like a tacit or unconscious acknowledgment of his own inability to do so. The mirror he wants drama to hold up to nature will, one presumes, show "virtue her own feature, scorn her own image" (26–27) only in a Platonic sense. It will portray the ideal forms of these qualities, not their mixed, ambiguous realities in the world of becoming which is Denmark.[22] Will it not, we wonder, resemble that magic one which shows the ugly witch not herself, but the beautiful Snow White?

In his soliloquy after the Pyrrhus speech, however, Hamlet seems almost willfully to reject the reality of dramatic illusion, even as a mirror, in favor of his own "motive and . . . cue for passion." He insists on the baselessness of the Player's performance ("all for nothing" 593) and rejects the reality of Hecuba ("What's Hecuba to him, or he to Hecuba" 595). Yet the splendid ambiguity of the Player's performance is such that we cannot be sure of what Hamlet assumes, that the actor's tears are the result of a mere forcing of the soul (589). If the speech is spoken well, it will seem quite possible that the dramatic illusion has assumed a reality sufficient to cause tears; or the Player may be suiting the action to the word quite literally. There is no way to tell. Dramatic illusion is more real, or at least more complex, than Hamlet allows. Under pressure of a clear command to murder a king who is a player, Hamlet seems to view drama only as a tool, a "thing / Wherein [to] catch the conscience of the king" (643–44). His earlier words about actors being "the abstracts and brief chronicles of the time" (557) are replaced at the end of the scene with narrower comments on "the very cunning of the scene" (629) as a means of obtaining "grounds / More relative" than the Ghost's mere command (642–43). He rejects acting in favor of action, or at least he intends to.

"The Murder of Gonzago" and the various characters' responses to it provide a central focus for the different ideas of action— and acting—that we have considered so far. Significantly, this focus is itself another story of king killing. The single most important fact about the play within a play is that, as everybody

22. The similarity between this and the mirror episode in *Richard II* is obvious but significant.

knows, it is performed twice. The dumb show version is as essential as the spoken version to its effect, the two together posing a double test for Claudius, only half of which he can pass.[23] The two versions are informatively different. The dumb show has all of the unflinching directness of a wordless repetition of the murder Claudius committed. Briefly, but without any qualification or comment, we see a king murdered and his wife won by the murderer. But this version also has a certain indefiniteness, a lack of any specific identification. Human complexities like motive, resistance, and rationalization are also missing. The dumb show presents regicide pure and simple, an archetype of secret murder. It offers only the first third of what constitutes full drama—action, but not character or poetry.

Character and poetry are largely reserved for the second version, which has very little action because it is broken off by Claudius's collapse. The spoken version is the opposite of the dumb show: here all is extended speech, qualification, rationalization, and human weakness.

The opening speeches on lasting love exchanged by the Player King and Queen evoke the same images and values as were associated with old Hamlet's and Gertrude's love:

> *Player King.* Full thirty times hath Phoebus' cart gone round
>   Neptune's salt wash and Tellus' orbed ground,
>   And thirty dozen moons with borrow'd sheen
>   About the world have times twelve thirties been,
>   Since love our hearts and Hymen did our hands
>   Unite commutual in most sacred bands.
> *Player Queen.* So many journeys may the sun and moon
>   Make us again count o'er ere love be done!
>
> [III.ii.167–74]

The classical imagery matches that which in Hamlet's speeches has come to surround old Hamlet; the sense of an orderly uni-

23. Again I skirt the troubled waters of Dover Wilson (*What Happens in Hamlet?* [Cambridge: Cambridge University Press, 1935], pp. 138–97) arguing that Claudius misses the dumb show, and of S. L. Bethell (*Popular Tradition*, pp. 151–60) arguing that Claudius sees a *different* dumb show from the one we see. The most obvious solution is the best: Claudius can stand seeing his murder performed only once.

verse as the home of an orderly and tender love reminds us of
the Ghost's speeches and Hamlet's comment on Hyperion—"so
loving to my mother / That he might not beteem the winds of
heaven / Visit her face too roughly" (I.ii.140–42). The Player
King's words about love uniting hands and hearts are also reminiscent of old Hamlet's comments on his love, which

> was of that dignity
> That it went hand in hand even with the vow
> I made to her in marriage.
>
> [I.v.48–50]

But then the Gonzago play takes an important turn which
aligns it more closely with the plot of *Hamlet*; the Player Queen
comments:

> But, woe is me! you are so sick of late,
> So far from cheer and from your former state,
> That I distrust you.
>
> [III.ii.175–77]

Suddenly the Hyperion world of Neptune and Tellus is replaced
with the decaying realities of Elsinore; the orchard is replaced with
the unweeded garden. The verse changes too. Despite some continued formality, a new flexibility appears. The Player Queen
tries to account for her worries ("For women's fear and love holds
quantity"—"Where love is great, the littlest doubts are fear" 179–
83), and we begin to glimpse the woman underneath the royal
robes. Rather earlier than Gertrude, we sense that the lady
protests too much, especially in contrast with the quiet warnings
of her husband.

After his first speech, the Player King too no longer sounds like
old Hamlet, but rather a bit like the Claudius of the council
scene, urging moderation, compromise, "realism," and acceptance.
He accepts what the Ghost was revolted by—the way time
changes love. But he goes even further than Claudius, erecting a
whole philosophy of change, transience, and sorrowful acceptance.
His words—"what we do determine oft we break" (199)—apply
to nearly every character in *Hamlet*, but when he makes this into
a proscriptive rather than merely descriptive statement, the color
darkens:

> Most necessary 'tis that we forget
> To pay ourselves what to ourselves is debt;
> What to ourselves in passion we propose,
> The passion ending, doth the purpose lose.
>
> [III.ii.204–07]

The first two lines go even further than Claudius's advice on accepting the deaths of fathers by generalizing the acceptance. The last two lines bring to mind the soliloquies of Hamlet and anticipate Claudius's words to Laertes in act IV ("Time qualifies . . . for this 'would' changes . . ." 112–24). The Player King continues his worldly advice, commenting on grief following joy, the relative powers of love and fortune, friends' desertion of the fallen man; and then he concludes,

> But, orderly to end where I begun,
> Our wills and fates do so contrary run
> That our devices still are overthrown,
> Our thoughts are ours, their ends none of our own.
>
> [III.ii.222–25]

His tone is different—sadder and wiser—than Claudius's, but the general tenor of his argument with its acceptance of the disjunction between thoughts, actions, and consequences resembles the king's. Especially the last line quoted above echoes Claudius's frequent reiteration of time's changes.[24] The Player Queen, in any case, responds to each of her husband's sad warnings with increasingly extreme vows of loyalty.

Shakespeare has presented thus far something very like a map of the play. The dumb show reiterates the shape of the murder in visual terms which parallel the confident rage and disgust of the Ghost at what happened to him; it is hardly more melodramatic than the Ghost's description of his death (I.v.59–80). The spoken version begins in the key of old Hamlet but shifts to a debate, unidealistic realism versus unrealistic idealism, in which we can hear echoes of Claudius versus Hamlet. The dumb show attacks the

---

24. To my ear the Player King's concern with ending where he began, with turning a neat speech, also recalls what Claudius implicitly tried to do in I.ii.

eye with all the clarity of "proof ocular," while the spoken version assails the hearing, traditionally a less lucid sense. The first version shows us a murder which is rendered more horrible by disloyalty, while the second version hardly gets to the murder but, like Claudius, overwhelms us with the naturalness of decay and death. In other words, precipitated out of their normal solution, we have in this Gonzago play not only summaries of the old and new kings, but also the essential dual aspects of the dramatic experience itself: the symbolic action with its generalizing tendency and the human psychology in speech with its involving detail.

Acting is here not used to show inauthenticity, lack of clear identity, or essential unreality, as it was earlier in *Hamlet* ("They are actions that a man might play" 1.ii.84). Nor has drama been merely useful, as Hamlet intended, or merely distracting, as Claudius hoped (iii.i.24–25). Rather, drama has, as a form, become a way to clarify the dramatic issues and perspectives of *Hamlet.* "The Murder of Gonzago," a play about regicide, has cast light on the structure, dynamics, and meanings of killing the king. It functions like a very complex Chorus, alerting us to the double nature of everything in Denmark.

When Claudius breaks down and leaves the stage, we watch a basic breakdown in the dramatic experience. In their different ways, Claudius and Hamlet have both lost not only the name of action but also the name—and meaning—of acting. Each, under the weight of his special burden, has focused his attention on being a stage manager rather than a spectator or an actor.

Hamlet in the play scene has chosen, rewritten, and staged a play to drive home a single point to particular spectators. He is counting on personal involvement—one of the two responses necessary for the appreciation of good drama—to the complete exclusion of the other (aesthetic distance). His behavior here mirrors his behavior through act iv. He is always using people and events in an attempt both to protect himself and to plague Claudius. As with the moralist, everything becomes grist for his mill—everyone, too, and four people become his victims before the play ends.[25]

---

25. I mean Polonius, Ophelia, Rosencrantz, and Guildenstern. I have left out Laertes and Claudius, since they are killed only after making direct attacks on Hamlet.

The man who loved theater before (II.ii.345–480), when "there were no sallets in the lines to make the matter savoury, nor no matter in the phrase that might indict the author of affection" (470–73) has abused that love and that theater.

However, it is Claudius's reaction that most clearly reveals the function of the Players and their play in exploring the meaning of killing the king. An audience that responded like Claudius would murder wives after seeing *Othello*: all aesthetic distance collapses, and the meaning—murder—is understood without regard to the form—a play. Claudius is, of course, right, the play *is* directed at him, but Gertrude's response appears to have been placed by Shakespeare precisely where it would point up the aspects of a play which Claudius can no longer appreciate. Asked by Hamlet, "Madam, how like you this play?", she answers, "The lady doth protest too much, methinks" (241–42). Assuming this is not merely an expression of boredom like Polonius's earlier "This is too long" (II.ii.529), Gertrude has responded to the psychological realism of the Player Queen's extreme vows and has noticed their excessiveness. The main point is that—either bored or involved— Gertrude has noticed things other than the archetypal pattern of the play. Though she has failed to perceive in the Player Queen any comment on her own behavior, she has at least listened to the spoken version.

Claudius appears to be stuck on the level of dumb show. The man who perfectly stage-managed regicide, and slipped into the throne and "incestuous sheets" with equal dexterity, now is reduced to passivity and confusion by a poor parody of his crime. Character and verse mean nothing to him, he can see only the plot.

Shakespeare has, in effect, translated his central theme of killing the king into theatrical terms, or, somewhat more accurately, he has forged a perfect union of theme and form. Nothing could convey in the theater more clearly the essential psychological meaning of regicide—the imprisonment in the mind that can result from attacking external authority—than the image of the spectator who can no longer discriminate between his crime and that of a dramatic character, between nature and art. Likewise, the central political meaning of killing the king is presented in the decline of the efficient stage manager who manipulates everyone, to

the haunted tyrant who can trust no one, and, finally, to the be-
sieged paranoiac who is exposed by his own fear. Hamlet suffers
less distortion, since revenge is not quite the same as murder, but
the effects of his having to kill a king, even in revenge, are clearly
explored in the play within a play as well.

This is serious drama at its best: Shakespeare has shown happening at a play something that could happen at a performance of
Hamlet, were the play less good or a spectator as guilty consciously as the popular Oedipal theory would have us all unconsciously. Our fuller, more balanced response to the whole play is
invoked to cast light on a particular character and event—Claudius at Hamlet's play—while our response to that event guides our
response to the whole play. The dynamics of the theatrical experience are relied on to help develop the fullness of the characters
and the meaning of regicide. Our detachment is implicitly called
upon to help judge Hamlet's single-minded utilitarianism, Gertrude's naive observation of detail at the expense of the larger
meaning, and Claudius's guilty, indiscriminate involvement in the
artifice as if it were real.

Lodged in the middle of all these vivid scenes with the Players,
which so thoroughly involve the audience in the serious business
of dramatic artifice, is a speech that, were it any other, would simply be forgotten in the excitement. The famous soliloquy of act III
("To be, or not to be . . .") marks, obviously, an even deeper disillusionment than that revealed in act II with Rosencrantz and
Guildenstern or in the previous soliloquy right after the Pyrrhus
speech. Now Hamlet displays a despairing uncertainty based on
the pervasive ambiguity of life and action (which the Players trig-
ger in his and our minds) not only in Denmark, but in the world
at large. A remarkable feature of this soliloquy, as many have observed, is its purview over "the thousand natural shocks / That
flesh is heir to" (III.i.62–63) from things which Hamlet has experienced ("The pangs of disprized love" 72), to things which, so far
as the play informs us, he has not experienced ("the law's delay"
72), to generalized shocks that all men encounter ("the whips and
scorns of time" 70). Here, contemplating suicide, he expands his
personal dilemma into universal proportions, mirroring the expan-
siveness of the play:

> Thus conscience does make cowards of us all,
> And thus the native hue of resolution
> Is sicklied o'er with the pale cast of thought,
> And enterprises of great pitch and moment
> With this regard their currents turn awry
> And lose the name of action.
>
> [III.i.83–88]

His words function as a general comment on the human condition. The passage moves in many directions at once: losing the name of action implies the clotted ambiguity in Elsinore, thought destroying resolution implies some kind of moral loss, but conscience imposing its controlling power may imply some moral gain. For all its clarity—thought stalls great enterprises—the passage remains fundamentally ambiguous by raising the question whether it is by conscience that such resolution is "sicklied o'er," and whether Hamlet himself is indeed a coward for losing the particular resolution in question.

I have noted how, after the play scene, Hamlet departs to his mother's chamber with a speech (" 'Tis now the very witching time of night . . .") which seems to portend clear action impeded by no conscience or coward-making thought. But after vowing that he feels capable of drinking hot blood, he continues,

> Let me be cruel, not unnatural:
> I will speak daggers to her, but use none;
> My tongue and soul in this be hypocrites.
>
> [III.ii.414–16]

Here we are thrown back once more on complexity and ambiguity, with an obvious breach between words and deeds, tongue and soul, and a moral atmosphere such that even to attempt good one must play the hypocrite, or, as Hamlet will later put it, "be cruel, only to be kind" (III.iv.178). When he comes upon Claudius praying, his initial impulse to kill is speedily sicklied o'er with the cast of thought, though it is hardly conscience that stops him. Critical debate about this scene merely reflects its purposeful ambiguity. On the one hand, we are struck with the irony of Hamlet's decision when Claudius complains, "My words fly up, my thoughts remain below" (III.iii.97)—he has not been able to pray, as Hamlet mistakenly thought. On the other, our sense of irony is balanced with a certain admiration for Hamlet as he refuses to cut down from behind a man at prayer. Even though Claudius murdered old Hamlet in his sleep—or, indeed, because of this—young Hamlet's decision to spare him brings a certain relief. Our admiration is typically, however, qualified with dismay, or even with revulsion, at his intent to catch the king "about some act / That has no relish of salvation in't" (91–92).[26]

Prefaced as it is with various displays of a pervasive irony and ambiguity of motive, thought, and word as well as confused, mistaken actions, the actual confrontation of mother and son comes as a kind of summary of the preceding scenes before the final and fatal rush of events. It opens bluntly with Hamlet's first direct action, the slaughter of Polonius. But galvanic as it is, his thrust is not open like Richard's in prison but through an arras, and suddenly the hands of one who wanted to sweep cleanly to his revenge are covered with blood, like those of Bolingbroke and Claudius. Yet, as he talks with his mother, he ignores the complexities which his mistaken murder has just revealed so fatally and narrows his attention to describe Gertrude's remarriage in terms of absolute villainy:

> oh, such a deed
> As from the body of contraction plucks
> The very soul, and sweet religion makes
> A rhapsody of words.
>
>   [III.iv.45–48]

He shows her the pictures of her two husbands, turning, in a manner reminiscent of the Ghost, one into a god ("the front of Jove himself" 56) and the other into "a mildew'd ear, / Blasting his wholesome brother" (64–65). The whole speech is unrelentingly myopic, laying down absolute rules ("at your age / The hey-day in the blood is tame" 68–69) and almost eagerly expanding Gertrude's "sin" to the proportions of another Fall.

This explosion of vivid rhetoric ("In the rank sweat of an

---

26. Again we may, perhaps, legitimately detect Hamlet's longing for some clarity, even the clarity of total corruption.

enseamed bed . . ." 91–101) has two remarkable effects. First, Hamlet's outrage awakens a broader, more complex awareness in Gertrude. His brutal presentation of her remarriage turns her "eyes into [her] very soul" (89). For the second time in the play,[27] Gertrude becomes an internally dramatic character, like Claudius in his scenes of conscience (iii.i and iii.iii). She becomes capable of interior struggle, seeing "black and grained spots" (90) in her own soul. And at this precise moment, as if to signalize a second effect of Hamlet's savage rhetoric, the Ghost appears, as he says, to whet Hamlet's "almost blunted purpose" (111) but also commanding him to help Gertrude, to "step between her and her fighting soul" (113). The representative of the old order of downright thoughts and actions proves himself more gentle and responsive to human compromise than Hamlet. The prince's greater awareness does not, it appears, bring with it any greater humanity. The complicated son can be more cruel than the betrayed father. Shakespeare does not encourage the sentimental notion that Hamlet has reformed his mother, awaking her to new moral responsibilities: the scene is contrived so that he and we see the Ghost, whereas Gertrude does not, claiming, "yet all that is I see" (132). Hamlet is cruel, but sees more than Gertrude, too.

As if in response to the new complexity revealed by the Ghost in demanding both revenge and mercy, Hamlet now speaks once more with that breadth of vision he displayed earlier. He still sounds priggish and too confident in his own rectitude, but he displays an awareness of the confusion in Elsinore that no other character shares.

> Forgive me this my virtue,
> For in the fatness of these pursy times
> Virtue itself of vice must pardon beg.
>
> [iii.iv.152–54]

This is a wiser, more somber version of Polonius's motto, "By indirections find directions out," yet a consciousness of the enigmatic character of experience pervades both. Hamlet then recommends an approach to virtue perfectly suited to a world of ambiguities and appearances:

27. The other is at ii.ii.56–57.

Assume a virtue, if you have it not.
That monster, custom, who all sense doth eat,
Of habits devil, is angel yet in this,
That to the use of actions fair and good
He likewise gives a frock or livery,
That aptly is put on.

[III.iv.160–65]

There is a long tradition behind this advice, going back at least to
Aristotle's *Ethics*, which is here combined with a Renaissance conception of serious "playing." Hamlet's recommendation treads a
giddy path between wisdom and hypocrisy, but his words ("That
monster, custom, . . . is angel") reflect a reassuring awareness
that it *is* giddy. The difference between this position and his vow
on the battlements to "wipe away all trivial fond records . . . all
pressures past" (I.v.99–100) emphasizes how much he has
changed. Custom is now seen for what it is, both monster and
angel, and its power recognized. It is a far more serious thing than
the facile "thinking" which Hamlet said in act II could make
things good or bad.

In act IV, Shakespeare shows us for the last time the two extremes of Hamlet's temperament and in these two extremes the
competing views of action and thought on which the play turns.
Questioned by Claudius about the location of Polonius's body,
Hamlet's words (IV.iii.20–34) echo his earlier conversation
with Rosencrantz and Guildenstern about kings and beggars
(II.ii.265–73), this time taking a literal approach that foreshadows
the Gravedigger's and leads him to the same conclusion: "your fat
king and your lean beggar is but variable service, two dishes, but
to one table" (IV.iii.24–26). Here, Hamlet's wit is at its most
strained and brittle, his antic disposition—though more necessary
than ever before—at its most abrasive. Later, the stirring passage
of Fortinbras's army, though not free of ambiguities (as we saw),
effects a certain clearing of the air and tightening of nerves. Action remains possible if one is either resolute enough or insensitive
enough (characteristically, the two conditions are as impossible to
distinguish clearly in Hamlet's world as in our own) to pay its
price: "My thoughts be bloody, or be nothing worth" (IV.iv.66).

This is followed, in turn, by the letter that Horatio receives, with its account of an action undertaken *without* thinking too deeply on the event: "and in the grapple I boarded them" (IV.vi.19). We become anxious for the hero's return.

When we see Hamlet next, in the graveyard, all of the old terms reappear, but with a difference. For the first time, he is primarily the connoisseur of puns, not the punster. His meditation on Yorick's skull is quiet and controlled, a balanced mixture of affection ("a fellow of infinite jest, of most excellent fancy" 203) and disgust ("my gorge rises at it" 206) that we have not seen before. His tracing of Alexander to the stopper for a bung-hole recalls all the previous references to the ways in which time qualifies, but shows a detachment that is new. His explosion at Laertes's ostentatious grief is extreme, but then he admits later, "I am very sorry . . . That to Laertes I forgot myself" (v.ii.75–76).

In the last scene, Hamlet indirectly reveals the basis of his new confidence and command: "The interim is mine" (v.ii.73). There is occasion for action, but that occasion and action will be necessarily limited. Giving up his extreme desire for a total cure of Denmark's woes, Hamlet can discover the limited possibilities that are actually his. It is only by abandoning the letter of old Hamlet's command that he is able to accomplish the spirit. The point is not, of course, that he now has a simple solution to the ambiguities and corruption in Elsinore, but that he displays an attitude ready to accept what partial solutions become possible. Shakespeare loads the last act with tiny indications of these partial solutions and limited occasions. Hamlet describes, for instance, how his fair penmanship helped him despite the fact that he once held it "A baseness to write fair" (34)—old learning turned by chance to good effect. He also now sees that "Our indiscretion sometimes serves us well" (8). The readiness is indeed all, but the unknown and anticipated will play their parts: "I had my father's signet in my purse . . . even in that was heaven ordinant" (48–49).

The unknown and the unanticipated lead to Hamlet's success and to his death. There is a splendid poetic aptness in his spontaneous double murder of Claudius. The thrust of the sword with which Hamlet cuts down the king brings to mind the

heroic individualism of old Hamlet's defeat of the elder Fortinbras (though, appropriately, flexible foils have replaced the
heavier weapons of the past). The poisoned cup, on the other
hand, which Hamlet now forces on Claudius—death disguised
as celebration—is thoroughly a product of Claudius's deceitful
rule, a final dramatization of the way indirections can, and must,
find directions out in the murky atmosphere of Elsinore. The
Ghost's command has been done, though not as directly as he
desired, and the villain has been "Hoist with his own petar"
(III.iv.207). Both the world's call for revenge and evil's own
tendency toward self-destruction are balanced in the symbolism
of this double killing with sword and drink.

Horatio's summary of the play as a story seems to cover most
of the events, but is obviously inadequate.

> Of carnal, bloody, and unnatural acts,
> Of accidental judgments, casual slaughters,
> Of deaths put on by cunning and forced cause.
>   [v.ii.392–94]

The middle ground, the performance of an inflexible, principled
command in a shifting, protean world, Hamlet's interim "readiness"—this has all already disappeared. The ending, with Hamlet
naming Fortinbras to succeed him and Fortinbras bursting on
stage with a shower of commands, dramatically concludes this
play of indecision, but resolves little. In fact, it seems to liquidate
altogether the painful equilibrium of forces, emotions, desires,
and actions that Hamlet had finally managed to achieve. It certainly marks the disappearance of Hamlet's obsessive and impressive internal struggle. Shakespeare seems to have been conscious
of this and, at the very end, takes care to turn the audience's attention backwards and inwards[28] to the heart of the play, back
from Fortinbras's bright confidence to the confused skein of

---

28. These last two words, and probably something more, come from
Louis Martz, *The Paradise Within* (New Haven: Yale University Press,
1964), e.g. p. 140. Another element directing us backwards, if not inwards, is Horatio's farewell to Hamlet, "Good night, sweet prince" (370)
which recalls quite clearly Ophelia's "Good night, sweet ladies" (iv.v.72),
transferring some of the shattering pathos of her death to Hamlet's
tragedy.

action and thought that filled acts II and III. We are not to look to the future, he seems to assure us, or to any fuller "explanation" than his own. It is in the story—that Hamlet wants told and that the audience has just watched being retold—that enlightenment must be found.

> You that look pale and tremble at this chance,
> That are but mutes or audience to this act,
> Had I but time (as this fell sergeant, death,
> Is strict in his arrest) oh, I could tell you—
> [v.ii.345–48]

Structurally, the whole of *Hamlet* can be seen as an expansion of the last scene of *Richard II*: the effects on a new king and his court of the death of the old king. But there the likeness ends. Certain questions are posed by *Richard II* that seem to cry out to be resolved in the following plays—most obviously, the question whether Bolingbroke is essentially protean or merely expedient, and the question whether his vigor and energy have any real relationship to Gaunt's conception of Christian service. To *Hamlet*, however, future events would add nothing. The story is complete and most of the characters are dead.

More important, the play is imaginatively complete. It has taken an action—the murder of a king—and has worked out the meanings and consequences of this action in complete detail. Furthermore, it has added to the study of regicide a different kind of king killing, a consequential revenge. Obviously the "facts" of received Renaissance history would not have allowed Shakespeare to show vengeance being taken on Bolingbroke, had he wanted to. And though such speculation is always uncertain, it would appear that when Shakespeare wrote his second historical tetralogy, he was interested in a different kind of revenge for regicide, not personal and local, but political and historical. The vengeance that constantly threatens Bolingbroke from Aumerle to the Archbishop of York (2 *Henry IV*) is closer to that pictured by Carlisle in *Richard II*, and closer to the Tudor myth of the consequences of rebellion, than it is to the deeply personal and philosophic revenge of Hamlet. In the Danish court, the religious, philosophic, political, familial, personal, and psychic dimensions of the initial

murder and the immensely more complex reaction are all explored. What the story fails to show about one aspect, the poetry
does show. The central questions of action, responsibility, motive,
intention, will, consequences, roles, identities have all been raised,
and with respect to gods, kings, soldiers, courtiers, fathers, children, lovers, friends. *Hamlet* is almost bewilderingly complete.

And yet, discernible throughout is the tripartite structure we
have traced, rather like that in *Richard II*, of an old world of set
ideas and confident identity, a new world of masks, manipulation,
and human complexity, and a poor, battered but courageous
Hamlet wandering and wondering between them. Underneath
the infinite variety of battlements and arrases, fathers and sons,
kings and servants, there is this basic "geography" which makes
all Elsinore, even all the world, have effect on, and seem to
resonate to, Hamlet's questing and questioning.

But no, or very few, answers are given. The overriding question, whether anything is "either good or bad, but thinking makes
it so" or whether "foul deeds will rise, / Though all the earth
o'erwhelm them, to men's eyes" (i.ii.256–57) is left hanging. No
very clear resolution is offered to the enigma of action, and indeed
the end, with death in game and victory in defeat, merely complicates the matter. The question of human responsibility is raised
but not settled. Above all, the most personal of questions, the one
which underlies all religious, metaphysical, and moral problems,
the question of conscience, is unresolved. Does conscience make
cowards of us all or is it man's "chief good and market of his
time" (iv.iv.34)? Can it transform regicide into revenge? Who
best understood the meaning of regicide, the Ghost with his call
for revenge or the prince with his complicated response?

In the figure of its hero the play commends an imaginative
flexibility that casts light on all the issues it encounters. Hamlet
does very little, accomplishes successfully even less, but encounters imaginatively practically the whole range of possible
experience. Unlike Richard II, who develops deep, internal
awareness only under the pressure of suffering and external
events, Hamlet displays this complex awareness from his opening
pun on "kin" and "kind." His final development is not increased
insight so much as a new sense of stability among old insights.
He achieves a balance which, acknowledging that the readiness

is all, can kill a king without committing the same overreaching crime that Claudius originally committed. In *Richard II*, killing the king meant the replacement of one conception of kingship with another, but, in *Hamlet*, killing the king exfoliates into action—action in all its meanings, public and private, physical and psychic, ranging from a secret murder to a mistaken stab through an arras, from a doubtful suicide to a public revenge. The dramatic growth of awareness that became a major aspect only in the last acts of *Richard II* occupies in *Hamlet* the whole play.

3

The Voice in the Sword

In *Richard II*, it is the garden scene (iii.iv) that catches in an emblem the main issues of the play; in *Hamlet*, it is the chamber scene (also iii.iv) with its contrasting portraits of the two kings and the immersing of the hero in the destructive element of guilt; and, in *Macbeth*, it is the banquet scene (again, iii.iv). The act and scene numbers of these episodes—garden, chamber, banquet—are, of course, coincidental and critically unimportant, since in most cases our modern divisions come from the First Folio and not from Shakespeare directly, but some such summary and foreshadowing scene at roughly the same point in the play does appear to be a fairly consistent aspect of Shakespeare's tragic orchestration. In this instance, as in the other two plays, we come upon a scene that summarizes clearly the main moral and imaginative issues and foreshadows important developments to come.

Though only one banquet is actually staged in *Macbeth*, the idea and imagery of banqueting are richly developed, as a number of critics have observed, with the result that this scene assumes a significance far surpassing its importance in the plot. The earlier gathering at Duncan's castle at Forres (i.iv) had concluded with a reference that associates the mutuality of feasting to the mutuality inherent in any benign social order, where loyalty and gratitude have the importance and almost the palpability of food.

> True, worthy Banquo: he is full so valiant,
> And in his commendations I am fed;
> It is a banquet to me.
>
> [i.iv.54–56]

Significantly, Macbeth's soliloquy debating the murder of Duncan (i.vii.1–28) takes place in the wake of a procession indicated in the folio stage direction as "*Enter, and pass over the stage, a Sewer, and divers Servants with dishes and service.*" The contrast between the gregariousness of feasting and the willful solitude of murderous thoughts is thus underlined as Shakespeare frames Macbeth's soliloquy between this procession and Lady Macbeth's entry to say, "He has almost supp'd. Why have you left the chamber?" (I.vii.29). Similarly, the massive retaliation of cosmic forces against Macbeth after he has killed his king is foreshadowed immediately after the murder in the famous lines on sleep, also seen in terms of feasting.

> Sleep, that knits up the ravell'd sleave of care,
> The death of each day's life, sore labour's bath,
> Balm of hurt minds, great Nature's second course,
> Chief nourisher in life's feast.
>
> [II.ii.36–39]

From the very first, social imagery of banqueting is balanced against actions of anarchic individualism. Duncan's lines about being nourished in and by the commendations of Macbeth follow immediately on Macbeth's "let that be, / Which the eye fears, when it is done, to see" (I.iv.52–53). The banquet at Inverness, taking place offstage, as we have seen, is balanced by Macbeth, alone on stage and alienated, considering murder. Likewise, in the banquet scene proper, Macbeth is unable to join the feast because he has cut himself off from the society of mutual trust and obligation that is represented there: first he is prevented by the Murderer's entrance, then by the Ghost's appearance, and finally by his wife, who breaks up the gathering (III.iv.117–20). The "broken feast" thus becomes a vivid metaphor of the play's political action to this point and at the same time prepares us for the antifeast of the witches with their "hell-broth" in the next act (IV.i.19). Even this perverted "banquet" becomes something like a broken feast as the witches' "gruel" (32) sinks in the cauldron at Macbeth's insistence on certain answers.

What the Gardener in *Richard II* does with his instructions about gardens that are also kingdoms and what Hamlet does with his two lockets (or perhaps merely with a pair of verbal portraits) in his mother's bedroom occurs visually in *Macbeth* when the Murderer enters during the feast. For here on stage before us is a powerful depiction of the antithetical natures of the play's two kings: the feasting fellowship of the lords that looks back to Duncan and the murderous complicity of Macbeth with the

Murderer. The Gardener in *Richard II* has to develop the imagery which contrasts Richard with the ideal king, but in *Macbeth* the difference is presented wordlessly. We see suddenly—contraposed —the mutuality of feasting and an obsessive, self-centered appetite no feast can gratify.

Macbeth welcomes his guests, it has been often noticed, in the language of an established order: "You know your own degrees" (III.iv.1). The confidence that each man will know his own degree—testimony to an order that is durable and clear—is also testimony in this case to its frailty, since none knows better than Macbeth how easily "degree" can be and has been broken.[1] Underlining this note of irony, Macbeth greets the Murderer not as he greeted his guests, with an insistence on degree, but with an intimation of anarchy: if the assassin has killed Fleance as well as Banquo, he is "the nonpareil" (18). The movement of the scene is thus from the rejection of degree in Macbeth's mind— implicit ever since the first murder and here recapitulated in an attitude that relates it to his rejection of, and also his rejection from, "the good meeting" (108)—to chaos in the company at large. For Lady Macbeth, it will be recalled, is soon to urge the guests to "Stand not upon the order of your going. / But go at once" (118–19), explicitly reversing the terms in which they have been welcomed.

All this is, of course, accentuated in the theater. We are aware, first, of guests taking their accustomed seats at a feast which we realize is essentially a mask for the ultimate breach of degree, regicide. Then there is an interruption by the new king's hired assassin, reporting his murder of one who was both thane and friend, after which the new king, discovering that his place at table has been filled by the murdered man, becomes hysterical. At the end the whole society disintegrates in disorder—although, as we see in the next scene (III.vi),[2] the disruption of the banquet signals the emergence of a counterforce that will eventually bring reintegration to Scotland. We have only to suppose, further, that the "state" (5) intended for Macbeth and his lady in this scene

1. This unites Macbeth with Claudius who, as we saw, having poisoned old Hamlet, pays elaborate lip service to the divinity that hedges a king.
2. I am assuming, with most modern editors, that III.v is not authentic.

is a pair of thrones, one of them being subsequently assumed by Banquo, on his second entrance, to see how much stress is laid here (or is capable theatrically of being laid) on the emptiness of Macbeth's achievement at all levels. He can no more assume the throne than he can maintain a good society. Duncan may be dead in his body natural but in his body politic he yet lives on in Malcolm. Banquo too is dead, but he lives on both as a ghost and in Fleance, whose posterity will be kings.

Another important theme, or pattern of contrasts, to which the banquet scene gives special prominence is that of isolation versus companionship—the solipsism of criminal self-will. Duncan, we recall, is never seen alone; he is always, even in sleep, surrounded by loyal servants. Macbeth's isolation, on the other hand, is intense from the beginning. His progress through the rebel army in act I is described as if he were a lonely woodsman cutting through undergrowth (I.ii.19), and when at last he slays Macdonwald, his triumph is seen in terms that rather oddly call attention to civilities unindulged:

> he fac'd the slave;
> *Which ne'er shook hands, nor bade farewell to him,*
> Till he unseam'd him from the nave to th' chops.
> [I.ii.20–22; italics mine] [3]

Immediately upon seeing the witches he retreats into an interior solitude to which Banquo several times draws attention with phrases like "Look, how our partner's rapt" (I.iii.143). Later, at Forres, though he is among many, we sense his actual isolation both in his aside about the stars that must not be allowed to see his "black and deep desires" (I.iv.51) and in the grim irony of his pledge of loyalty just thirty lines after his "horrible imaginings" (I.iii.138) of murder. His benumbed isolation before, during, and right after Duncan's murder is one of the most vivid memories of every spectator, and we can see him in the same abstraction again among the loyal mourners (II.iii) after the murder has been discovered. Throughout, except in his earliest scenes with Lady Macbeth, he is spiritually a man apart. Even

---

3. The prebattle ceremonies of old Hamlet and old Fortinbras, described by Horatio (I.i.80–95), offer an interesting contrast.

when with his wife, he seems somewhat isolated by his profounder feelings, and just before the murder of Banquo further sets himself apart: "Be innocent of the knowledge, dearest chuck, / Till thou applaud the deed". (III.ii.45–46).

In the banquet scene this all-pervasive alienation receives clear expression in Macbeth's peculiar situation of being alone in company and in company (the company of his wife and the Ghost) when alone. Any echo here of the regal scene at Forres, such as the chair or chairs of state already mentioned, will accentuate yet more the fact that he has brought his isolation from the edge of that scene to the very heart of this one, where (apparently) he never occupies *his* "state" at all. The scene is pivotal, moreover, in that up to this point we have always seen Macbeth alone against the others, whereas here "the others"—first in the form of the Ghost—begin to engage together against him. Soon, in the persons of Lennox (III.vi), a Messenger (IV.ii), Macduff, Siward, and Malcolm (IV.iii), and nearly all of Scotland (V.ii), the balance will shift until all companies and companions are set against the king. Either way he is isolated among crowds, unable to participate at life's feast. The final stage in his spiritual starvation—"I have almost forgot the taste of fears . . . I have supp'd full with horrors" (V.v.9–13)—will recall us to this moment in the banquet scene, and also to that other moment, as he stood withdrawn in his house from another banquet, set for Duncan, when in his hunger for power and security his humanity began to starve.[4]

A feature of this scene that relates intimately to the isolation of Macbeth is his growing realization (to recur to the terms used in the preceding chapter) that "Heaven *will* direct it," that "foul deeds *will* rise, / Though all the earth o'erwhelm them, to men's eyes" (italics mine). In the banquet scene, the rising of foul deeds under heavenly direction shifts from being internally to being externally manifested. Macbeth's words to the Murderer on learning that Fleance has escaped perhaps hint that much has happened to him psychically of which he is not yet himself aware.

4. The image is kept alive in between these limits, as at III.vi.35, IV.i.32, IV.iii.81–82.

> I had else been perfect;
> Whole as the marble, founded as the rock,
> As broad and general as the casing air:
> But now, I am cabin'd, cribb'd, confin'd, bound in
> To saucy doubts and fears.—But Banquo's safe?
>
> [III.iv.20–24]

His images of perfection, we notice, differ enormously from those associated with Duncan in the latter's well-known colloquy with Banquo about the approach to Inverness.

> *Duncan.* This castle hath a pleasant seat; the air
>   Nimbly and sweetly recommends itself
>   Unto our gentle senses.
> *Banquo.*   This guest of summer,
>   The temple-haunting martlet, does approve,
>   By his loved mansionry, that the heaven's breath
>   Smells wooingly here: no jutty, frieze,
>   Buttress, nor coign of vantage, but this bird
>   Hath made his pendent bed, and procreant cradle:
>   Where they most breed and haunt, I have observ'd
>   The air is delicate.
>
> [I.vi.1–10]

And earlier at Forres: "our duties / Are to your throne and state, children and servants" (I.iv.24–25); "I have begun to plant thee, and will labour / To make thee full of growing" (28–29); "There if I grow, / The harvest is your own" (32–33). Duncan's form of kingship is expressed as generation, growth, and harvest; Macbeth's as rock, marble, and casing air—symptoms, one supposes, of an invulnerability that is becoming inhuman because it would be more than human.

At this early point in the scene, despite his distress at Fleance's escape, Macbeth appears to sense in it only a new frustration of his hopes, one more in the throng of "saucy doubts and fears" that have plagued him ever since in imagination he saw Duncan dead. But this attitude is soon to give way to a more desperate one, to which the ghost of Banquo will be vehicle. The appearance of the Ghost is one of those occasions when Shakespeare exploits theatrical convention for powerful effect: we and Macbeth together see the Ghost, whereas he alone saw the dagger leading him to Duncan.[5] The difference is important since, as we learned in the chamber scene of *Hamlet*, the effect of having audience and hero see together what others on stage are blind to establishes a bond of understanding or at least common experience that prevents our interpreting the Ghost as mere illusion.[6] The Ghost is actually, we realize, a preliminary version of the rising of foul deeds—already substantial enough, Macbeth learns, to fill his place at table, but not yet visible to others and effective, so far, only internally on himself. His appearance clearly prepares, however, for a reaction to crime that will be more substantial and that will be effective externally on the criminal.

The first moment of a new and appalling apprehension in Macbeth's mind is brilliantly captured by his taut, still half-unbelieving whisper, as if he were a man trying to digest the fact that he has become the victim of a cosmic joke:

> the time has been,
> That, when the brains were out, the man would die,
> And there an end; but now, they rise again,
> With twenty mortal murthers on their crowns,
> And push us from our stools.
>
> [III.iv.77–81]

Here is everything he had fearfully imagined as he sought to dissuade himself from the murder of Duncan (I.vii). Here are "Bloody instructions" (I.vii.9) returning, as he had anticipated, though in an unanticipated way, to plague the inventor. Here is "even-handed Justice" giving a foretaste of the moment when it

5. These are the obvious theatrical solutions since a floating dagger would have been difficult to portray on Shakespeare's stage even if he had wanted this. But, as Lear's vision of Goneril in a joint stool shows, it would have been possible to have Banquo's ghost invisible—the effect suggesting more madness, less danger.

6. Lady Macbeth, of course, equates the ghost with "the air-drawn dagger" (61) and confidently asserts, "When all's done, / You look but on a stool" (66–67), sounding something like Gertrude. Her particular image for Macbeth's "flaws and starts" as things appropriate to "A woman's story at a winter's fire" (62–64) revives the notion of a peaceful, ordered quiet at the very moment of greatest confusion and despair. Cf. also *Richard II*, v.i.40–50.

will commend "th' ingredience of our poison'd chalice / To our own lips" (10–12). Here is innocence, in this case Banquo's, pleading (after the fact) "like angels, trumpet-tongu'd, against / The deep damnation of his taking-off" (19–20). And visible, as he had feared—not only in all of these, but in the present circumstance that "now, they rise again, / With twenty mortal murthers on their crowns, / And push us from our stools" (III.iv. 79–81)—looms the dread evidence that his is not a world where action terminates upon "this bank and shoal of time" (I.vii.6), but rather one in which "the Powers above," as Malcolm soon will phrase it, "Put on their instruments" to shape it (IV.iii.238–39).

Further evidence is forced upon him when the Ghost appears for the second time. He tries to assure himself that death is all-sufficient.

> Avaunt! and quit my sight! let the earth hide thee!
> Thy bones are marrowless, thy blood is cold;
> Thou hast no speculation in those eyes,
> Which thou dost glare with.
>
> [III.iv.92–95]

But an intuition much more fearsome keeps breaking through.

> What *man* dare, I dare:
> Approach thou like the rugged Russian bear,
> The arm'd rhinoceros, or th' Hyrcan tiger;
> *Take any shape but that,* and my firm nerves
> Shall never tremble: or, *be alive again,*
> And dare me to the desert with thy sword;
> If trembling I inhabit then, protest me
> The baby of a girl. Hence, horrible *shadow!*
> *Unreal mock'ry,* hence!
>
> [III.iv.98–106; italics mine]

Macbeth is significantly more moved at the second appearance, and his language shows clearly his recognition that what cabins, cribs, confines, and binds him is not simply, as he had hoped, his own rebellious doubts and fears but another order of reality. Moreover, he now loses altogether the balance that he had partly maintained the first time, uttering his hysterical fancies only to Lady Macbeth in asides. This time he makes it clear to all the company that he is seeing or imagining a *man* ("with thy sword" 103), and then he publicly praises Lady Macbeth because she

> can behold such sights,
> And keep the natural ruby of your cheeks,
> When mine is blanch'd with fear.
>
> [iii.iv.113–15]

When Rosse inquires "What sights, my lord?" (115) it is obvious despite Lady Macbeth's rapid breaking up of the feast that the foul deeds are rising now to *all* men's eyes.

After the company has dispersed, Macbeth states what is essentially the "metaphysical" moral of the scene.

> It will have blood, they say: blood will have blood:
> Stones have been known to move, and trees to speak;
> Augures, and understood relations, have
> By magot-pies, and choughs, and rooks, brought forth
> The secret'st man of blood.[7]
>
> [iii.iv.121–25]

Almost instantly, however, the moment of truth fades: he lets slip the full meaning of his intuition that blood will have blood and makes it rather an exhortation to more murder. His closing speech dramatically traces this shift as he raises the issue of Macduff's absence from the banquet, plans to learn the future from the witches (is it his new consciousness of the challenge to his plans by another order of reality that inclines his mind so rapidly to have recourse to them?), vows "For mine own good, / All causes shall give way" (134–35), makes the stunning comment that returning from where he is steeped in blood "were as tedious as go o'er" (137), and then concludes with a bold and excited assertion of activity:

7. Only 150 lines later, Macbeth asserts boldly, "That will never be: / Who can impress the forest; bid the tree / Unfix his earth-bound root?" (iv.i.94–96), undercutting his perception here.

Strange things I have in head, that will to hand,
Which must be acted, ere they may be scann'd.

[III.iv.138–39]

But though it is lost almost as soon as found, for one moment Macbeth holds a full perception of the real nature of the plot he is caught in: blood will have blood. Foul deeds *do* rise; heaven *does* direct it.

The contrast of *Macbeth*'s "moral"—less a moral than a way of looking at experience—with those communicated in the corresponding scenes of *Richard II* and *Hamlet* helps us see more clearly, I think, the characteristic colorings of the play as a study of king killing. In *Richard II*, the obvious lesson of the garden scene is the necessity for vigorous pruning in a healthy state, nature's unruliness having ever to be shaped by man's controlling art. In *Hamlet*, in the chamber scene, the problem shifts from the external and political arena to the internal, personal one of psychic motivation. Nature and the physical world (Richard II's "Dear earth," for example) seem distant and the central struggle lies within—between a commanded action and Hamlet's discovery of action's paralyzing complexities and ambiguities. The banquet scene in *Macbeth*, incorporating both the mental dimension of *Hamlet* and the political dimension of *Richard II*, reaches a perception in "blood will have blood" that is primarily neither political nor personal, but, as already mentioned, metaphysical.

The settings of the three plays are plainly in tune with this difference of emphasis. *Richard II* takes place in an England that is fully historical, where all the issues are correspondingly political, and the paradigms of more profound experiences, when they exist at all, exist peripherally as allusions, like Richard's own enactment at Gaunt's house of the role of Willful Youth Rejecting Good Counsel. *Hamlet* takes place in a Denmark that has a genuine political orientation, but where fable has moved closer to the heart of things and the normal activities of a court can be adjusted so as to throw into high relief the intensely personal struggle of Hamlet and Claudius. To give a second instance of the change, the Christian background in *Richard II* forms the basis for the whole conception of Christian service;

whereas in *Hamlet,* an equally "religious" play, the explicitly Christian background has a far more psychic and even mythic cast. It supplies what keeps the hero from suicide, what pricks the conscience of the king, and it supplies also the paradigm of the ruined garden to which so many of the play's actions may be referred, both as they exist in their own right within the play and as they suggest a parable of moral experience everywhere.

Macbeth takes place—imaginatively as well as literally—half way between England and Denmark in a country where the Christian background remains important, and the kings remain (to an extent) historical, but where psychology has been re-examined and raised to a higher power. Shakespeare uses his setting in this case not to enclose and justify a gallery of indifferent children of the earth, as in *Hamlet,* but to throw one character into overwhelming relief and place his every action in a political and metaphysical pattern, all parts of which converge to illuminate the central study of a crime and its punishment. In a special "poetical" way, Macbeth is as fully conceived a character as Hamlet. The latter has all the indefinable complexity and completeness of a real human being encountered and watched in action, though he is also clearly a symbol; the former has all the clarity and completeness of a perfect symbol (in his own world we do not ask for more meaning than he gives us), though he is also realistic enough to excite our interest and admiration. In production, his reality comes through loud and clear.

In all these areas, the banquet scene enforces the special qualities of the play. Here is no clear urging to vigorous action along known lines (as in *Richard II*), nor an insistent psychic dilemma about how to act (as in *Hamlet*): here, rather, is a scene in which action is contemplated only to escape from larger questions, and in which the psychic dilemma is far overshadowed by metaphysical dilemmas about the nature of crime—not the criminal—and about the structure of the universe in which crime takes place. If *Richard II* deals with the history of killing the *king* and *Hamlet* with the tragedy of needing to *kill* the king, *Macbeth* confronts the full tragedy of *king killing;* religious, political, and personal dimensions combine to piece out the full meaning of regicide; emphasis falls evenly on the action, the actor, and the figure acted upon. Somehow the actual killing of

Richard has become almost irrelevant by the time it occurs, for the old kingship has been dying from the opening scene; somehow the fact that Claudius is king is no more important than that he has murdered his brother and seduced his brother's wife. But in *Macbeth,* everything is pruned, shaped, and focused to dramatize king killing in all its moral, political, metaphysical, and *symbolic* horror.

Macbeth, it has been sometimes said, is *Hamlet* told from Claudius's point of view. To see it so may be an exercise worth performing, but it can also blind one to important differences. The possible resemblances of Duncan to old Hamlet, Macbeth to Claudius, and Macduff to an avenger are far less significant, obviously, than the fact that *Macbeth* has no counterparts of Polonius, Ophelia, Laertes, Rosencrantz and Guildenstern, Osric, the Gravediggers, or the Players, and that *Hamlet* has no counterpart of the witches, the great storm, Birnam wood, and men not born of women. The unique nature of *Macbeth,* in fact, makes it helpful in discussion to approach the play as if it were two different plays, for more than either *Richard II* or *Hamlet* it exists from start to finish on two levels and excites simultaneously two responses—as is perhaps inevitable considering that it has a hero-villain. Our first play, of course, is the familiar morality of crime and punishment; the second is a more personal tragedy of self-destruction. The morality play involves, as we might by now anticipate, an older, idealized order of kingship, embodied in Duncan, which is attacked and destroyed by the villain-hero. There is reaction by the forces of legitimacy—as if the Aumerle plot had succeeded in *Richard II*—and the "new" man is soundly defeated. These are the dry bones that Shakespeare again makes live in *Macbeth.*

Duncan, developed in a way dramatically reminiscent of Gaunt and old Hamlet, is more idealized than they, pastoral images of natural growth, as noted a moment ago, replacing Gaunt's images of vigorous control and old Hamlet's images of Olympian authority. But structurally all three figures have a similar role evoking an ideal order, simplicity, and clarity that is shattered by the dramatic events of the play. Like his counterparts, Duncan fulfills what seems to be a common Shakespearean need (expressed throughout his career in figures as different as the Henry of the *Henry VI* plays and Gonzalo in *The Tempest*) for a character representing an essentially nostalgic idealizing view of the world.[8] Unlike them, he prepares us for certain special qualities in the play to follow. In *Richard II*, Gaunt is not king, and we only hear about the kingship of Richard's ideal grandfather; in *Hamlet*, the king has been killed before the play opens; but in *Macbeth*, Duncan *is* king, and hence we see idealized out of the dramatic mixture at the very start of the play the pure lyrical form of the good ruler actively ruling. When he has won the battle against the rebels, he is surrounded with happy harvest imagery. After his death, as Wilbur Sanders has pointed out,[9] the associations in which he is enveloped join sanctity to nature: he is "The Lord's anointed Temple" (ii.iii.69), "the gracious Duncan" (iii.i.65 and iii.vi.3); with him "renown, and grace, is dead" (ii.iii.94). Loved, loving, trusting, generous, surrounded with images of fertility and divine grace too numerous to count, he is presented to us, in a brief glimpse, as the ideal king for an ideal world.

Even before we see Duncan, however, Shakespeare has hinted at an ominous disjunction between him and the world in which he reigns. We have seen the witches, and we no sooner see the king than his first words—"What bloody man is that?" (i.ii.1)— introduce us to the antifertile or black harvest theme of blood and death that echoes against the images of fertility until the end of the play. Moreover, as every spectator and critic notices, Duncan's "O valiant cousin! worthy gentleman" (i.ii.24)—uttered on hearing of Macbeth's feats in the battle—jars oddly against the violence it approves: a man "unseam'd . . . from the nave to th' chops" (22). We need not follow the modern critics who read the whole imaginative balance of the play in the light of these startling lines to feel their harshness.[10] Even allowing for strong-stomached Elizabethan reception of a traitor's defeat, this is still a savage picture. It warns us that Shakespeare has placed his ideal

8. Desdemona and Cordelia can be added to the list, with some qualifications. Such figures do not appear in the Roman plays, where everything is mixed and modern.

9. *Received Idea*, pp. 257–58.

10. The most recent and brilliant of such readings is that by Sanders, *Received Idea*, pp. 253–307.

king in a dramatic context that foreshadows and almost guarantees his ruin. Our task as audience, therefore, is to remain sensitive to both. Either aspect taken alone will distort the balance of the play and result in a mistaken view of Duncan's murder and his murderer.

Antithetical to all that Duncan represents in the play, realistic, ambitious, and competitive, viewing power as something to be seized and life as something to be waged, unvisited by the weird sisters yet somehow more demonic than they in her singleness of purpose, stands Lady Macbeth—the Lady Macbeth of acts I and II. What have been slightly ambiguous hints of rebellion and brief glimpses of dark power and unnatural ambition collect, the moment we first see her, in a full and positive portrayal of great natural forces abused. For maximum contrast, this sense of her is given us immediately after the scene of harmony at Forres. In her soliloquy (in I.v) there is no ambiguity whatsoever, every image of health is rejected ("thy nature . . . is too full o' th' milk of human kindness" 16–17), every scruple overthrown ("Thou . . . Art not without ambition, but without / The illness should attend it" 18–20), every natural order inverted ("Come, you Spirits . . . unsex me here" 40–41). Nature itself is opposed ("That no compunctious visitings of Nature / Shake my fell purpose" 45–46), and the darkness, inner as well as outer, invited and cherished ("Come, thick Night, . . . That my keen knife see not the wound it makes" 50–52). In this one speech, Shakespeare conveys everything that we are to understand is opposed to Duncan's world of loving trust, all the patterns of images—analyzed by many[11]—that will later inform the play with the horror of his murder: blood, perversion of nature, slaughter of children, disease, darkness, confusion, disruption of time, ominous birds.

There is no need here to follow out these patterns in detail. As is sufficiently well known, from the opening lines of paradox and hurly-burly the play quickly fills with evidences of evil, all of which gather around the Macbeths and their act of murder.

11. Among others, Holland, *The Shakespearean Imagination*, pp. 50–71; G. W. Knight, *The Wheel of Fire* (London: Oxford University Press, 1930), pp. 140–59, and *The Imperial Theme* (London: Oxford University Press, 1931), pp. 125–53.

Confusion, hunger, sleeplessness, disorder, and frustration haunt them. The order of loving trust is blotted out and (for a time) in its place come murder, sterility, and chaos. For in *Macbeth* the usurper cannot rule. In *Richard II* and *Hamlet*, he who kills the king is himself an effective king, but Shakespeare even deviates from his source to eliminate all evidence that Macbeth is politically successful. We see him, in fact, almost exclusively as murderer, not as governor or even as soldier, from the end of i.iv till the very end of the play. The loyal thane of the opening scenes becomes a brooding (i.vii), frightened (ii.i), bloody (ii.ii), lying (ii.iii), scheming (iii.i), smug (iii.ii), raving (iii.iv), gullible (iv.i), frantic (v.iii), despairing (v.v) ruin. The man in whose commendations his king was fed becomes the hunted monster of the last act whose only supporters are enforced and whose whole nature has been reduced to that of a beast "tied . . . to a stake," who can only mindlessly "fight the course" (v.vii.1–2). All this is the reverse of what has been shown in Duncan.

From the last scene of act III on, the growth of a counterforce opposed to Macbeth, different in character, opposite in the actions and images associated with it, can be clearly traced. This movement has been foreshadowed as early as ii.iv, the scene immediately after the discovery of Duncan's murder, when Macduff refuses to go to Macbeth's coronation and we hear the Old Man muse: "God's benison go with . . . those / That would make good of bad, and friends of foes" (ii.iv.40–41).[12] The escape of Malcolm in ii.iii has guaranteed it an eventual rallying point, and its stirrings multiply with each new scene. The great storm and the eclipse show that Duncan's death has been registered by mysterious forces somewhere; Banquo senses the evil that has been done; Fleance escapes the death planned for him; the Ghost plagues the king publicly; Lennox and another Lord inform us that all of Scotland now knows the murderer of Duncan and Banquo, that Malcolm has found favor at the court of Edward the Confessor,

12. Even the Old Man's syntax marks a way to resolve the paradoxes that opened the play: lost *and* won, fair *is* foul, are now good *of* bad, friends *of* foes. A direction is given to the terrible equilibrium of the witches' paradoxes.

and that Macduff has gone there to raise, if possible, an English invasion. Perhaps there is further evidence in the fact already noted, that even the unnatural world seems to shudder when the witches' cauldron sinks at Macbeth's question: "shall Banquo's issue ever / Reign in this kingdom?" (IV.i.102–03).

In all this, Shakespeare prepares us for the highly controversial, but, in my view, crucially important scene in the English court between Malcolm and Macduff (IV.iii). True, if the whole play were like this, *Macbeth* would be prosy, even dull; but omitting the scene, as has habitually been done in performance, turns the end of the play into an unexplored moralitylike victory of the counterforces, whereby a smug young prince simply supersedes a more interesting villain, as at the end of *Richard III*. In this long scene, the counterforces are given a chance to reveal their nature and motives. Malcolm's long charade attributing to himself the evils of voluptuousness, avarice, and "the division of each several crime" (IV.iii.96), and his subsequent reversal, "[I] here abjure The taints and blames I laid upon myself" (123–24), though altogether unrealistic psychologically, are emblematically serviceable as a way of summarizing Macbeth's vices ("bloody, / Luxurious, avaricious, false, deceitful, / Sudden, malicious . . ." 57–59), and identifying the opposing virtues ("Justice, Verity, Temp'rance, Stableness, / Bounty, Perseverance, Mercy, Lowliness, / Devotion, Patience, Courage, Fortitude" 92–94) before the countermovement gets under way.[13] Moreover, in addition to describing the widespread effects of Macbeth's rule, the interview guarantees both Macduff's idealism—"Fit to govern? No, not to live. . . . These evils thou repeat'st upon thyself / Hath banish'd me from Scotland" (102–13)—and Malcolm's prudent scepticism (especially as Macduff has been so far suspiciously free of Macbeth's harassments).

> Macduff, this noble passion,
> Child of integrity, hath from my soul

13. Several of these points about IV.iii have been made by Eugene Waith, "Macbeth: Interpretation versus Adaptation," in *Shakespeare: Of an Age and for All Time*, ed. Charles Prouty, The Yale Shakespeare Festival Lectures (Hamden, Conn.: Shoe String Press, 1954), pp. 101–22.

Wip'd the black scruples, reconcil'd my thoughts
To thy good truth and honour.

[IV.iii.114–17]

It also guarantees Malcolm's genuine concern for his country's
welfare: "What I am truly, / Is thine, and my poor country's, to
command" (131–32). The scene is filled, too, with powerful at-
mospheric images. The passage about angels being "bright still,
though the brightest fell" (22) adds Shakespeare's usual analogic
glow to the tale of king killing: in *Richard II*, the Garden, Adam
and Eve, Judas, and Pilate; in *Hamlet*, again the Garden, a serpent, and a brother's murder. The passage also recalls, in Malcolm's line "Yet Grace must still look so" (24), Duncan's "There's
no art / To find the mind's construction in the face" (I.iv.11–
12). But the difference is impressively stressed by the context:
Duncan trusted, and was slaughtered; Malcolm, who is cautious,
lives to restore peace. We are being shown a less idealistic world,
but also a more secure one.

The following episode in the scene, that of the English Doctor
who tells of Edward's curing "the Evil" (146) is also important
and effective. Here certainly for the first time in the play, and
perhaps for the first time in all of Shakespeare, we hear of actual
supernatural goodness in a king. When Richard taunted Gaunt—
"Why, uncle, thou hast many years to live"—he was answered,
"But not a minute, King, that thou canst give." Now for the first
time we have a king who *can* give time to men. Of course we are
not allowed to see him; his appearance would be theatrically ques-
tionable if not disastrous. In the first place, we would expect Edward to perform a miracle, and miracles on stage tend to be comic,
however seriously done. Furthermore, like old Hamlet or Edward
III (in *Richard II*), he is more effective through remaining an
image, his appropriate type of dramatic existence. He can be
praised in lyric poetry but is saved from having to face the essential ironies of stage presentation. But the mention of his curative
prowess in connection with Malcolm, who will soon heal his suffering Scotland of its Macbeth—evil which is a "king's evil" in a
different sense—adds a hint of otherworldly perfection to Malcolm's pragmatic realism. The fact that Edward's miraculous touch
is passed down in orderly succession further contrasts with Mac-

beth's vain attempt to invade this succession with his childlessness. The news of the slaughter of Macduff's family, which is reported at this point, is something I shall return to in a moment.[14]

I have lingered on the Macduff-Malcolm scene because here the imaginative roots of a new conception of kingship, the third in the play, are laid bare, and the twin agents of the new forces are developed from being merely "other lords" into the angry, suffering, and (to Scotland) loyal Macduff and the shrewd prober and unspoiled practitioner of royal virtues who is Duncan's son. After this scene, the action moves rapidly to the eventual clash with Macbeth, whose death, brutal and decisive, follows almost at once. At the end of the play, order has been restored, crime punished, and Malcolm accredited as a healer king.

As Tillyard has suggested, Malcolm is a "representative" character of a sort that Shakespeare uses frequently: he "provides little interest in himself but a great deal in what he stands for." [15] Devoted to the good of his country, keeping tight control of his passions, Machiavellian in distrust of others until they prove their integrity, "he is . . . the ideal ruler"—not the ideal man!—"who has subordinated all personal pleasures, and with them all personal charm, to his political obligations. . . . As a subordinate character he fits perfectly in the play and does not risk letting his creator down, as Henry V had done." [16] Here Tillyard has, I think, caught precisely the quality and limits of the counterforces to Macbeth. Shakespeare's Malcolm is a mixture of lion, fox, and pelican—a mixture and *balance* that are probably more authentically Elizabethan (remembering the protean flexibility and variety of the Queen who gave her name to the Age) than the later romantic conception which called for singleness of being.

Tillyard's comparison of Henry V and Malcolm raises many interesting questions that cannot be dealt with here. For our pur-

---

14. At the start of iv.iii Malcolm sounds like Richard II in act iii: "Let us seek out some desolate shade, and there / Weep our sad bosoms empty" (1–2), and Macduff just like Carlisle: "Let us rather / Hold fast the mortal sword" (2–3). By the end of the scene however, Macduff is brooding, Malcolm urging him on like Carlisle: "Let's make us med'cines of our great revenge" (214).

15. *History Plays*, p. 317.

16. Ibid.

poses, the important similarity is that each represents a strong therapeutic and unifying force emerging to control the forces of division. In *Henry V*, despite certain qualifications that seemed to emerge when Gaunt's lyricism was actually dramatized, the king managed to put things to rights in practically every sphere of life, eliminating, or at least suppressing, the warring contradictions that plagued his father. In *Macbeth*, we seem to have a similar movement at the end of the play back toward a simpler vision of kingship and order. Malcolm and Henry V are both more flexible, expert, and successful than the kings they replace. In both plays, there is an obvious movement away from the divisions, tensions, and corresponding impression of a variety of "life" under the rebel king. The reaction and restoration at the end of *Macbeth* is as essential to its shape and meaning as *Henry V* is to the shape and meaning of the tetralogy it concludes.

The morality *Macbeth*, at which we have so far been looking, will not of course do. Macbeth, though a murderer and toward the end something like the monster he is called, is obviously a great deal more than this, as Shakespeare forces us to recognize by means of Malcolm's summary at the play's close: "this dead butcher, and his fiend-like Queen" (v.ix.35). We understand why Malcolm and his followers should feel and speak so, and within limits we know them to be right. But only within limits. This is *their* Macbeth; it is not quite ours. Our Macbeth is hero as well as villain, and our response to him is multiple. Though it has been argued that "we cannot adopt [Macbeth] selectively, feel oneness with some parts of him and reject others," [17] I believe this view is unacceptable. True tragic identification seems to require detachment as much as it requires engagement. And in these terms, Macbeth is an extreme and very clear example: our admiration for him is intense but also distant; it is admiration in the word's root sense—a wondering at.

The quality in Macbeth that most engages us is not, I think,

17. Robert Heilman, "The Criminal as Tragic Hero: Dramatic Methods," *Shakespeare Survey* 19 (1966):14. Though I disagree with this one point, Mr. Heilman's argument is brilliant and informative. He too sees Macbeth shrinking in the play from—to use his terms—multilateral to unilateral being.

his acute imagination, though this has often been proposed. More accurately, it is his deep, almost inarticulate sense of levels beyond our limited experience to which his imagination gives him, and us, some sort of intuitive access. Everything, for the Macbeth of the first two or even three acts, has reverberations, has *mana*. Everything, moreover, vibrates for him somewhere outside the world of time and beyond the human senses as well as within them, and therefore shakes him (the phrase is Hamlet's) "with thoughts beyond the reaches of our souls." For playgoers, probably the best remembered evidence of this faculty in Macbeth is the murder scene itself, where the reverberations that reach him from the owl, the cricket, the blood, and the voice crying "Sleep no more" are altogether lost on his wife. She cuts through the anxieties caused by his inability to say "Amen" and by his imagined murdering of sleep with the practical advice, "Go, get some water, / And wash this filthy witness from your hand" (II.ii.45–46). Leaving to return the daggers, she confidently adds,

> If he do bleed,
> I'll gild the faces of the grooms withal,
> For it must seem their guilt.
> [II.ii.54–56]

As the assured tone and grim pun on "gilt" suggest, she is unworried by the blood except as it may be a "witness."

But as soon as she has left, and the knocking offstage has announced, as DeQuincy was the first to see,[18] the emergence of some sort of nemesis from within but also from beyond the temporal, he looks at his hands uncomprehendingly: "What hands are here?" (58) and then, in a new key echoes her command.

> Will all great Neptune's ocean wash this blood
> Clean from my hand? No, this my hand will rather
> The multitudinous seas incarnadine,
> Making the green one red.
> [II.ii.59–62]

---

18. "On the Knocking at the Gate in Macbeth," *London Magazine,* October 1823.

Again her easy literalism is replaced with a wildly imaginative apprehension of a kind of reality in which blood has moral and not simply literal status. Then this too is set aside by her confident repetition as she returns from replacing the daggers: "A little water clears us of this deed: / How easy is it then!" (66–67). We have met with the washing image before. It occurs at crucial moments in both *Richard II* and *Hamlet*. Obviously, for Shakespeare it had the usual connections with Christian purification from sin, but also a special connection with tragic insight. Here, in *Macbeth*, it can hardly be coincidental that the only time we see Lady Macbeth reveal any internal stress or strain (in the sleepwalking scene) the washing reappears—and in Macbeth's sense of it: "Out, damned spot! out, I say!"—"What, will these hands ne'er be clean?"—"Here's the smell of the blood still: all the perfumes of Arabia will not sweeten this little hand" (v.i.34–35).

Macbeth's intense consciousness of something that lies beyond the pale of our normal Aristotelian city—where, as Auden says, "Euclid's geometry / And Newton's mechanics would account for our experience, / And the kitchen table exists because I scrub it"[19]—becomes apparent on our first acquaintance with him.

> If good, why do I yield to that suggestion
> Whose horrid image doth unfix my hair,
> And make my seated heart knock at my ribs,
> Against the use of nature? Present fears
> Are less than horrible imaginings.
> My thought, whose murther yet is but fantastical,
> Shakes so my single state of man,
> That function is smother'd in surmise,
> And nothing is, but what is not.
>
> [i.iii.134–42]

These lines are remarkable, as everyone remembers, both for their intuition of some profound inner assault by anarchic forces

---

19. "For the Time Being," *Collected Poetry of W. H. Auden* (New York: Random House, 1945), lines 1477–1479.

on his humanity, his "single state of man," and for their apprehension of a buried life within that can under the proper stimula-
tion rise to efface the life of which he is routinely conscious:
"And nothing is, but what is not." How far Shakespeare has come
in his exploration of the unexplorable may be seen by looking
momentarily back to *Hamlet*. The Prince's first soliloquy, like
Macbeth's here, immediately opens his character to our view.
But there what we see is a man musing on external events in the
face of which he must set a clear limit on his actions, "but I
must hold my tongue." Here something altogether different
happens. As the external reality, Macbeth's new title, Thane of
Cawdor, fades almost from his view, his introspections dominate
completely—possess him as if he were simply their instrument.
It is the difference between thoughts aroused by external and
those aroused by internal "events"—thoughts which in fact become their own events. Not his new title but "horrible imaginings"
and a "horrid image" take over his consciousness, while out of
his internal agitation dawns suddenly the fully developed, if still
fantastical, will to murder. There has been nothing to prepare
us for this; it seems to be Shakespeare's way of indicating that
some mysterious world and life are carrying on their own business
beneath the surface of Macbeth's public character.

The difference between this genesis of the idea of king killing
and its genesis in *Hamlet* is also revealing. There, too, the "command" comes suddenly and surprisingly. That something requires
revenge is mentioned in the Ghost's sixth line, and the actual
command—"Revenge his foul and most unnatural murther"—
is our first indication that a crime has been committed. But again
the distinction is what matters. Between the external, visible
Ghost in *Hamlet* and the mysterious inner impulse in *Macbeth*,
the gulf is wide. Even if we argue that Hamlet's Ghost is simply
symbolic of his own internal desire and need for vengeance, this
must not blind us to the vast difference in tone, dramatic effect,
and meaning between hearing a father's ghost command his son
to avenge his murder and hearing the will to murder, fully formed
in all its horrid particulars, surge up from within. It will not do
to say that in *Macbeth* Shakespeare merely does by internal
means what in *Hamlet* he does externally, for though this is

partly true, the way things are done in the theater is, inevitably, a large part of what they mean.[20]

Macbeth, then, appeals to us, even as he repels us, by his unspoken and perhaps unspeakable intuitions of a life within himself and beyond himself to which we too respond, and tremble as we do. What he experiences seems to go much deeper than the predictable hypocrisies of the villain, whether stage or real. When he participates, for a moment, in Duncan's world, falling into its idiom—"The service and the loyalty I owe, / In doing it, pays itself" (1.iv.22–23)—and imaging his duties to Duncan as "children and servants" (25), we have no right to be sure, as too many critics have been, that he is merely hypocritical. Much more plausibly that world is yet a possibility for Macbeth, a potentiality in him, like the valorous service he has just shown in battle against the invaders, the "milk of human kindness" in him to which his wife calls attention, and the scruples that beset him in his soliloquy outside the banqueting chamber at Inverness— not to mention the moral sensitivities that after the murder enable his ears to hear the voice crying sleep no more and his eyes to see the murder sticking to his hands along with the blood. Yet always from somewhere inside him (though also outside him, as the Sisters attest, for they are as visible to us and to Banquo as to him) comes the other urgency, and it floods in now, powerfully, as Duncan speaks to create Malcolm his heir.

> Stars, hide your fires!
> Let not light see my black and deep desires;
> The eye wink at the hand; yet let that be,
> Which the eye fears, when it is done, to see.
>
> [1.iv.50–53]

The last line of that passage—which we realize marks some sort of progression in this possession by a life within and yet beyond himself—appropriately hints at a further mystery in his experience to come. For this, though we are only in the fourth scene, is unquestionably the last occasion in the play when Macbeth will

---

20. The answer to the perennial question, Do the witches "cause" Macbeth's murder? lies hidden in the quotation marks: a clear answer requires too many assumptions about the very questions the play is exploring—such as what is a man, a deed, a cause, a consequence—to be very helpful.

be able to refer to a deed done or being done without exciting vibrations in us. Though I think there is much to be said for those who protest the modern tendency to assume that audiences respond to (or even notice) a repetition in the last act of a word used in the first,[21] in some of Shakespeare's plays repetition occurs so insistently and so impressively, that an attentive audience simply cannot miss it. "Honest" in *Othello* and "nothing" in *King Lear* are probably safe examples. So are "deeds," "do," and "done" in *Macbeth*. Not only do these terms pervade the play, but in at least eleven instances they appear emphatically in pairs or triplets and always in striking situations.

But in a sieve I'll thither sail,
And like a rat without a tail;
I'll do, I'll do, and I'll do.

[I.iii.8–10]

thou'dst have, great Glamis,
That which cries, "Thus thou must do," if thou have it;
And that which rather thou dost fear to do,
Than wishest should be undone.

[I.v.22–25]

In every point twice done, and then done double.

[I.vi.15]

If it were done, when 'tis done, then 'twere well
It were done quickly.

[I.vii.1–2]

I dare do all that may become a man;
Who dares do more, is none.

[I.vii.46–47]

After five such pairings in the first act, the idea of doing and the limits of doing become charged with implication, and in a sense

21. A good example is a refreshing review article by Matthias Shaaber in *Studies in English Literature* 7 (1967):351–76. Still it remains true that we recognize in a play what we bring with us the capacity for recognizing. An unread Laplander might attach no significance to the garden image in *Hamlet* because he would have no way of doing so—but this image is still there for the rest of us.

what Shakespeare does thereafter throughout the play is to
release this charge at telling moments, most often with ironic
force. In the murder scenes, for example:

> I am afraid to think what I have done;
> Look on't again I dare not.
>
> [ɪɪ.ii.50–51]

In the banquet scene, this theme expands. Macbeth's statement
to the Murderer seems to imply a conception of clearly achiev-
able deeds.

> Yet he's good that did the like for Fleance:
> If thou didst it, thou art the nonpareil.
>
> [ɪɪɪ.iv.17–18]

But then the Ghost's appearance makes him wonder, in lines
already quoted, whether nowadays murders can be "perform'd"
(76) as they could "i' th' olden time" (74) or whether now the
victims always "rise again" (79). By the end of the scene, he
seems confident once more that deeds *can* be done, that plans he
has "in head . . . will to hand" (138), and concludes ominously,
with a loss of insight that we will not appreciate fully till later:
"We are yet but young in deed" (143).

In her own less conscious way, Lady Macbeth follows a similar
psychic arc, but with one crucial difference. When she comes
looking for Macbeth after Banquo's departure on his last journey,
she expresses her concern at his recent behavior in the same flat
terms she had used in the murder scene.

> How now, my Lord? why do you keep alone,
> Of sorriest fancies your companions making,
> Using those thoughts, which should indeed have died
> With them they think on? Things without all remedy
> Should be without regard: what's done is done.
>
> [ɪɪɪ.ii.8–12]

Later, during the banquet, she handles the phrase again, quite
oblivious to its implication, like a child handling an explosive.

> Why do you make such faces? When all's done,
> You look but on a stool.
>
> [ɪɪɪ.iv.66–67]

When she uses it for the last time, she will be sleepwalking, re-living forever a murder that in one sense is never "done" and in another even more painful sense is "done" beyond recall.

> To bed, to bed: there's knocking at the gate. Come, come, come, come, give me your hand. What's done cannot be un-done. To bed, to bed, to bed. [v.i.62–65]

An important turning point in the development of Macbeth's character, as I interpret it, occurs in the soliloquy he utters out-side the banqueting hall at Inverness, which gives a paradigm in little of his general movement in the play from intense psychic activity in anticipation of an action to the stripping away and narrowing down that every action entails as it creates its own devouring vortex.

> If it were done, when 'tis done, then 'twere well
> It were done quickly: if th' assassination
> Could trammel up the consequence, and catch
> With his surcease success; that but this blow
> Might be the be-all and the end-all—here,
> But here, upon this bank and shoal of time,
> We'd jump the life to come.
>
> [i.vii.1–7]

The metaphysical uneasiness that becomes explicit here has been gestating since the opening lines, when a battle could be "lost and won." The ambiguities are in neither case merely linguistic; it is not merely a matter of a battle lost by one and won by another, though that happens, or of a deed not being finished when it appears complete. The ambiguity goes deeper, is metaphysical, even supernatural. Macbeth both wins that battle in act 1 and, by winning, loses—because of the temptations his victory and honors bring him. Likewise, he contemplates in the soliloquy the gap between the performance of a deed and its consequences as a deed performed, but soon all deeds begin to show an ultimate in-completeness. Murders require further murders, and dead men rise. His world increasingly reveals itself as a place in which no settled definitions of man exist, no final deeds, done and over with. It manifests its unpredictableness at every turn, in crises and in trifles—as when Banquo asks the witches, "are you aught / That man may question?" (i.iii.42–43), or when the Porter talks about drink's ambiguous effects on deeds, "it provokes the desire, but it takes away the performance" (ii.iii.29–30). Behind the solid front of Scottish politics, even behind murder and its discovery, we sense that something yet more momentous stirs.

In this soliloquy outside his banquet hall, Macbeth manages to meditate his way out of murder, only to be shamed back into it by his wife's "When you durst do it, then you were a man" (i.vii.49). His own earlier demurrer—"I dare do all that may become a man" (46)—a demurrer springing from a still complex awareness of all that it requires to be human—shrinks in just thirty lines, under her prodding, to signify solely courage: "thy undaunted mettle should compose / Nothing but males" (74–75). What the rest of the play then offers in Macbeth's character is an uneven but continuing retrogression from the earlier full awareness to a condition in which all faculties are attenuated to a male and murderous courage, noble and admirable only as the beast of prey is noble and admirable. Macbeth's tragedy, in short, as this soliloquy shows us, is of decreasing internal awareness, and this is what sets him so clearly apart from Richard II and Hamlet, and most other Shakespearean heroes.

The dagger soliloquy follows in ii.ii and again traces in little Macbeth's decline from his characteristic full awareness to a limitation, almost blindness, self-imposed. First of all it establishes the primacy of the visual sense both in the play and in its hero: "I have thee not, and yet I see thee still" (ii.i.35). The dagger is a "fatal vision" (36) and is only seen, not clutched, making the eyes either "the fools o' th' other senses, / Or else worth all the rest" (44–45). In phrase on phrase—"I see thee yet . . . I see thee still . . . to mine eyes" (40–49)—Shakespeare emphasizes the visibility of the dagger, partly, I suppose, because it is the instrument of powers that will repeatedly—with blood, daggers, ghosts, and every insidious form of apparition—work on Macbeth's sight ("But no more sights!" iv.i.155), and partly too because its appearance at this moment defines with characteristic ambiguity (is it in fact "vision" or hallucination?) the complex kinds and sources of experience to which Macbeth as tragic hero is sensitive.

The witches were visibly on stage whatever their function symbolically as embodiments of his ambition, and were seen by Banquo; the dagger, though invisible for us and untouchable for
him, nevertheless leads toward Duncan's bedroom: "Thou mar-
shall'st me the way that I was going" (42). Evil is allowed a
supernatural aggressiveness and reality in this play. It is not the
evil masking as good which we saw in Claudius, but an evil that
expresses itself openly in visible forms. And yet—Shakespeare
habitually taking away most of what he gives—the dagger is and
remains invisible to us, and Macbeth himself concludes: "There's
no such thing" (47).

Shakespeare handles the rest of the soliloquy in such a way as
to make us feel that Macbeth is wiser and more perceptive in
seeing the invisible dagger than when he rejects it as unreal.
Immediately upon rejecting it, he describes the night.

> Nature seems dead, and wicked dreams abuse
> The curtain'd sleep: Witchcraft celebrates
> Pale Hecate's off'rings; and wither'd Murther,
> Alarum'd by his sentinel, the wolf,
> Whose howl's his watch, thus with his stealthy pace,
> With Tarquin's ravishing strides, towards his design
> Moves like a ghost.
>
> [ii.i.50–56]

This is a remarkably vivid evocation of an infernal sympathy
between nature, night, and evil. Much more vividly than in
Hamlet, evil seems here to have its own dominations, thrones,
and powers, as in Milton's hell. For though they are only images,
a projection of the moral weather Macbeth has inside him, like
Duncan's harvest and Banquo's description of Dunsinane as a
procreant cradle (i.vi.3–10), the black vision does take over the
stage, suiting, as Macbeth says, his dark deed and repudiating
light—a repudiation intensely dramatic as he dismisses his servant,
who bears the only torch. The rejection of light, like the rejection
of the earlier multi-consciousness, is affirmed in Macbeth's calm
"I go, and it is done" (62). What has happened to the probing
mind that wondered *if* deeds were done when done? For the
second time we have a hint—though only a hint—that the evoca-

tion of an order of evil, a conspiracy of nature, may be simply
the other face of a narrowing of awareness, and the rejection of
vision and "sights" a simplifying of existential complexity.

This was certainly a possibility hinted at—even more obliquely
—in Hamlet's dark speech:

> 'Tis now the very witching time of night,
> When churchyards yawn, and hell itself breathes out
> Contagion to this world; now could I drink hot blood,
> And do such bitter business as the day
> Would quake to look on.
>
> [*Hamlet,* III.ii.407–11]

It will be remembered that this picture of cosmic conspiracy, with
its obvious parallels in image and tone to Macbeth's and Lady
Macbeth's speeches, immediately preceded Hamlet's dizzyingly
rapid double mistake of sparing Claudius by thinking too precisely and cutting down Polonius by not thinking at all. We had
watched Hamlet struggle throughout to suit the action to the
word, and it seemed that arms were "Black as [their] purpose" and
"Thoughts [were] black, hands apt, drugs fit, and time agreeing"
(III.ii.269) only in plays like "The Murder of Gonzago." In the
real world of Elsinore, such sinister harmony was difficult if not
impossible to achieve. Here, as Macbeth girds himself for regicide,
we are seeing the conspiracy of nature spread like an evil yeast
through not only the body natural of its next king but through
the whole body politic of Scotland. We saw Richard II turn the
traditional sympathy of nature for the king into a similar conspiracy (III.ii), but this remained essentially a private, internalizing, imaginative operation marking, if anything, the beginnings
of an *increase* in Richard's internal awareness. What makes *Macbeth* such a different kind of play is that the conspiracy view
ceases to be the imaginative construct of Hamlet's play or
Richard's nightmare and becomes real, filled with blood and a
strange dynamic power. We are seeing in graphic detail what
Marlowe only symbolized loosely in comic trickery: the world
that is bought with the sale of one's soul to the devil.

This experience is further anatomized when, in the next scene,
the deed of murder drives Macbeth back to a frenzy of psychic
division and wild imagining, contrasted almost favorably with

Lady Macbeth's unwavering singleness of being. "Amen" sticks in his throat, a voice cries out his name, his own hands essay to "pluck out mine eyes" (58). Carried on the flood of these mysterious and quasi-supernatural intuitions, some of the referents of the good order do return: "'God bless us'" (26), "the innocent Sleep" (35), "Nature's second course" (38), "life's feast" (39). But they return as realities lost, possibilities cancelled out by the act of killing the king.

The murder scene is, of course, a second important turning point. After this, Macbeth makes no major recovery, though he long retains some residue of the sensibility that was his at the beginning. At the discovery of the murder, he plays the dull hypocrite with no real flair and is all but discovered. The interest shifts now from questions about the inner meaning of his actions to questions about whether he will succeed. Many of the most interesting elements in the scene—the Porter, Banquo's quiet response, Lady Macbeth's swoon—seem hardly to make contact with his consciousness at all. When he speaks, he speaks like Duncan earlier ("There's no art / To find the mind's construction in the face" I.iv.11–12)—far truer than he knows.

> Had I but died an hour before this chance,
> I had liv'd a blessed time; for, from this instant,
> There's nothing serious in mortality;
> All is but toys: renown, and grace, is dead;
> The wine of life is drawn, and the mere lees
> Is left this vault to brag of.
>
> [II.iii.91–96]

We recall a time when he *was* capable of balance, as he wrestled with himself the night before, when he asks:

> Who can be wise, amaz'd, temperate and furious,
> Loyal and neutral, in a moment? No man:
> Th' expedition of my violent love
> Outrun the pauser, reason.
>
> [II.iii.108–11]

But now, I think for the first time, he sees less than we do. In this too he stands at the opposite pole from Richard and Hamlet, who, though embraced by irony at the start, become less and less open

to it as their plays wear on. As Macbeth loses his complex awareness, the audience gains it in a new ironic attitude.

The Macbeth of act III is indeed a diminished thing, under-
going what may be called the tyranny of the deed, different from
the ambiguity that surrounded action in *Hamlet*—for here the
deed performed has achieved a mysterious agent-capacity of its
own. What Macbeth contemplated as a metaphysical problem, "If
it were done . . . ," now returns to hound him as an inescapable
task and reality. In *Hamlet,* the Ghost called for blood; here,
blood itself will have blood, the deed done will have another deed.
  The direction in which Macbeth is now so clearly heading
is emphasized after Banquo's departure in III.i, in a soliloquy
whose details ideally should be compared, item for item, with
those which occupied Macbeth's mind during the banquet at
Inverness (I.vii). Suffice it to point out, in lieu of such comparison,
that though something of the old language persists, it is now sung
to another tune. Where formerly we had the baroque energy of
"angels, trumpet-tongu'd," and "Pity, like a naked new-born
babe, / Striding the blast," and "heaven's Cherubins hors'd / Upon
the sightless couriers of the air" to "blow the horrid deed in every
eye" (the imagery, unlimited and uninhibited, of a free imagination), we have now the constraining pressures of the practical
and expedient—what must be done because something else was
done and cannot be undone.

> To be thus is nothing, but to be safely thus:
> Our fears in Banquo
> Stick deep, and in his royalty of nature
> Reigns that which would be fear'd; 'tis much he dares;
> And, to that dauntless temper of his mind,
> He hath a wisdom that doth guide his valour
> To act in safety. There is none but he
> Whose being I do fear: and under him
> My Genius is rebuk'd; as, it is said,
> Mark Antony's was by Caesar. He chid the Sisters,
> When first they put the name of King upon me,
> And bade them speak to him; then, prophet-like,
> They hail'd him father to a line of kings:

Upon my head they plac'd a fruitless crown,
And put a barren sceptre in my gripe,
Thence to be wrench'd with an unlineal hand,
No son of mine succeeding. If't be so,
For Banquo's issue have I fil'd my mind;
For them the gracious Duncan have I murther'd;
Put rancours in the vessel of my peace,
Only for them; and mine eternal jewel
Given to the common Enemy of man,
To make them kings, the seed of Banquo kings!
Rather than so, come, fate, into the list,
And champion me to th' utterance!

[III.i.48–71]

Even the reference to "the vessel of my peace" and "mine eternal jewel"—fragments, we might say, still surviving from the earlier outlook—have become now an argument for more murder to be "safely thus."

We are not, therefore, surprised to find that the conversation with the murderers, which follows immediately, contains nothing that might not have been anticipated of the commonest villain on the Elizabethan stage. As with Bolingbroke, Shakespeare begins increasingly to set ironies at the edges of Macbeth's speeches: when the king claims to have demonstrated Banquo's villainy "To half a soul, to a notion craz'd" (82), he describes better than he intends the sort of person who would murder on the basis of his strained allegations. Even the catalogue of dogs, in its own curious way a reflection of the hierarchical principle that Macbeth has already violated, serves here merely to rate men with beasts and the best men with those who kill best.

When Lady Macbeth enters in the next scene, we realize that the two of them are attuned in a way they have never been before. She echoes the ideas we have just heard him speak in his soliloquy:

Nought's had, all's spent,
Where our desire is got without content:
'Tis safer to be that which we destroy,
Than by destruction dwell in doubtful joy.

[III.ii.4–7]

Her "safer" matches even his "safely." Then, in turn, he echoes
her words, though she spoke them before his entrance:

> Better be with the dead,
> Whom we, to gain our peace, have sent to peace,
> Than on the torture of the mind to lie
> In restless ecstasy. Duncan is in his grave;
> After life's fitful fever he sleeps well;
> Treason has done his worst.
>
> [III.ii.19–24]

There is a fitful flash, it may be, of the old distinction between
them, she laboring to assure him and herself that "what's done is
done" (12) and he realizing that "We have scorch'd the snake,
not kill'd it" (13)—but again the intuition of something beyond
the mundane and temporal is implicit as this image evaporates
under the tyranny of the new deed that he has already imple-
mented. And once more, as earlier in the dagger speech, his mind
fills with emblems of a conspiracy in nature which may be the
other face of a shrinkage of sensitivity, the fading of his "eternal
jewel."

> Come, seeling Night,
> Scarf up the tender eye of pitiful Day,
> And, with thy bloody and invisible hand,
> Cancel, and tear to pieces, that great bond
> Which keeps me pale!—Light thickens; and the crow
> Makes wing to th' rooky wood;
> Good things of Day begin to droop and drowse,
> Whiles Night's black agents to their preys do rouse.
>
> [III.ii.46–53]

"That great bond" sounds something like the even-handed Justice,
double trust, and golden opinions which defined what a man, and
especially a host, should do in I.vii. But, whereas these ideals were
there shattered by Lady Macbeth, here Macbeth himself turns
the bond into something that merely keeps him "pale." As his
more delicate and complex virtues are cut out one by one, the
last crude virtues of courage and a desire for clarity increase.

As the focus of the play shifts from what Macbeth thinks and says to what happens to him, our view of him becomes detached, our attitude toward him increasingly ironic. This effect is striking in the scene of his last visit to the Sisters (IV.i). Two main elements here compel us to see him in a new light. First, at the opening of the scene, the remarkable increase in seriousness of the witches.[22] For the first time these mysterious creatures sound like true demonic powers as they mix their horrible fragment-feast. Creatures who before had nothing better—or worse—to do than to beg chestnuts from a sailor's wife now speak lines that make the mind recoil, revealing in their conjuration the fragmentation of man and deed, the dismemberment and disjunction of all things, that we have been tracing in Macbeth's interior drama and that set the real nature of Macbeth's murders before us. Whether they have caused or merely reflect these evil actions, the witches introduce a group of images that recall Macbeth's and Lady Macbeth's earlier evocations of a universe of evil and also the murders they have committed.

They announce Macbeth's arrival—"By the pricking of my thumbs, / Something wicked this way comes" (IV.i.44–45)—and for the first time, I think, we come close to accepting this as a reasonable judgment. We may still be fascinated by Macbeth's quest for certainty and some horizon where a deed is "done," but we are also increasingly aware of its absurdity. When he asks them what they do, they answer with a phrase that perfectly describes his own doing: "A deed without a name" (49). We have been here before. But now Macbeth insists on finding the deed's name, and for a fourth[23] time his desire to contain and circumscribe what can never be circumscribed and contained ("I am bent to know, / By the worst means, the worst" III.iv.133–34) brings with it images of a conspiring cosmos.

> Though you untie the winds, and let them fight
> Against the Churches; though the yesty waves

22. I am assuming, again, that Hecate's silly lines are spurious.
23. This pattern is almost constant with Lady Macbeth before act v. I am counting only its occurrences in Macbeth's speeches (I.vii.73–75, II.i.49–60, III.ii.46–55).

Confound and swallow navigation up;
Though bladed corn be lodg'd, and trees blown down;
Though castles topple on their warders' heads;
Though palaces, and pyramids, do slope
Their heads to their foundations; though the treasure
Of Nature's germens tumble all together,
Even till destruction sicken, answer me
To what I ask you.

[iv.i.52–61]

Here too, as simplicity replaces complexity, chaos replaces the earlier figures of supreme control—the naked newborn infant striding the blast, the "hors'd Cherubins."

A second aspect of the scene that detaches us from Macbeth and envelops him in our irony is Shakespeare's use of the same theatrical conventions he had called on in the dagger speech. There *we* did not see what Macbeth saw—a situation, at that time, of greater mysteriousness than irony. We might have concluded that he was mad, or that he was supernaturally perceptive—but at least he saw more, not less, than we. Furthermore, while vividly describing the dagger, Macbeth himself constantly debated its reality and meaning. We were likely to become engaged with him in contemplating the mystery of this dagger. Here (in iv.i) Shakespeare exploits our senses in a manner less mysterious than ironic. We hear *and* see the witches' apparitions, whereas Macbeth seems only to hear. Put more accurately—when he looks at the apparitions, he fails to understand what he sees. The apparition that warns, "None of woman born / Shall harm Macbeth" (80–81), is a bloody child, of course related to the babe "from his mother's womb / Untimely ripp'd" (v.viii.15–16)—that is to say, to the threat posed by Macduff. Neither we nor Macbeth can at this point know this, but we in the audience should and do note the disparity between the apparition's looks and words. Even a modern high-school audience invariably asks what the bloody child means. The point is that Macbeth does not ask. Where before he found two truths in one experience, the deed that was not done when done, he now leaps anxiously at one truth in two experiences, one verbal, the other visual.

The same thing happens, with an even more mocking irony,

in the case of the third apparition—"*a child crowned with a tree
in his hand.*" Here the verbal message is simply that Macbeth need
not fear being vanquished until Birnam Wood shall come to
Dunsinane. Again he hears the words but does not sufficiently
wonder at what he sees. It does not take a terribly perceptive
spectator to suspect that he has just been shown precisely how
Birnam Wood *will* come to Dunsinane—as branches in the hands
of Malcolm's troops—and to feel accordingly superior to Macbeth.
If the spectator happens to remember the vivid image Macbeth
himself used after the banquet, "Stones have been known to move,
and trees to speak," the effect of detachment will be stronger still.
For if ever a tree "spoke," it is the one carried by the crowned
child, yet Macbeth does not even suspect what before he knew.
The striking character of both images inclines one to believe that
Shakespeare intended us to notice a connection and to see in it
decisive evidence of Macbeth's waning awareness. In the same
way, when Macbeth next says, "Rebellious dead, rise never" (97),
he seems not to remember what we recall: that he and we have
already seen one dead man rise.

Finally, as if to draw attention to the gap that has opened between a hero who hears only and an audience that both hears
and sees, Shakespeare presents a last apparition, who says nothing.
It is Banquo, preceded by the "*show of eight Kings.*" Our attention
is explicitly drawn to the visual nature of this episode: "Show his
eyes, and grieve his heart" (110), "Thy crown does sear mine eye-
balls . . . Start, eyes! . . . I'll see no more . . . some I see . . .
Horrible sight!—Now, I see, 'tis true," (113–22).[24] Forced in this
case to understand what he sees, Macbeth becomes angered and
rejects everything the witches have shown him—"damn'd all those
that trust them!" (139). Our own response to this is likely to distance us still further from Macbeth as we wish he would now
"trust them" enough to take their warnings, or had not trusted
them in act 1. We still care about Macbeth and wish he would or
could save himself, but we are no longer able to overlook the
abyss that has opened between ourselves and him.

Appropriately, the scene ends with the play's last extensive
exercises on the "deed" that is impossible to be "done." Macbeth's

24. The emphasis on vision echoes ii.i.33–49.

lines here are a remarkable example of how complex a poetry may
be written to communicate a diminished and gradually emptying
consciousness.

> Time, thou anticipat'st my dread exploits:
> The flighty *purpose* never is o'ertook,
> Unless the *deed* go with it. From this moment,
> The very firstlings of my *heart* shall be
> The firstlings of my *hand.* And even now,
> To crown my *thoughts* with *acts,* be it *thought* and *done:*
> The castle of Macduff I will surprise.
>
>   [IV.i.144–50; italics mine]

We need not listen very hard to hear echoes here of Hamlet's
fourth soliloquy ("How all occasions do inform against me . . .")
which worked its way to an equally passionate climax. Hamlet's
conclusion, "From this time forth / My thoughts be bloody or be
nothing worth," closely parallels in syntax and intensity Macbeth's
"From this moment, / The very firstlings of my heart shall be / The
firstlings of my hand." But whereas Hamlet speaks of "thoughts"
and quietly leaves for England, Macbeth speaks of hands and,
immediately after, we see the Macduff family slaughtered.

What Shakespeare seems to be doing here is to recall Macbeth's
earlier hesitant meditations by using the same antithetical terms
that were characteristic of him then. But now all these antitheses
are challenged, not pondered. This is not the man who meditated
on the peculiar "undoneness" of things done; this is the language
of his wife when she prayed that no natural compunctions should
"keep peace" between her fell purpose and its effect (I.v.45–47).
At this late point in Macbeth's progress the "deed" is paired with
the "purpose," the "hand" with the "heart," "acts" with "thoughts"
and "done" with "thought" only that the second of each pair may
be surpassed by the first. The full power of a style thick with
balancing antitheses is employed, almost paradoxically, to support
a narrowing single awareness; complexity exists in the rhetoric but
only to be rejected in favor of simplicity in the meaning.

The effects of this deterioration are reflected not only in the
brutal killing of the Macduffs, but more subtly in the conversation
between Lady Macduff and Rosse (IV.ii). Under the pressure of

fear and despair Lady Macduff, like Macbeth, uses syntactically balanced pairs in each of which one term has simply replaced the other: "When our actions do not, / Our fears do" (IV.ii.3–4), "All is the fear, and nothing is the love" (12), "little is the wisdom . . . against all reason" (13–14). Fear, lack of wisdom—these are the operative motives for her husband's being in England, Lady Macduff argues. Attention is drawn, however, to the one-sidedness of this judgment by Rosse, who refuses to take her extreme stance, reminding her that many motives may be involved: "You know not, / Whether it was his wisdom, or his fear" (4–5). Yet even Rosse has to admit, in a crowning antithesis that does not differentiate but join: "cruel are the times, when we are traitors, / And do not know ourselves" (18–19). Left alone after the messenger's urging to flee, Lady Macduff wonders:

> Whither should I fly?
> I have done no harm. But I remember now
> I am in this earthly world, where, to do harm
> Is often laudable; to do good, sometime
> Accounted dangerous folly.
>
> [IV.ii.72–76]

She picks up in "harm . . . laudable" and "good . . . folly" the paradoxical antithesis so dominant from the play's first scene. But there is also here a pathetic Ophelia-like note ("But I remember now . . .") that sets a human standard by which the ensuing violence can be measured.

For a whole act after his departure from the witches, we do not see Macbeth. His absence is even longer than Hamlet's at the same point in the action and serves a similar function, preparing for the final confrontation of the hero with his fate. But whereas Hamlet on reappearance is no less in control of events than before, and far more in control of his own personality, Macbeth, when he reappears, is less in control of both. Shakespeare's success is that we keep a portion of our sympathy for Macbeth despite his resemblance to a bear tied to a stake, for the most part merely reacting to the initiatives of others.

One of the ways the play achieves this is by the sleepwalking of Lady Macbeth. Her continuous reliving of the past, her pathetic wish to be clean of the "spot," her clinging now, when it is too late, to the "light"—all these things remind us of and enact before us a remorse that we may suppose Macbeth (at some subconscious level like this one) shares. And even if we choose not to make the supposition, they move us nonetheless through our memories of a man who murdered at his wife's bidding only to have her, and the deed itself, come to this. We may even choose to believe that awake she is still the brutal force we saw in act I. But, at the same time—since Shakespeare ever creates double and triple effects—the fact that these visions of blood, ghosts, weakness, and guilt occur in her sleep stresses the deep authenticity of the realities and moral scruples they represent. While, from one point of view, it is only in sleep that Lady Macbeth is weak enough to suffer the pangs of conscience, from another point of view it is only in sleep—sleep which a murder murdered—that such profound moral realities can be faced directly. Lady Macbeth, haunted and probing in her sleep, offers an internal correlative for the counterforces which we have just seen preparing in England.

To take a final look at these forces of reaction, we must first note what there is about them that makes *Macbeth* unique in structure among Shakespeare's plays and what makes the two "plays" we have now discussed into the single tragedy—*Macbeth*. I have traced a progressive narrowing of Macbeth's awareness, a gradual trend toward the simple, external "solution" to what was previously seen as a complex problem with both psychological ("full of scorpions is my mind, dear wife!") and metaphysical ("blood will have blood") dimensions. When we see him again in act v, he reacts with ferocity to external events, commanding "Bring me no more reports" (v.iii.1), exulting in the spoken prophecies of the apparitions, and mercilessly insulting the bringer of news about the English. But in the long scene at the English court (iv.iii), something new and impressive was added to the play.

In the one aspect of the scene which we passed over before—Macduff's reception of the news of his family's slaughter—Shakespeare momentarily revives the style of complex awareness as he lets us glimpse in Macduff a man who has it in him to develop from the role of messenger into the role of patriot, father, and sympathetic human being, and who can perhaps kill *this* king without repeating Macbeth's act of bloody overreaching. Macduff's reaction to Rosse's news is placed in a context calculated to focus attention on his situation. Earlier in the scene, he has been shown to be brave, loyal, honest. Rosse has described Scotland as a place of sudden death—"good men's lives / Expire before the flowers in their caps" (171–72)—and has called the news he bears so bad that "No mind that's honest / But in it shares some woe" (197–98). Before he has had time to speak, Macduff already senses what is coming—"Humh! I guess at it" (203)—preparing us, I think, for some startling reaction.

The bad news out, Macduff's reaction is startling indeed in its stark simplicity and impressive sincerity: "My children too?" (211), "My wife kill'd too?" (213), "Did you say all?" (217). Though Shakespeare must achieve the effect quickly and by sleight of hand, we are plainly meant to feel that a deep, internal meditation and realization is taking place within Macduff. This in the revenger balances what we saw in the rebel in act 1, when Macbeth suddenly turned inward to his imaginings of murder (1.iii.139). In both cases, Shakespeare manages to suggest what he does not actually dramatize—a secret, hidden life of the feelings and the mind.

When Malcolm tries to cheer Macduff, his words are hearty and in the wrong key, the more so as he uses a by now powerfully charged word: "Dispute it like a man" (220). Macduff's answer contrasts radically.

> I shall do so;
> But I must also feel it as a man:
> I cannot but remember such things were,
> That were most precious to me.—Did Heaven look on,
> And would not take their part? Sinful Macduff!
> They were all struck for thee.
>
> [iv.iii.220–25]

This richly dramatic moment stands out sharply in a scene of ruse, mistrust, charade, and the cataloguing of royal vices and virtues. Here, once again, is the mixed style of double awareness, complicated and genuine. "But I must also feel it as a man": this is the way we wish Macbeth had answered his wife. The "also" is the crucial qualification. Macduff accepts the need for *both* responses, both definitions of man. We feel ourselves, for just a fleeting moment, back with the full consciousness that Macbeth displayed in acts I and II.

Furthermore, we find ourselves back with the modes of thinking that underlay conceptions like the king's two bodies, discussed in the Introduction. Malcolm here urges a response appropriate to the body politic; Macduff agrees but reminds him of the reality and needs of the body natural. The body natural is the flawed part ("Sinful Macduff!"), but it is also the part that excites the most immediate dramatic interest. The good prince cannot afford the luxury of deep feelings, the need for restorative action is too great ("Be this the whetstone of your sword" 228). But his ordinary human supporter and instrument—the good man—can afford to feel deeply, and indeed the play could not afford to be without this moment of anguished silence and sorrowful humility, which matches in the opposing party the subterranean anguish we are soon to see in Lady Macbeth. Many criticisms of the play stem from a belief that Shakespeare has not made enough of these personal feelings—that body natural—in the forces of reaction against Macbeth, and perhaps the criticisms are right.

The last act of *Macbeth* is like a good baroque suite: the interest is less in the richness of any chord than in the way the various voices sound against each other. We see little of the hero, and yet it becomes his tragedy in this act; the morality theme of crime and punishment is worked out, though it remains somewhat external; the most fascinating moments are the glimpses of Macbeth and Lady Macbeth, and yet the play refuses to be seen as a personal tragedy in the same way as *Hamlet* and *Othello*.

As the short scenes follow rapidly on one another, our attention and interest are kept shifting from Macbeth and his wife to their attackers. As I have noted, the scene of Lady Macbeth sleepwalking (v.i) focuses many themes and moods: the horror of the murders, the pitiable internal suffering of the criminals, the way murder "will out" sooner or later, the mysterious resistance to murder even within an ambitious queen. This is followed by a scene that shows us the psychic forces that are internally gnawing at Lady Macbeth, and by extension at Macbeth himself, in their *outward* habit of encounter in the form of the Scottish soldiers under Lennox.

> *Angus.*   Now does he feel
> His secret murthers sticking on his hands;
> How minutely revolts upbraid his faith-breach:
> Those he commands move only in command,
> Nothing in love: now does he feel his title
> Hang loose about him, like a giant's robe
> Upon a dwarfish thief.
> *Menteth.*   Who then shall blame
> His pester'd senses to recoil and start,
> When all that is within him does condemn
> Itself, for being there?
>
> [v.ii.16–25]

Set next to this, we encounter Macbeth at Dunsinane reduced to observation of experience rather than reaction to it.

> I have liv'd long enough: my way of life
> Is fall'n into the sere, the yellow leaf;
> And that which should accompany old age,
> As honour, love, obedience, troops of friends,
> I must not look to have.
>
> [v.iii.22–26]

He is now a commenter, no longer a pioneer. The insight remains, but the moral fight is over. The only resistance in him now is outward: "I'll fight, till from my bones my flesh be hack'd" (v.iii.32). The Doctor's suggestion that Lady Macbeth's cure is not to be had from medicine but only from within is greeted by Macbeth with "Throw physic to the dogs; I'll none of it" (47). Reversing the Doctor's view, he wants some external nostrum to cure the internal war.

> Canst thou not minister to a mind diseas'd,
> Pluck from the memory a rooted sorrow,
> Raze out the written troubles of the brain,
> And with some sweet oblivious antidote

Cleanse the stuff'd bosom of that perilous stuff
Which weighs upon the heart?

[v.iii.40–45]

And his conception of the external war is again similarly mis-
guided: "what purgative drug, / Would scour these English
hence?" (55–56).

The cure for Scotland will, in fact, be external, because the
disease has become external. What began in Macbeth's mind
(i.iii) has spread throughout his kingdom, as Siward insists, and
must be fought there: "Thoughts speculative their unsure hopes
relate, / But certain issue strokes must arbitrate" (v.iv.19–20). In
some ways, this is the heart of Macbeth's tragedy—first that this
insight is not his but Siward's; and second that it should come to
"strokes." Macbeth has so thoroughly drained himself of *internal*
significance that he must be dealt with in the way he dealt with
Macdonwald. He will have to be unseamed from the nave to the
chops. The psychic and spiritual energy he brought with him has
merely festered. It is almost, in fact, as if we have been witnesses
to an evolutionary failure: Duncan's singleness of being was replaced with a new capacity for tense, ironic, multiplicity of being,
but the new capacity went berserk; its possessor had to be cut
down; and the species reverts to something more like the original
creature than the deviant. In other words, there is nothing very
heartwarming about the forces of reaction in the play. Apart
from their motive, which is genuine love of Scotland, they are
soldiers who will kill and be killed, like Macbeth. Apart from
Macduff, they are impersonal and abstract. We wish them well,
but they belong to an emptier world than the one we know.

In our last glimpse of Macbeth before the final battle, we see
the man who has emptied that world and, along with it, himself.
He is no longer even the Tantalus figure he resembled in acts iii
and iv, when he hoped one murder more would suffice, and would
"make assurance double sure" (iv.i.83). Now he has fallen away
even from that. Like the prisoners in Satan's mouth in the ninth
circle of Dante's hell, he is frozen, spiritually immobile, eternally
trapped.[25] What Dante presents in an allegorical tableau, Shake-

25. It is not coincidence that the inhabitants of this lowest circle are
those "treacherous to lords and benefactors."

speare has shown us happening step by painful step. Before, Macbeth nourished his king and started at his horrible imaginings; now he has "almost forgot the taste of fears" (v.v.9), "Direness . . . Cannot once start [him]" (14–15). He has "supp'd full with horrors," he is all but impervious to the death of his wife, and in the great bleak words that Shakespeare now gives him ("Tomorrow, and to-morrow . . ." 19–28), he is the spokesman of all despairs.[26] Appropriately, his dismissal of life as a poor player leads him to the final despair of wishing the whole charade cut short:

> I 'gin to be aweary of the sun,
> And wish th' estate o' th' world were now undone.
>
> [v.v.49–50]

This is quite different from his earlier willingness to see "Nature's germens tumble all together" (iv.i.59). That sprang from a frantic interest in his fate, this from a wish to be freed of it.

Challenged directly in v.vi–ix, Macbeth recaptures at least a beleaguered animal's activity as he faces his enemies. And it is interesting, I think, that his revival seems to be connected imaginatively with conscious *rejection* of the idea of life as a poor player. The motive behind his resurgent courage in the face of death is clearly shown to be a determination to avoid being merely an "actor" on life's stage. Like Cleopatra, he will not see his greatness boyed or his nature trivialized by the predictable suicide of the Roman stoic: "Why should I play the Roman fool, and die / On mine own sword? Whiles I see lives, the gashes / Do better upon them" (v.viii.1–3). Macduff threatens him,

> Then yield thee, coward,
> And live to be the show and gaze o' th' time:
> We'll have thee, as our rarer monsters are,
> Painted upon a pole, and underwrit,
> "Here may you see the tyrant."
>
> [v.viii.23–27]

26. There is a general similarity between Macbeth's final monologue ("To-morrow, and to-morrow . . .") with its images of creeping, dust, and meaningless sound and fury, and Satan's final condition in *Paradise Lost* as a serpent crawling in the dust, supped full with ashes, met by a universal meaningless hiss.

And he answers:

> I will not yield,
> To kiss the ground before young Malcolm's feet,
> And to be baited with the rabble's curse.
>   [v.viii.27–29]

He will not "perform" either as Roman fool or baited bear. His life may signify nothing, but it will not be that of a player strutting and fretting. Then—the final irony—he storms off fighting with Macduff, an actor after all in Malcolm's revenge play.

On stage now come the smaller, paler figures of Malcolm, Rosse, and Siward. Siward's son, whom we have seen Macbeth cut down like wheat, is found and barely lamented. When Malcolm says, "He's worth more sorrow" (v.ix.16), his father fiercely counters, "He's worth no more" (17). We are back in that dry, principled, but not quite fully human world in which York begs for his son's death out of loyalty to the new king. Siward's response seems too unfatherly to be satisfactory. Yet we have just seen in five acts what the opposite of loyalty to the king can lead to. Though neither is reassuring, Siward's loyalty is clearly less horrid than Macbeth's rebellion. This is a tragedy and we are learning what to make of a diminished thing.

Macduff enters the scene of this arid victory with Macbeth's bleeding head. "The time," he says, "is free" (21). But what he carries and what he says do not fit easily together. A huge and bloody price has been paid for this "freedom," and the other freedom that could think of angels trumpet-tongued and Pity striding the blast has been forfeited forever. There is not going to be any satisfying soldier's funeral here, as there was in *Hamlet*. This is a darker, harsher play, despite its greater emphasis on the order which is victorious at the end.

What unites the two "plays" we have traced in *Macbeth*—one of crime and punishment, one of internal awareness—is their common, tragic resolution. Macbeth's degeneration and disintegration are tragic; so, in a different more moralistic way, are his defeat and "punishment." The replacement of nostalgic vision by expedient realism which we noticed in *Richard II* is here changed. Now expedient realism allies itself with representatives of nostalgic vision to destroy the diseased embodiment of a more complex form of consciousness. Structurally, it is as if Claudius were to be allied with old Hamlet against the prince. This structure was latent in *Richard II*, where Bolingbroke was allied with Gaunt as a vigorous leader, as Richard was not. But to a significant degree *Richard II* was, appropriate to a history play, successive in its parts: first, Richard was shown to us in various lights, then he and Bolingbroke collided like mighty opposites, and finally Richard took over the play while losing first the body politic and finally his natural life. *Macbeth's* innovative shape—two simultaneous rather than two successive plays—is the result of moving the "villain" to the center: Bolingbroke and Claudius remain on the fringe. The effect, however, is to make the tragedy darker. Richard II and Hamlet both achieve personal victories as well as genuinely tragic deaths—the old values are at least partially and momentarily restored within them at the end of each play. But in *Macbeth* both "plays" move away from the momentary victory in act 1 when Macbeth rejects the idea of murder. The hero's own awareness *and* the external forces that oppose him move inexorably to the brutal and wholly physical clash that closes act v. Thus the play concludes on an altogether external note, whereas *Richard II* and *Hamlet* both end with emphasis on the inner precincts of the mind.

Ideal figure, selflessly saving his country, Malcolm begins the last speech of the play by promising rewards to those who support him. This is traditional at the end of tragedy, but it comes as an anticlimax after the horror which we have just seen and which still occupies some corner of the stage in the form of Macbeth's severed head. Malcolm then mentions his projects, "planted newly with the time" (31), and this may carry our minds back to Duncan's trusting plans at Forres. This time the predicted harvest seems more practicable, for we have observed Malcolm's shrewdness, his careful testing of apparently loyal promises, and his effective marshaling of the assault on Macbeth. Still one senses—rightly?—a certain shallowness of comprehension in the lines. No one seems quite to see what we have seen—that weeds grow faster and stronger than flowers, that Macbeth was far worse, but also far greater than any of the survivors. I have referred earlier to Malcolm's summary reference to "this dead butcher, and his

fiend-like Queen" (35). If Macbeth is not, as Malcolm thinks,
worth more sorrow, he is at least worth more concern. Something
great and horrible has happened and something profoundly disturbing in a political sense has been removed. But the profundity
of the disturbance in other and more important senses has been
ignored. *Macbeth* is a tragedy only for the audience; for the
surviving characters it seems to remain a history.

When Macduff at last meets Macbeth, he says to him:

> I have no words;
> My voice is in my sword: thou bloodier villain
> Than terms can give thee out!
>
> [v.viii.6–8]

The voice of almost everything human speaks in Macduff's sword,
but it is still a sword, and, as such, must forever lack the poet's
fully human voice of understanding and sympathy to which we
in the audience have been listening. For it is not necessary to
sentimentalize Macbeth to perceive what a handful of dust we
are left with after he is gone. The new world is ordered, but
bare; healthy but bland. Macbeth made himself into a monster,
but lived on a level to which no Malcolm or Macduff can attain.
The voice in the sword says what must be said, but that does
not keep it from adding to the tragedy: blood asks ever for
more blood.

Thus there is nothing optimistic about the end of *Macbeth,*
but there is nothing pessimistic either. *Macbeth* ends with a
restoration of order that is unmatched in fulness and dramatic
weight in the other tragedies. Yet no words can quite describe
the hard, somber mood of the end of this play. In simplest terms,
what has been shown is that killing the king is *almost* inevitably
to be attempted and yet is *almost* inevitably unperformable. The
king can be killed, but the whole world, human, natural, and
supernatural, reacts to offer a new king. Regicide is finally in some
strange way impossible, for better and for worse. At a profounder
level, what we have been shown is the destruction of a soul,
whose intuitions of a life beyond life are his glory and become
his ruin; we go from the savageries within a man to the savageries
of the battle that cuts him down, from a hero who sees more
deeply into the abyss than we do to a villain who, like his op-

posers, sees far less. Regicide easily becomes a mysterious sort of suicide, spiritual and physical.[27] It is this ironic distance between us and the protagonist and also between us and the antagonists that lends the somber though reassuring tone to the play's end. In Northrop Frye's terms,[28] *Macbeth* is an autumn tragedy heading toward the winter of irony, whereas *Richard II* and *Hamlet* bestride the middle of the tragic spectrum, equidistant from ironic winter and romantic summer.

27. This sense of regicide as a form of suicide links the plays I have here considered with *King Lear,* and even, by extension, with *Othello* in ways that need still to be explored. Albert Camus brilliantly summarizes this movement in a passage describing a different king killing and alluding to Brutus, but obviously applicable to Macbeth: "[he] who must kill himself if he does not kill others, begins by killing others. But there are too many; they cannot all be killed. In that case he must die and demonstrate, yet again, that rebellion, when it gets out of hand, swings from the annihilation of others to the destruction of the self." See *The Rebel,* trans. Anthony Bower (New York: Random House, 1956), pp. 128–29.

28. *Anatomy of Criticism* (Princeton: Princeton University Press, 1957), pp. 158–239.

4

Merely Players?

In many ways, we have come full circle. We are, at the end of *Macbeth*, closer to the place where we began in *Richard II* than at any point in the interval. Closer in images and tone, that is, to that vision of vigorous, heroic, national service which was developed behind the main action in the first two acts of *Richard II*. Destroyed from within, order in Scotland and a stable version of kingship have to be restored from without. This external, pragmatic, and healing order triumphs in Scotland in much the way old Gaunt had pictured England victorious at the sepulchre of "stubborn Jewry." The fact that in *Macbeth* this victory is a return home as well as an example of Christian service makes the success more splendid.

At the end of the play we feel, however, that we must look both forward and backward. The new body politic of Scotland has been connected with images of powerful forces in the universe at large (storms, ghosts, miraculous cures, prophecies calculated to deceive the usurper, a protector with an extraordinary history —Macduff) and therefore has a solid dramatic reality and interest; but Macbeth's personal journey from loved defender to hunted beast has uncovered truths and aspects of human nature that no one else in the play is aware of. Part of the peculiar mixed tone at the end of *Macbeth* stems, I suspect, from the very similarities between Malcolm's order and Gaunt's vision. Before, in Shakespeare, such visions have usually been dying, or are already dead, while here is one growing, and flourishing. Though we emotionally welcome Malcolm and join the celebration, we sense that something has changed, that the times are now different since the appearance of Macbeth—and Richard, Bolingbroke, Claudius, and Hamlet. What seemed ideal when sung about in the nostalgic lyric past by a choric remnant like Gaunt becomes more complex and debatable when made to live and move under the bright lights of actual dramatic existence. We wonder if we can go home as simply as Malcolm asserts.

What has forced these questions upon us are the violent deaths of the kings. Richard, old Hamlet, Claudius, Duncan, Macbeth have all been cut down. And with them, by imaginative extension in Shakespeare's allusions, have fallen Adam, Eve, Cain, Phaëthon, Hyperion, Lucifer, and Christ. Constant, repeated attacks on kings—historical, mythical, religious—have successfully been made in the plays.

In each of the three plays we have considered, killing the king has been treated in somewhat different ways. Richard II, the bad king ruining England economically and politically, having gone too far in injuring a powerful nobleman, is opposed and crushed by a conventional revolt of the barons. This is virtually Holinshed's story and if Shakespeare had followed his source, his play would resemble the *Henry VI* plays more than it does. But Shakespeare, who had already written *Richard III* and probably *Romeo and Juliet,* had, as we have seen, other things in mind. First, he made the killing of Richard into a symbol for the death of a whole conception of the universe and man's ordered place in it. Richard has abused but still represents this order; Bolingbroke, so far as the play shows us, is hardly aware of it. The second addition that Shakespeare made to Holinshed's pragmatic regicide is the developing portrait of Richard as he gradually becomes aware of himself as both king and common man. The effect of this personal development is to make the act of king killing stand out not only as the cause of but also as an attack on awareness, the victory of a narrower, though more effective and disciplined, power over growing imagination and understanding.

Another addition to the simple regicide plot is the pervading ambiguity that Shakespeare insists on in Bolingbroke. In retrospect, from the vantage point of *Hamlet* and *Macbeth,* this might be the most important of the additions, for it takes the first steps in exploring the mystery of the king killer. In the later plays, this internal mystery will become a dominant theme, but it begins in Bolingbroke, who is not merely a political rebel, or, rather, whose mystery is not removed by calling him a political rebel; for although it remains a secondary theme, precisely what makes a political rebel is one of the issues in the play. Shakespeare leaves Bolingbroke's motivation unresolvably ambiguous, giving up political clarity in favor of imaginative richness. In the *Henry VI* plays, we frequently hear full and clearly expressed reasons for attacking the king, and however much we may question their justice or wisdom, they have little mystery. But Bolingbroke is never shown openly or consciously plotting to kill Richard—or even to unseat him; all his actions are shrouded with mystery. There is even possibly an indication that if he had himself seen clearly through this shroud of mystery, he might never have killed Richard.[1]

> The guilt of conscience take thou for thy labour,
> But neither my good word nor princely favour.
>   [v.vi.41–42]

Bolingbroke, however, remains a minor character in comparison with Richard and the death of the king an essentially political event with mythic overtones deriving from the Fall and tragic overtones deriving from Richard's increasing awareness and decreasing power.

In *Hamlet*, of course, the personal outweighs the political. The fate of Denmark is important, but the experience and reactions of Claudius and Hamlet are far more so. Claudius clearly states his motives for killing old Hamlet: "those effects for which I did the murder, / My crown, mine own ambition, and my queen" (III.iii.54–55), so that what was ambiguous and political in Bolingbroke becomes personal, sinister, and upsettingly clear in Claudius. Furthermore, in the council scene (I.ii), we see in him an attitude that makes killing the king not only possible, but easy. Claudius's description of nature and reason, "whose common theme / Is death of fathers" (I.ii.103–04), and his simple, almost eager, comment on death, " 'This must be so' " (106), both help define a personal attitude out of which regicide in his case sprang. The effects of having killed old Hamlet are mercilessly por-

---

1. Two plays later, on his deathbed, Bolingbroke still demonstrates the same uncanny ability both to state and to blur the truth: "God knows, my son, / By what by-paths and indirect crook'd ways / I met this crown" (*2 Henry IV*, IV.v.183–85). Awareness of guilt is balanced by a euphemistic indirection in "met." Similarly Henry V speaks the night before Agincourt of the fault his father made in "compassing the crown" (IV.i.300), another evasive euphemism.

trayed. What we just caught a glimpse of in Bolingbroke in the final scene—the sense of imprisonment in a role not freely chosen, or at least not fully understood—plagues Claudius throughout. Hamlet, identically plagued, is no Aumerle, easily caught, safely spared: he poses a dangerous problem for the king. An equally interesting threat, however, comes to Claudius from within. Despite his espoused view of life as merely a progress toward death, something inside him rebels at his own rebellion. An upsetting sense of the disparity between ideal and actual seems to come with killing the king:

> The harlot's cheek, beautied with plastering art,
> Is not more ugly to the thing that helps it
> Than is my deed to my most painted word.
>
> [III.i.51–53]

The murder has two main effects on Claudius: one is a new sense of irony, inauthenticity, and role playing; the other is the loss of his ultimate efficiency. Though an effective public ruler, he cannot rule himself or Hamlet. The man who could quietly kill old Hamlet, win his wife, and take over his throne now is unable to accomplish any of his personal schemes. His decoys fail, his plots are foiled, and, most important, his vision of life as merely a progress toward death is taken over and rehabilitated by Hamlet as he muses on Alexander and Yorick in the graveyard in act v. The virtuoso performer of act i ends up a total failure, a bringer only of death, and a woodcock caught in his own springe (I.iii.115; v.ii.317).

Killing the king thus becomes more complicated than it was in *Richard II*. The actual act of regicide remains dismayingly easy, but the nature of the resistance to the death of a king is changing. In *Hamlet*, not only does the crown sit more uneasily on the new king's head than it did on the old, but supernatural forces seem to oppose the rebel king and personal internal division plagues him more than it ever did Bolingbroke.

All this, however, is kept a minor issue in *Hamlet*, as the main stress is on the different king killing demanded by the Ghost—an act of revenge. Again, the killing itself is relatively easy—Hamlet passes up one sure chance; easily, if fatally, succeeds in the other. But the internal resistance to regicide grows, despite the traditional justifications for king killing. The difference between simple regicide and the avenging of a father's murder which happens to involve regicide ought, one might think, to make the deed easier. That it does not testifies to the increasing difficulty with which killing the king seems to be surrounded in Shakespeare's mind. Further testimony to this is that Hamlet can only bring himself to kill as a last, extreme gesture, after he knows he has been fatally wounded. What was expediently and exultingly accomplished with no internal tension in the *Henry VI* plays now either returns to plague the killer (Henry IV somewhat; Claudius greatly) or poses so many problems of awareness and value that action is rendered almost impossible (Hamlet). Hamlet finally achieves a certain liberation through killing a king, but it is a tragic liberation like Brutus's: he is used up in the process.

In *Macbeth*, killing the king reaches its most fully symbolic proportions. Though the political and personal questions remain important, in Macbeth's experience we come to see killing the king as a dramatic correlative for the thrust of anarchies of every kind against authority both external and internal. We never learn from precisely where the evil will to regicide reached Macbeth, but we follow in great detail what happens when a man violates a mode of traditional authority that turns out to be, in fact, an aspect of his own moral and spiritual health, thereby extinguishing in himself not merely the reality but even the dream of such a unity between microcosm and macrocosm as the old, nostalgic vision proposed.

One word will describe the process Macbeth undergoes: imprisonment. This is the interior punishment exacted by his political crime. Having lost Duncan, the trusting king who allowed freedom and growth to all, Scotland becomes slave to the tyrant rebel who attributes his own motives to all, trusts no one therefore, and brings only death to his country. The personal story of Macbeth runs parallel. Having rejected all the traditional bonds which ordered life, however imperfectly (they did not keep Cawdor from rebelling, but did help defeat him), he becomes a slave to the narrow view of man and man's priorities held by his wife and by a part of himself. He becomes imprisoned in the tyrannical authority of his own unrestricted egotism or self-will.

This is a profound psychological insight, as is Shakespeare's awareness that once such internal tyranny of self-will is established, it cannot easily be broken from within. Man cannot alone save himself from damnation; help must come from without— as his romances will show:

> And my ending is despair
> Unless I be reliev'd by prayer.
>
> [*The Tempest,* Epilogue, 15–16]

In the terms of tragedy, the tyrant hero must be cut down for the good of the world at large. Though this is a loss, anything else would be worse. Furthermore, all of the resistances to regicide which he encountered, even as he overrode them, would appear to have been only the fantastical visions of a deranged mind if he were not in turn to be attacked. Macduff's final act of regicide— so far as we know, the last in Shakespeare's works—confirms in a harsh, unflinching way the true existence of all those values and forces whose importance is proved negatively in the career of diminution and imprisonment that follows Macbeth's attempt to ignore them.

Killing the king gradually becomes then, in Shakespeare, a kind of lens in which all manner of political, social, moral, psychological, metaphysical, and religious questions are focused. What was perhaps implicit in the act in *Richard II* takes on explicit dramatic substance in *Macbeth*. In three separate plays, Shakespeare explores in rich detail the paths marked out by Marlowe at the start of the great age of English theater in *Tamburlaine* and *Doctor Faustus*. Both these plays took for their subject an act of rebellion against authority and its effects.[2] Shakespeare, I suggest, learned from but quickly rejected the essentially external and episodic approach of the *Tamburlaine* plays. *Faustus* was another matter. All three of the plays we have dealt with can be seen as complex versions of that play's theme: the fascination and destructive folly

2. There are, of course, three plays, if we take the two parts of *Tamburlaine* separately. A helpful article by A. Bartlett Giamatti, "Reading Marlowe and *Doctor Faustus*," in *Report of the Fifteenth Yale Conference on the Teaching of English* (New Haven, 1969), explores Faustus's progression in terms of language. Mr. Giamatti's terms—the use and abuse of the Word and of words—offer an interesting parallel to my view of king killing as cause of both awareness and disintegration.

of the overreacher. In Bolingbroke at the very end, and in Claudius and Macbeth progressively, we can see mirrored Faustus's imprisonment in his own self-will. Richard, whose abuse of the royal power is both a kind of regicide and a kind of suicide, is literally imprisoned but escapes, at least partially, the prison of self-will through the power of self-awareness. Hamlet, of course, finds all Denmark a "goodly" prison since his father's death. His victory— for which he deserves at least soldiers' music and the rites of war— is precisely that he finally avoids the imprisonment we have seen threatening him from without and within throughout the first four acts. He does this by achieving a balanced awareness and control that gives new, "modern," and dramatic meaning to that warm picture of one on whom every god seemed to have set his seal.

At the same time, whether it comes in the form of Tamburlaine's melodramatic sickness just twenty lines after his verbal attack on a religious "king" or in the mental anguish of Faustus, Richard, Bolingbroke (v.vi), Hamlet, Claudius, and Macbeth, there is something in the universe as portrayed in all these plays that does not accept either the overreacher or the supreme act of overreaching, which is regicide.

In the three plays treated here, the "nostalgic" world is easily deprived of whatever actual existence it may have had, but the dream of order on which it is based refuses to die. Authority and order in their actual embodiments seem almost to invite attack— by ignoring responsibilities, or sleeping in an orchard, or blindly trusting an ambitious supporter—and this attack is generally softened, even justified, for the audience by the fact that it brings into being the kind of unsure, complex, and ironic world we live in all the time. But what our three plays seem to reveal with increasing clarity is that while the Faustian cycle may be inevitable, it is inevitably tragic. We may in some ways welcome the shift from the old epic world with its hierarchies and inflexibilities to a new, dramatic world of mask and manipulation. But the shift is painful, wasteful, and irreversible for those involved.

As Robert Frost once said, emending his own poem, "something there is that doesn't love a wall . . . and something there is that does." Likewise, something in man seems to drive him to challenge authority and limitation, while something at the same time, in the world and within the challenger, makes the action painful and destructive as well as exhilarating and informative.

The image that captures this mixture of pain and exhilaration, destruction and freedom, is that of acting. And images of acting have surfaced repeatedly throughout the preceding pages in the quotations from the plays as well as in the discussion. We need badly a careful yet speculative study of Shakespeare's use of images of acting and of the theater.[3] However, for my purposes a brief glance at a few of the moments when acting becomes essentially involved with the act of regicide and with ideas of kingship will suffice, I hope, to conclude this study of king killing and to point in the direction where I suspect a great deal is to be learned about the way tragic identification is created and controlled in Shakespeare's greatest plays.

We have already seen that in *Hamlet* the image of acting—like everything else in that almost too-rich play—refuses to remain an image, like York's "well-grac'd actor" (v.ii.24) or Macbeth's "poor player" (v.v.24), but comes bustling on stage in act II to change the entire complexion of the play. The presence of admitted actors on stage makes inescapable comparisons of Hamlet's antic disposition, Claudius's plots, Polonius's arrases, and of course the Player King's status. This last figure is clearly labeled only in our printed editions of the play: on stage he will simply be another man acting another role, though this time everybody knows "it is only a play." We have seen how the Players cannot be located with the terms used to distinguish old Hamlet's heroic simplicity and Claudius's deceitful manipulation. The Players are carriers of the heroic past, yet masks and illusion are their way of life. Like the play that contains them, they are open to use, abuse, and

3. From the almost unending collection of books and articles on this relationship, only three stand out as very helpful. Two are books: Anne Righter, *Shakespeare and the Idea of the Play* (London: Chatto & Windus, 1962); and Robert Nelson, *Play within a Play* (New Haven: Yale University Press, 1958). A still more speculative and suggestive approach is taken in a tightly argued piece by Alvin Kernan, "Hamlet and the Nature of Drama," in *Report of the Thirteenth Yale Conference on the Teaching of English* (New Haven, 1967).

interpretation from many points of view. They function as a touchstone of authenticity that both *increases* the realism of *Hamlet* since it can contain a play called "The Murder of Gonzago" and *undermines* the realism of all the characters by reminding us that they too are merely actors playing roles like the Players. This undermining effect is especially severe on Claudius since we are reminded by the Player King not only of the actor playing Claudius but also of the fact that *within* Elsinore Claudius is only a player king since the real king has been murdered and his expected heir pushed aside.

We have also seen, furthermore, how fully Shakespeare is able to use "The Murder of Gonzago" to map the basic tensions of his larger play and to draw out in terms of the theater some of the effects of killing the king. It is a critical commonplace to show that a play within a play forces us in the audience to ask where the acting ends, and to see the larger play that includes us as well as everyone on the stage. But Shakespeare here does something subtler and more daring still: he invokes our full response to his play—a mixture of involvement and detachment caused respectively by awareness of psychological realism and symbolic structure—to enable us to judge out of our own present experience the behavior of others. He not only counts on our seeing "The Murder of Gonzago"—even both versions together— as an inferior kind of play to *Hamlet,* but further he demands from us a more complex response to his play than Hamlet, Claudius, Gertrude, or poor uncomprehending Ophelia can give to Hamlet's "Mousetrap." Killing the king is not only shown to have political and personal effects, but these effects are imaged for us on stage in terms of the theater's own dynamics. Our complex mental state in the theater is called upon by Shakespeare to help us feel and experience the meaning of killing the king. Regicide is explored in terms of acting.

Like so many things, this can be seen rather less clearly in *Hamlet* than in *Richard II* where acting remains an image (rather than bursting on stage) and where we can watch the awareness of acting, the sense of role playing, develop under the pressure of an attack on the king. The image of acting in *Richard II* emphasizes primarily the inauthenticity, the fiction, of acting and of the theater in general, as is appropriate in a play about the death of a clear, settled order that entertains no uncertainties about its identity, has no place for role playing. In Gaunt's view—which we have seen Richard progressively adopt—the king rules not by personal choice or even by popular support of his social role, but rather as God's surrogate. Kingship is not a role but a sacramental function. Like the religious reformers of the sixteenth century, Bolingbroke does not challenge the ideals and assumptions of his father's view, but merely their abuse by Richard. Again, however, like the reformers', his actions speak louder than his words, and the pattern is set for all men—Aumerle, Hotspur, Northumberland, Cambridge, Scroope—to follow in rebellion. Historically, this was not first learned in 1399, of course, but Shakespeare presents in *Richard II* the imaginative birth of this new, secular, and pragmatic view. Suddenly any man can become king if he has the power.

But when a man has wrested the crown from the king, he is no longer able to be king in the old sense, because of his very act. A crown seized is a different crown; now the king must *play at* being king. We have already noted that Bolingbroke seems to sense that he is playing a role in the first scene after he becomes king, when he gracefully—but significantly—points out, "Our scene is alt'red from a serious thing" (v.iii.77). Richard had sensed essentially the same thing under the pressure of rebellion in act III when he described Death as "allowing him a breath, a little scene, / To monarchize" (III.ii.164–65). In each case, reference to the theater serves both to underline the triviality of a situation and to show a certain mastery of that situation through ironic acceptance. When York describes Bolingbroke and Richard's entry into London in theatrical terms the effect is more complicated, since our reaction to York's description becomes blurred by our reaction to his theater image.

> As in a theatre the eyes of men,
> After a well-grac'd actor leaves the stage,
> Are idly bent on him that enters next,
> Thinking his prattle to be tedious . . .
>
> [v.ii.23–26]

Mention of actors and a stage in connection with kings can simultaneously indicate a new, less authentic kind of kingship and can heighten our sympathy for the less "well-grac'd" actor, Richard. Furthermore, implicit in York's words is an equation of the good king with the good actor and the bad king with the "tedious" actor. This is a crucial equation, implying a wholly new standard of kingship, different from either the two bodies kind of thinking or the Christian service ideal of Gaunt. Kingship is not an identity or a God-given position anymore. It is not even a complex in-stitutionalized fiction like those of the Middle Ages traced by Kantorowicz and Edward Peters.[4] Rather, it is a role to be played by an actor with skill and illusion. Kingship is coming to have the flexibility of the actor—*he* is always separate from his mask—but it is also suffering the essential inauthenticity of the theater. The play can only go on—in Court and theater alike—as long as the "show" is interesting, realistic, and powerful enough to encourage a certain suspension of disbelief in the audience. And the sense of the transience of the theater and its "two hours' traffic of our stage" is pervasive in English Renaissance drama.[5]

Faced with death, Richard II thinks immediately of acting, playing "in one person many people" and echoing Henry VI's thoughts just before he too was killed ("What scene of death hath Roscius now to act?" 3 *Henry VI*, v.vi.10).[6] But, as we saw before, the various roles leave him in "none contented." The image of an actor unable to play his—or any other—role is a perfect way of portraying the death of a king or of an idea of kingship. The engaged, frail, and suffering mortal body—the actor—cannot support the weight of the detached, unchanging, olympian body politic—the role. The royal identity, once settled and unself-conscious, has now become a thoroughly self-conscious part to be played and in the process has become, for Richard, unplayable. Bolingbroke is the better actor.

In prison, Richard comes to recognize the appropriateness of

4. Kantorowicz, *Two Bodies*; Peters, *Shadow King*.

5. For a penetrating, brief discussion of this sense, see the introduction to *Classics of the Renaissance Theater*, ed. J. Dennis Huston and Alvin Kernan (New York: Harcourt, Brace & World, 1969), pp. 3–25.

6. Significantly Richard III—whose career has been filled with images of acting—does not end with them. Perhaps this is because Richard is at his least authentic when a king, and his most authentic and heroic when involved ın battle as at Bosworth Field.

"acting" as an image for the destruction of the old unity of
kingship.

> Thus play I in one person many people,
> And none contented. Sometimes am I king,
> Then treasons make me wish myself a beggar,
> And so I am. Then crushing penury
> Persuades me I was better when a king;
> Then am I king'd again, and by and by
> Think that I am unking'd by Bolingbroke,
> And straight am nothing.
>
> [v.v.31–38]

He sees king and beggar as equally possible and equally unsatis-
factory roles. Deprived of his throne—and with it goes his assured identity—he comes to see that he is essentially separate and
separable from any particular role.

The recognition by Richard of his new relationship to his kingship puts on stage in a character's consciousness the double awareness the audience has been accepting throughout the play.
Suddenly, all the moments of awareness of the play as production,
the character as actor, the speeches as calculated poetry, are seen
not to be merely irrelevant distractions, but to have some meaning
in the play itself, some meaning for understanding Richard. For
the first time, we can see clearly that Richard's painful experience
of kingship—caught between real personal feelings and ideal public responsibilities—has been mirrored in our aesthetic experience
of the play, as we watch this actor on stage cope, or try to cope,
with his role. Richard's dilemma, the sense of a role which does
not fit and yet without which he "straight [is] nothing," has
fascinated us partly because we have had on the stage before us
a concrete embodiment of a parallel "dilemma" in the actor. It
surely is this flesh and blood example of the actor and our involvement in his efforts as well as in the role he is playing which is part
of what makes live theater essentially different from film. In film,
as in the novel and the lyric poem, the unforeseen has been virtually eliminated. It is a safer, less existential medium. The inability to do the things that film does—zoom close up, cut from
one angle to another, take a scene again—is what makes a play
so exciting and the tragic hero so appealing. We, like him, are

involved in a drama—the drama of the theater becomes a part of the drama on the stage. Of course, we trust the actor will succeed where Richard must fail, but the very conventions and limitations of the dramatic form alert us to the personal meaning of Richard's struggle toward deeper awareness.

Richard's view that he is content with no role is crucially different from Macbeth's view of life as merely a bad play, because the former maintains the fundamental distinction between actor and role that the latter rejects. While Macbeth throws out both in favor of a cynical monism, Richard wrestles on with his role as king until it is snatched away with his life on the point of Exton's sword. And it is just possible that a part of the glow we feel when Richard fights his assassins stems from the fact that at the very end of a play that has detailed the growing disparity between king and man, between role and actor, Richard acts in a way that suggests that there may be finally some basic connection between actor and role—that, although deposed, in some sense Richard is still a king. We are as relieved finally to see Richard succeed as we are to see the actor playing him succeed. For a moment, both plays—Richard's personal one and the larger one we are watching—turn together in complete harmony.

As we saw, *Macbeth* closes with references to acting which stress the inauthenticity, ridiculousness, and transience of theatrical illusion. Macbeth's immobility is conveyed by his willingness to see *all* life as a "poor player." He no longer makes distinctions between reality and illusion, acting and being, true kings and false. All merely strut and fret an hour upon the stage. Richard's painful awareness of the disparity between the king and the beggar shifts in Macbeth to a blurring of all distinctions. Macbeth goes beyond realizing that the king is also a man, or only a role. He concludes, in his hell-like vision, that "man" is himself only a role: the reality is a poor, bare, forked animal—even less, a walking shadow—caught up in the Hobbesian war of all on all. He opts for this "reality," giving up any understanding which the awareness of roles could have brought in his vain desire to escape the lack of clear identity implied in being an actor.[7]

7. The villain-hero is a remarkable dramatic creature requiring an exquisite artistic balance, and the references to acting at the end of

When Macbeth passes all life off as the "poor player / That struts and frets his hour upon the stage, / And then is heard no more" (v.v.24–26), Shakespeare is counting on our detachment to enable us to see that these are the distorted philosophical views of a king killer, while our involvement in the play *Macbeth* prohibits us from accepting his narrow, denigrating view of drama. This is indeed a daring venture on the dramatist's part: if we have, in fact, watched a poor player strutting and fretting his hour, these lines will be undercut with a withering irony; someone will be heard (or imagined) to mutter "You ought to know about poor players" to the *actor* rather than to the character; the balance will be destroyed. It is only Shakespeare's confidence that he has not presented a tale told by an idiot signifying nothing which allows him, with references to "acting," to draw attention to the close relationship between theme and form without fear of destroying the balance of realism and illusion that characterizes the form. Regicide is here imaged as a bad play, the evil *action* caught in terms of weak *acting;* the effect of an assault on human limitations described in terms of dramatic limitations. The narrowing of moral awareness is shown leading to a narrowing of aesthetic consciousness; life is deprived of its solid reality, art of its free illusion.

In all these varying forms, the acting image is capable of recognizing and accommodating, with considerable anguish and suffering, the now incompatible two things—actual and ideal, private and public, man and role—that previously were united in conceptions like Gaunt's "nostalgic" kingship, old Hamlet's rugged heroic simplicity, Duncan's governmental pastoralism. Though these unified conceptions have been shattered by different abuses, the double aspects which they reconciled remain as long as human life exists. The new substitute for the old doctrine—sensed instinctively by Bolingbroke, Claudius, and Malcolm (iv.iii), struggled for painfully by Richard and in his different way, Hamlet, and thrown away recklessly by absolute Macbeth—is this view of life as a play.

Macbeth are possibly essential parts of that balance, for they embody Macbeth's ultimate despair, which at once repulses us and elicits sympathy. Macbeth is both the hero who sees the truth of the world, and the villain who has made a vision of horror come to be true in that world.

In *The Praise of Folly,* Erasmus writes as follows:

If one at a solmne stage plaie, woulde take upon hym to plucke of the plaiers garmentes, whiles they were saiying theyr partes, and so disciphre unto the lokers on, the true and native faces of eche of the plaiers, should he not (trow ye) marre all the mattier? and well deserve for a madman to be peltid out of the place with stones? ye shoulde see yet straightwaies a new transmutacion in thynges: that who before plaied the woman, shoulde than appeare to be a man: who seemed youth, should shew his hore heares: who contrefaited the kynge, shulde tourne to a rascall, and who plaied god almightie, shulde become a cobler as he was before. Yet take awaie this errour, and as soone take awaie all togethers, in as muche as the feignying and counterfaityng is it, that so deligteth the beholders. So likewise, all this life of mortall men, what is it els, but a certain kynde of stage plaie? wheras men come foorthe disguised one in one arraie, an other in an other, eche plaiying his parte, till at last the maker of the plaie, or bokebearer causeth theim to avoyde the skaffolde, and yet sometyme maketh one man come in, two or three tymes, with sundrie partes and apparaile, as who before represented a kynge, beying clothed all in purpre, having no more but shyfted hym selfe a little, shoulde shew hym selfe againe lyke an woobegon myser. And all this is dooen under a certaine veile or shadow, whiche taken awaie ones, the plaie can no more be plaied.[8]

Nothing could more succinctly summarize the core of connections between kings and acting, and typify the fascination among imaginative writers—from Pico and Vives on—with a conception of roles replacing the idea of stable, unified identity. Erasmus captures perfectly the sense, so strong in the mature plays of Shakespeare, of a shifting, protean quality that characterizes not only kings, but finally all men. This same sense, with a similar bittersweet taste, is discernible in the quiet scene in *Hamlet* before the duel when the hero mulls over certain analogous ideas and focuses

8. Chaloner's translation, ed. Clarence Miller (New York: Oxford University Press, 1965), pp. 37–38.

them all on the action of killing a king. For what Erasmus is playing with is precisely what Hamlet says to Horatio in this final moment of meditation before the storm of the last scene. Folly is, as always, arguing for a peculiar wisdom which requires the finest balance of wit and irony. Hamlet, it seems to me, achieves just this balance in v.ii.

He has given up his earlier compulsion to stage-manage everything, to "plucke of the plaiers garmentes," to show the world that he "who contrefaited the kynge" was "a rascall." Indeed, there were moments when his efforts became so unpleasant and strained (as in iv.iii) that we might have wished the "madman to be peltid out of the place with stones." But he now accepts that a divinity shapes his ends, that "at last the maker of the plaie . . . causeth theim [whose roles are fulfilled] to avoyde the skaffolde." Although there is, in this part of the scene, only one explicit reference to acting—"Ere I could make a prologue to my brains, / They [Rosencrantz and Guildenstern] had begun the play" (v.ii.30–31) —it is quite obvious that the balance Hamlet has achieved is mirrored in the balance the *actor* must achieve and the *audience* must be alert to: that balance of freedom and limitation, between man's rough-hewing and the divine shaping, between the interim and the arrival of news, and, in theatrical terms, between the interpretation and the text. There is a balance of fatalism ("Let be" 235) and heroic rashness ("We defy augury" 229) in Hamlet's assertion that the readiness is all. He senses the danger in his acceptance of a role in the duel-play ("how ill all's here about my heart" 220–21), but he achieves in this role a visible, refreshing freedom—freedom to act without thinking too precisely, to apologize nobly to Laertes, to perform eventually his appointed revenge.

It is, I think, this acceptance of a role with its responsibilities, limitations, and freedoms that makes Hamlet so endlessly fascinating and appealing to audiences in all periods. There is a certain rashness in adopting any role ("And praised be rashness for it" 7), but, as Erasmus's Folly points out, "A foole in jeopardyng, and goyng presently where thynges are to be knowne, gathereth (unles I am deceived) the perfect true prudence." [9] Hamlet dis-

9. Ibid., p. 36.

plays this kind of prudence, the actor's rashness who accepts his mask. Here is none of Richard's intellectual dissatisfaction with all roles ("And none contented"), Macbeth's frantic attempts to avoid playing a role in Malcolm's play of restoration ("Why should I play the Roman fool, . . . be baited with the rabble's curse"). Hamlet's final stance is so thoroughly in tune with the dynamics of the theatrical experience that, when he looks out and addresses us "That are but mutes or audience," there is hardly a shock of recognition. We feel that we have been accepted before this. Here is no theater with a missing fourth wall, and Hamlet's confident willingness from the start of act v to play his appointed role of revenger in his own way has accentuated the traditionally prominent interaction between audience and stage in the Elizabethan theater. Not only is this interaction accentuated, but the whole play has drawn on it—explicitly in the Players themselves, implicitly in Hamlet's quest for a way to "play" the avenger—to involve all of us (Hamlet, actor, and audience) in a parallel effort at balance, control, and unification of disparate energies. Our involvement and detachment, the actor's text and interpretation, Hamlet's circumscribed interim to perform the Ghost's command in Claudius's world, all offer parallel and related dilemmas of balance. It is because we are involved so basically (that is *not* to say uncritically) that Hamlet remains a man for all seasons. Perhaps we can finally worship him or judge him, but, more important, for two hours we can *play at* being him while not giving up our detached perspective as audience. First through the Players, and then increasingly through Hamlet himself, the dynamics of our own experience at a play are employed by Shakespeare to increase both the depth and breadth of our experience of *Hamlet.* We are not mutes or audience, we are collaborators.

Hamlet is perhaps Shakespeare's only tragic hero who knows almost as much about the meaning of his action as we do. He has, and knows he has, single-handedly turned king killing into an action of spiritual freedom, rather than imprisonment—though in the tragic world he cannot escape death. And the terms that describe how he has been able to do this are his own—acceptance of a role before spectators—as are those terms which his words invoke ("There's a divinity"; "in that was heaven ordinant"; "there's a special providence in the fall of a sparrow" v.ii.10–230)—the service that is perfect freedom. The Ghost has his revenge; Hamlet's (and possibly heaven's) play of awareness and control ends triumphantly; but Claudius's play of poison and mask triumphs in its own fatal terms as well. The "nostalgic" world's command is reconciled with the "indifferent" world's requirements of irony and limitation, but the cost is life itself. Samson has fulfilled his role, he has united what regicide cut apart, but has been used up, *agonistes,* in the tragic process.

The only play which Hamlet does not see is that hidden "under a certaine veile or shadow, whiche taken awaie ones, the plaie can no more be plaied"—namely, the play Shakespeare wrote, which includes all the others. It is our awareness of this play that makes king killing something relevant to an age without kings, and Hamlet a hero outside Denmark. The aesthetic distance and freedom resulting from our awareness both of the playwright hidden behind the veil and of that veil's essential contribution to our awareness—it is this freedom from the pressures of Elsinore that Hamlet never has in the play, nor we in our daily lives, which makes Hamlet into everyman, his death into a kind of victory, and a four hundred year old play into living thought. Because—however much Hamlet has seen, and we through him—the one Erasmus calls "the bokebearer" sees more and saw it first.

Index

For both economy and clarity only the significant appearances of the various Shakespearean characters are recorded, always under the play title.

205

the king on trial, 58–63; the king killed, 64–69; Bolingbroke as king, 69–74; and *Hamlet*, 75–76, 85, 93–94, 135; tripartite structure, 136–37, 182–83; and *Macbeth*, 147–50, 154, 158, 186; acting in, 194–98

—Characters

Bolingbroke: his efficient realism, 34–42, 93, 199; his confidence, 52; and treason, 58; and Richard's mirror, 62–63; as king, 69–73; and Fortinbras, 85; and Claudius, 109, 130; and Macbeth, 169; his function, 186–88, 189; as a "new" man, 199

Carlisle, Bishop of: his view of kingship, 21; his prophecy, 39–40, 58, 135

Exton, 68–69; and Osric, 103–04

Gardener, the, 28–33; and *Macbeth*, 139–40

Gaunt: his view of kingship, 15–21, 66–67, 93, 135, 186, 199; and ceremony, 27–28; and conspirators, 36; and Henry IV, 71–74; and old Hamlet, 83–84; and Horatio, 89*n*; and Claudius, 109; and Duncan, 149–50

Groom, the, 67–68

Mowbray: his death, 25, 38; and Gaunt, 27, 71; and Lamord, 102

Northumberland: and conspiracy, 34–37; Bolingbroke's iron man, 39–40

Queen Isabel: in the garden scene (III.iv), 28–32; in Richard's absence, 48–50; and Ophelia, 98

Richard II: his development, 42–72, 187; and Holinshed, 42–44; Shakespeare's attitude toward, 43–44; in act 1, 44–46; his view of kingship, 46–48; and the king's two bodies, 52–

64; his internal awareness, 53–68, 115, 117, 164, 166; his metaphorizing, 56–67; his growing awareness, 59–69, 187–88; and Claudius, 109, 116; and Malcolm, 155*n*; and Macbeth, 166; and acting, 194–98, 202; as a "new" man, 199. *See also* Sympathy of nature

York, Duke of: his view of kingship, 21–22, 47–48, 50–51; like Siward, 182

—Scenes

Gaunt's death scene (II.i), 15–21, 33–37, 46–48

Garden scene (III.iv), 26–33, 75, 138–40; and *Hamlet*, 83–84, 105*n*; and *Macbeth*, 138, 147

Deposition scene (IV.i), 58–62

Pomfret Castle (V.v), 65–69

Richard III, 12, 13*n*, 20, 153, 187

Righter, Anne, 193*n*

Sancho II, King of Portugal, 3

Sanders, Wilbur, 20*n*, 68*n*, 150

Setting, 147–48

Shaaber, Matthias, 161*n*

Shakespeare, William. See *individual play titles*

Southcote, Justice John, 5

Spenser, Edmund, 1, 10*n*

Sprague, Arthur Colby, 66*n*

Sympathy of nature, 23–25, 63–64; and Richard's horse, 24–25; created by art, 32; and Ophelia, 99, 105*n*; and Richard, 105*n*; and conspiracy in *Macbeth*, 165–66, 170

Talbert, Ernest W., 55*n*

Tayler, E. W., 32*n*

Tempest, The, 94*n*, 150

Tillyard, E. M. W., 2, 21, 26, 30*n*, 60, 155

Time: linear and cyclical, 58, 72; in *Hamlet*, 93–99, 107–08, 111–15, 124–25, 133